Cloud Identity Patterns and Strategies

Design enterprise cloud identity models with OAuth 2.0 and
Azure Active Directory

Giuseppe Di Federico

Fabrizio Barcaroli

‹packt›

BIRMINGHAM—MUMBAI

Cloud Identity Patterns and Strategies

Group Product Manager: Mohd Riyan Khan

Publishing Product Manager: Mohd Riyan Khan

Senior Editor: Romy Dias

Technical Editor: Rajat Sharma

Copy Editor: Safis Editing

Language Support Editor: Safis Editing

Project Coordinator: Ashwin Kharwa

Proofreader: Safis Editing

Indexer: Manju Arasan

Production Designer: Nilesh Mohite

Senior Marketing Coordinator: Marylou De Mello

Marketing Coordinator: Ankita Bhonsle

First published: December 2022

Production reference: 1021222

Published by Packt Publishing Ltd.

Livery Place

35 Livery Street

Birmingham

B3 2PB, UK.

ISBN 978-1-80181-084-5

www.packt.com

To Valerio, who was born as I was writing the first chapter. He keeps pushing me to discover the real meaning of love on a daily basis.

– Giuseppe Di Federico

To my family and my future wife.

– Fabrizio Barcaroli

Contributors

About the authors

Giuseppe Di Federico started working for Microsoft in 2011, with previous experience working for IBM and Accenture in software development. He became an architect for cloud and hybrid solutions, serving customers in more than 10 countries across EMEA. He had the opportunity to lead multicultural teams, visit many multinational customers, and learn about different cultures, mindsets, and assets, which enabled him to also appreciate how organizations' structures impact their results. During his experience, he has been able to appreciate many identity patterns designed to last, to be reliable and secure. In June 2022, he accepted the challenge to join a new leading-edge team for the greatest service company in Italy.

I want to thank my wonderful family, Valerio and Luisa, for giving me the space and support I've needed to write this book during a tough period, with a child born, a transfer, a house renovation, and a job change. A special thanks to my parents as well, for providing me with all the tools I need in life.

Fabrizio Barcaroli (born in 1987) started his career as a consultant in Italy after obtaining a master's degree in computer science in 2012. In 2013, Fabrizio joined Microsoft as part of the Microsoft Consulting Services unit, where he developed his technical skills and helped customers achieve their business goals through the usage of Microsoft technologies. With the rise of the cloud era, Fabrizio specialized in cloud and identity solutions, and in 2020, he became a cloud solution architect, a technical advisor that helps close the gap between business needs and Microsoft technologies for big enterprises operating in the manufacturing, finance, and retail markets in Italy and across the globe.

I want to thank my whole family for always supporting me throughout my entire life: my father, Annibale, who has always been a role model for me; my mother, Rosa, whose unconditional love has always protected us; my sisters, Silvia and Federica, who always believed in me; and last, but not least, the love of my life, Giulia, who inspires me and bears with my bad temper every day.

Finally, I would like to thank Microsoft, for giving me the space to write this book, and the Packt team, for patiently guiding me and Giuseppe through this great journey.

About the reviewers

Gennady Shulman is an identity and access management architect specializing in single sign-on and multi-factor designs, implementations, and strategies. He has over 20 years of experience at Pfizer, eBay, and Guardian Life, covering the areas of architecture and pattern building for enterprises and external identities. During his tenure at Pfizer, he was able to identify multiple **common vulnerabilities and exposures (CVE)** related to implementations of federated services in multiple products, which required well-known vendors to re-architect or fix issues.

Gaurav Khullar obtained his B.E. (Honors) in information technology from Panjab University, India, in 2012. He currently works as a security consulting manager at Accenture UK&I, with a core focus on digital identity. He has been part of several digital transformations and has helped enterprises define and deliver their digital identity roadmaps. Gaurav is an expert in the field of **identity and access management (IAM)** and has been working in the industry for around 11 years. He started working in the industry as a full stack developer with an IAM vendor company headquartered in California, US. He has received several recognitions for delivering complex digital identity projects.

Table of Contents

Part 1: Impact of Digital Transformation

1

2

Part 2: OAuth Implementation and Patterns

3

4

5

Part 3: Real-World Scenarios

6

Trends in API Authentication   109

7

Identity Providers in the Real World   137

8

Real-World Identity Provider – A Zoom-In on Azure Active Directory   155

Preface

The world around us is changing faster than ever before. Technology is leading this change in a multitude of ways:

- Every company is a software company

- Big companies are restructuring themselves to be able to deal with such a fast evolution

- Start-ups are forging themselves around technology, building organigrams optimized to put technology at the center

- Architectural paradigms are evolving to produce cloud-ready scalable designs

All in all, enterprises that aim for an ambitious and sustainable time to market to stay ahead of the competition cannot deal with technology in the same way they would have done years ago.

This book leverages these concepts to focus on the impact of core technology that is paramount for an enterprise: its identity.

Focusing on how digital transformation is reflected in identities, with a broad view, this book will cover, among others, the following aspects:

- Enterprise identities that have a direct impact on employees' productivity

- Customer identities, consumed by the client, and the service an enterprise offers

- Application identities and the new challenges related to cloud-born applications which are distributed with independent microservices that requires mutual authentications

Besides business understanding, part of the book will be technically oriented and you will be guided in understanding why an identity strategy is important, the importance of protocols such as OAuth, and the different flows needed according to the scenario, as well as recommended identity patterns for distributed applications.

Who this book is for

The recommended audience for this book is enterprise architects and people with technical profiles.

What this book covers

Chapter 1, Walkthrough of Digital Identity in the Enterprise, covers basic concepts to support you in understanding the main challenges around digital identity.

Chapter 2, The Cloud Era and Identity, explains how the cloud and the modern architectural pattern add further challenges around the topic of identity

Chapter 3, OAuth 2.0 and OIDC, describes the most widely used identity protocol in cloud applications.

Chapter 4, Authentication Flows, provides an overview of different ways to adopt OAuth according to the context.

Chapter 5, Exploring Identity Patterns, looks at some basic patterns to be used with OAuth and also maps typical identity requirements with the related impact on application design.

Chapter 6, Trends in API Authentication, covers identity design from a high-level point of view: how an API portfolio of a company may look and how identity patterns can be implemented. It describes how new trends such as service meshes map with identity strategies.

Chapter 7, Identity Providers in the Real World, provides an overview of the various choices we have for IdPs by mentioning the most common ones in enterprise and high-level specifications.

Chapter 8, Real-World Identity Provider – A Zoom-In on Azure Active Directory, provides a zoom-in on the capabilities of a specific identity provider (Azure Active Directory). This will help you to understand the typical customizations and features available and how to leverage them to facilitate an identity strategy.

Chapter 9, Exploring Real-World Scenarios, focuses on the experience we have collected in the real world. The chapter covers the 360-degree impact of identity within an organization. It will also help you to understand how enterprise structure can affect strategic choices and how important it is to have the technical team connected with the business team for a long-term winning strategy within a company.

Download the color images

We also provide a PDF file that has color images of the screenshots and diagrams used in this book. You can download it here: `https://packt.link/U2PwD`.

Conventions used

There are a number of text conventions used throughout this book.

`Code in text`: Indicates code words in text, database table names, folder names, filenames, file extensions, pathnames, dummy URLs, user input, and Twitter handles. Here is an example: "The client application (a public client specifically, since a confidential client must specify the `client_secret` parameter too) requests an access token from the `/token` endpoint by sending the authorization code."

A block of code is set as follows:

```
GET /authorize?
response_type=code
```

```
&client_id=s6BhdRkqt3
&redirect_uri=https%3A%2F%2Fclient.example.org%2Fcb
&scope=openid%20resource_server_id
```

When we wish to draw your attention to a particular part of a code block, the relevant lines or items are set in bold:

```
POST /token HTTP/1.1
Host: authzserver.example.com
Content-Type: application/x-www-form-urlencoded
Authorization: Basic czZCaGRSa3F0MzpnWDFmQmF0M2JW
```

Bold: Indicates a new term, an important word, or words that you see onscreen. For instance, words in menus or dialog boxes appear in **bold**. Here is an example: "Select **System info** from the **Administration** panel."

> **Tips or important notes**
> Appear like this.

Get in touch

Feedback from our readers is always welcome.

General feedback: If you have questions about any aspect of this book, email us at customercare@ packtpub.com and mention the book title in the subject of your message.

Errata: Although we have taken every care to ensure the accuracy of our content, mistakes do happen. If you have found a mistake in this book, we would be grateful if you would report this to us. Please visit www.packtpub.com/support/errata and fill in the form.

Piracy: If you come across any illegal copies of our works in any form on the internet, we would be grateful if you would provide us with the location address or website name. Please contact us at copyright@packt.com with a link to the material.

If you are interested in becoming an author: If there is a topic that you have expertise in and you are interested in either writing or contributing to a book, please visit authors.packtpub.com.

Share your thoughts

Once you've read *Cloud Identity Patterns and Strategies*, we'd love to hear your thoughts! Scan the QR code below to go straight to the Amazon review page for this book and share your feedback.

https://packt.link/r/1801810842

Your review is important to us and the tech community and will help us make sure we're delivering excellent quality content.

Download a free PDF copy of this book

Thanks for purchasing this book!

Do you like to read on the go but are unable to carry your print books everywhere?

Is your eBook purchase not compatible with the device of your choice?

Don't worry, now with every Packt book you get a DRM-free PDF version of that book at no cost.

Read anywhere, any place, on any device. Search, copy, and paste code from your favorite technical books directly into your application.

The perks don't stop there, you can get exclusive access to discounts, newsletters, and great free content in your inbox daily

Follow these simple steps to get the benefits:

1. Scan the QR code or visit the link below

https://packt.link/free-ebook/9781801810845

2. Submit your proof of purchase

3. That's it! We'll send your free PDF and other benefits to your email directly

Part 1:
Impact of Digital
Transformation

This part will give an overview from the identity origin until the challenges that need to be tackled in a cloud design solution and why OAuth is needed in the cloud era.

This section contains the following chapters:

- *Chapter 1, Walkthrough of Digital Identity in the Enterprise*
- *Chapter 2, The Cloud Era and Identity*

Walkthrough of Digital Identity in the Enterprise

Business and the technology to support it are moving at a faster pace than ever before.

Digital transformation has disrupted the technology we used to deal with until recently. It is still occurring, and the evolution is not finished. The reason why this is happening can be summarized as follows: new technologies, trends, and tools supplied by the major cloud providers are helping companies to focus on business value rather than the surrounding complexity of an in-house data center.

Cloud and digital transformation cannot be seen anymore as the next step of **information technology (IT)** transformation; it is the present, and it is occurring right now. Many companies have already embraced this evolution and have transformed their data centers into cloud assets, and we need to expect most of the remaining companies' assets to leave on-premises data centers soon.

In other words, most companies are in the process of reinventing themselves. They are revisiting how they produce software assets, they are caring more about time to market, and they are understanding how much this can be directly proportional to the success of the company.

In this chapter, we are going to cover the following topics:

- Impacts of digital transformation on the market
- Why it is important to think about an identity strategy, what items an enterprise should not underestimate, and what the challenges are
- The importance of the UX and how it maps to the digital identity
- Common technical protocols for identity in the enterprise

Digital transformation – the impact on the market

The implication of digital transformation on identity impacted both the enterprise and the consumer market.

But let's take a step back and start with an overview of the two markets, how they differ, and their relationships with digital identities.

On one hand, we have the **consumer market**. The term consumer market, in this context, refers to the market that targets internet users. In other words, every time we consume a cloud service from a PC or a mobile (for example, Microsoft OneDrive or Google Drive) or we hit a website, we are in the consumer market. The consumer market includes social networks (for example, Facebook), search engines (for example, Google or Bing), e-commerce web applications (for example, Amazon, Zalando, or eBay), and, in general, everything consumable by a general internet user. In the consumer market, the service targets us, we represent the final user, and, most importantly, we represent the source of revenue. This revenue may come from our money, our data, (which can include both personal information and/or tracking and collecting our behavior on the web), or anything else that can be profitable.

From a very high-level standpoint, the typical objectives that service has on the consumer market are as follows:

- Increase traffic
- Encourage the users to access the service as much as possible
- Get money:
  - From advertising, if the business model of the application is ad-based
  - Increase the transformation rate in e-commerce applications
  - Any other profitable revenue that comes from the product service model

On the other hand, we have the **enterprise market**, a market where, historically, giants such as Microsoft, VMware, HP, Cisco, Oracle, and IBM competed to sell products to install and consume on top of servers in the customer's data center. These tech giants targeted the enterprise market by offering products to the IT department of a company. The IT department of an enterprise company, in turn, needed to create services on top of these products to be consumed by the end business. The result is that these tech giants have always been far from the end business; they have always been focused on boosting the internal IT departments of enterprises. This was the enterprise market that we knew until a few years ago.

The advent of the cloud in enterprises took this paradigm a step further. Today, some of these tech giants, such as Microsoft, Oracle, and IBM, have become enterprise cloud providers. They sell **Infrastructure-as-a-Service (IaaS)**, **Platform-as-a-Service (PaaS)**, or **Software-as-a-Service (SaaS)** cloud services to serve their enterprise customers that don't need a private data center anymore. Enterprise customers take advantage of cloud services by fueling external business and at the same time boosting internal employees' productivity. This has an important implication: offloading the IT complexity and data center management outside the enterprise by delegating it to the cloud providers and letting themselves focus more on their core business rather than on IT tasks and data center management.

Thanks to the enterprise cloud, which provides the capabilities of the past with less complexity and, most importantly, the new capabilities of the next generation, the next wave of the enterprise market is being created. Companies are constantly looking for new ways to improve their business with technology. The cloud market is young, and the efforts by the IT giants to onboard new customers (enterprises) at this stage to guarantee long-term revenue in the upcoming years are a top priority for them.

The portfolio of services that cloud providers provide to enterprises is huge. As anticipated, services span from simple servers (virtual machines) to web servers, to container hosting, storage, backup as a service, and much more. *Identity providers* are another important service offered to enterprises, and this is the core topic of this book.

In the context of digital identities, if we try to compare the consumer market with the enterprise, we will notice something. In the enterprise market, unlike the consumer market, there is a high level of complexity. The reason for that is that companies are supposed to manage their identity services for their employee. Identity, on the other hand, is consumed in the consumer market and managed by identity providers, such as Facebook or Google, just to provide two examples.

This concept has several implications. To properly use identity services, we need an enterprise-grade identity strategy that can simplify the complexity of this wide and critical topic.

Why an enterprise identity strategy?

The enterprise market and the consumer market are different, but there is one common factor: *simplifying the user experience*.

On the one hand, we have the consumer market, where the main KPI is to prevent the users who access the service from leaving too soon. The goal is to maximize the time spent on the service and, consequently, the service adoption.

On the other hand, we have the enterprise market, where companies want to maximize their business and improve employee productivity. In both cases, the adoption of a service and the onboarding of new users are important KPIs.

The **user experience** (**UX**) is paramount to achieving these KPIs.

When it's time to develop a service, regardless of the target market, one core item is mandatory: *a user-centric approach*. We may have heard this phrase many times, so let's contextualize it to see what it means.

A user-centric approach aims to produce a UX that is tailored to the user's needs to make interaction easier and improve productivity. When we talk about a user-centric approach, we also mean a service or a set of services that are built around the user. In the *Single sign-on* section, we are going to talk about the **single sign-on (SSO)** experience. Having SSO in place has the important benefit of preventing users from logging in with different sets of credentials to the different services: they just need to prove who they are once and everything else, including the ability to switch to a different service, is done transparently from a user perspective.

The concept of the user-centric approach can go even beyond this. The services know the user, and they can even enrich the user details and information together in a distributed way. This reduces the amount of time the user spends; for example, the user may be asked to provide their email address, phone number, and other information that can be instead provided by the **Identity Provider (IdP)** out of the box. There are two great advantages of a user-centric approach; one is technical and the other is more business oriented:

- Technically speaking, the application can offload some of the logic to the IdP, which results in easier development and maintenance of applications

- In the business area, the users can enjoy a custom experience that can increase user engagement

The following diagram is a graphical representation of services built upon the IdP. These services can be developed by offloading the identity's business logic to the IdP:

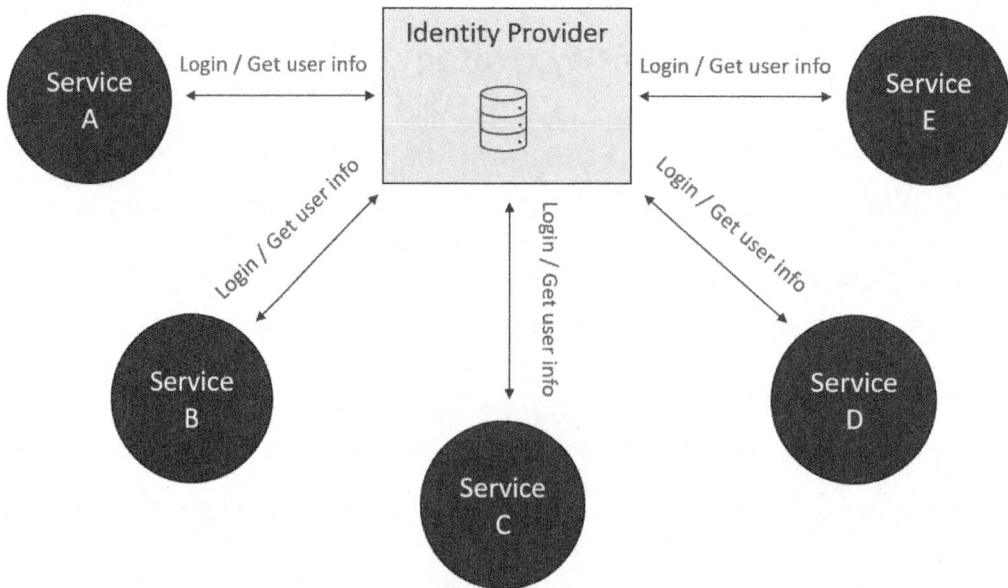

Figure 1.1 – IdP and service relationship

Of course, to implement services that cooperate to facilitate the UX, an enterprise-grade user management system design needs to be done upfront.

To have an idea of a fully user-centric approach, think about consumer services such as the cloud services from Google or Microsoft. Once you are signed in with your @gmail or @outlook email ID, you don't need to create a new user to manage calendars, maps, emails, or photos; you are the very same entity across all these services, and these services are going to share the details of your interactions to tailor the perfect UX for you across the cloud service. If you ask Google Assistant to remind you about something when you are back home, very likely you don't need to specify where your home is, so long as this information has been provided to a different service, such as Google Maps. This gives us an idea of the benefits that can be achieved from a user perspective and how productivity can be boosted with this approach.

To summarize, having a user-centric approach means that services are tailored around users to enable them to get the most efficiency and productivity.

The impact of identities on the UX

Recently, UX has become more and more important as the market understands that it is directly proportional to user satisfaction with the service. As a consequence, a lot of changes in blueprints and best practices have occurred.

The demonstration of this progress is visible every day. It's pretty hard nowadays to visit a website where we are forced to register as a new user with very long registration forms and many fields that may discourage the end user from finalizing the action and make them leave the service before they even start to use it. This practice was common in the web of the past generation:

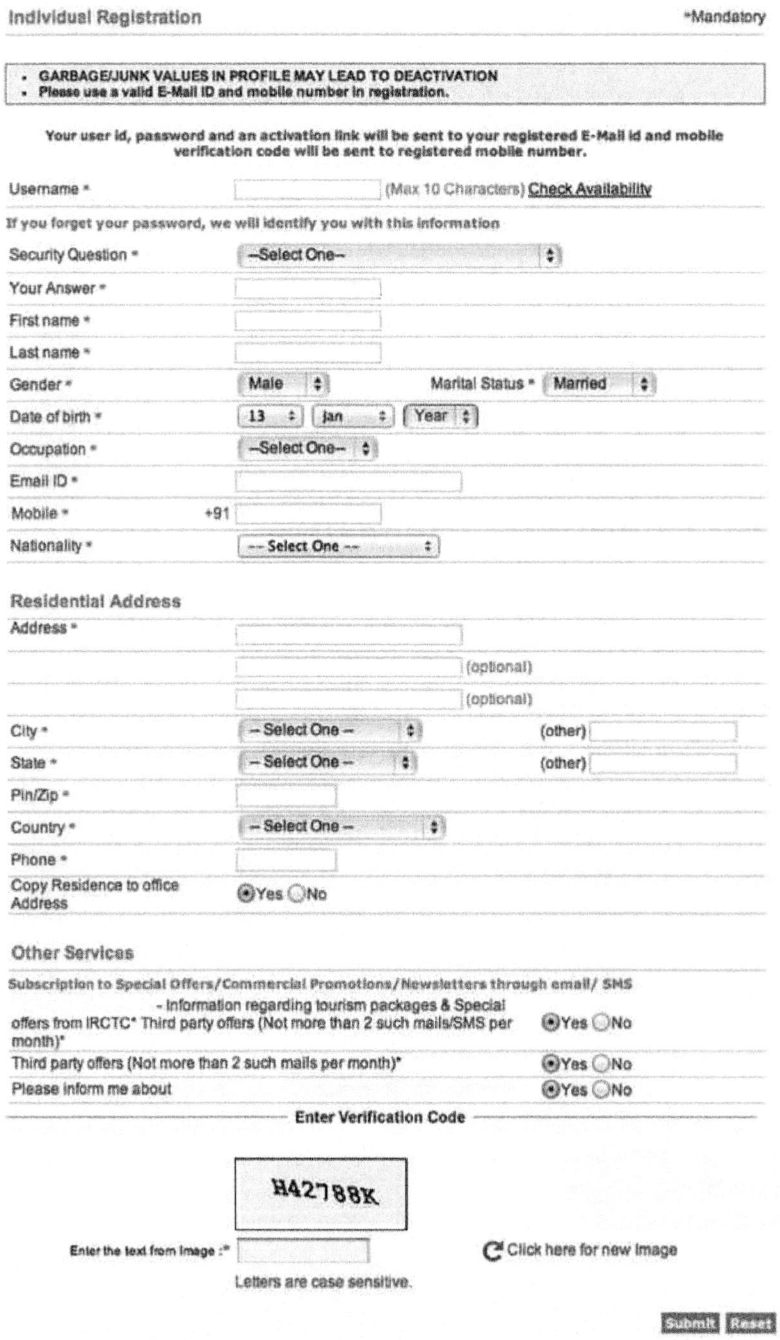

Individual Registration *Mandatory

- GARBAGE/JUNK VALUES IN PROFILE MAY LEAD TO DEACTIVATION
- Please use a valid E-Mail ID and mobile number in registration.

Your user id, password and an activation link will be sent to your registered E-Mail id and mobile verification code will be sent to registered mobile number.

Username * [_____] (Max 10 Characters) Check Availability

If you forget your password, we will identify you with this information

Security Question *	--Select One--
Your Answer *	
First name *	
Last name *	
Gender *	Male Marital Status * Married
Date of birth *	13 Jan Year
Occupation *	--Select One--
Email ID *	
Mobile *	+91
Nationality *	-- Select One --

Residential Address

Address *	
	(optional)
	(optional)
City *	-- Select One -- (other)
State *	-- Select One -- (other)
Pin/Zip *	
Country *	-- Select One --
Phone *	
Copy Residence to office Address	⦿Yes ◯No

Other Services

Subscription to Special Offers/Commercial Promotions/Newsletters through email/ SMS

- Information regarding tourism packages & Special offers from IRCTC* Third party offers (Not more than 2 such mails/SMS per month)*   ⦿Yes ◯No

Third party offers (Not more than 2 such mails per month)*   ⦿Yes ◯No

Please inform me about   ⦿Yes ◯No

――――――――――― **Enter Verification Code** ―――――――――――

H42788K

Enter the text from image :* [_____]   ↻ Click here for new image

Letters are case sensitive.

Submit   Reset

Figure 1.2 – Example of a long registration form, which is not so common nowadays

On the web, it is incredibly common to hit a service where part of the user management or the entire sign-up process is outsourced to external IdPs:

Figure 1.3 – Example of an external IdP signup

Outsourcing the onboarding process to an external IdP has been a game changer; it now takes a user a few seconds rather than minutes to register themselves for a specific web service, something that was challenging before OAuth.

The benefits of sign-up/sign-in outsourcing are multiple:

- Decreases the probability of a user leaving the service before they even start to use it
- Avoids asking for too many details from the user during registration for a service, which may raise privacy concerns and increase the probability of the user leaving the service
- Allows the user to spend their time using the service rather than on ancillary activities such as registering or completing their profile information
- Prevents bugs in the registration experience that prevent the user from accessing the service

There is another important achievement that OAuth brought to the world: a new security level for service-to-service communication. We will discuss the technical details in *Chapter 4, Authentication Flows*, but let's take a quick look at it in advance with an example. Suppose you are an architect and you need to create a new service for the consumer market. This service is supposed to enable user-to-user communication through web calls, such as Zoom, Microsoft Teams, or Google Hangouts. Let's call this service Contoso Video. One of the features of Contoso Video is integration with Google Calendar. This integration should enable users to check the calendar so that if User A wants to send an invitation to User B for a call, the Contoso Video service can check on the calendar whether User B is available at that time.

How can Contoso Video check the Google Calendar of a specified user (in our scenario, User B) without having the username and password of the Google account?

Before December 4, 2007, when the first version of OAuth was released, this wasn't possible. The service that needed to check the Google Calendar of a specified user needed to have the username and password to log in on behalf of the user to Google Calendar.

This is not good from a security perspective for the following reasons, among others:

- Contoso Video is an external service that needs to store the user's credentials; it can be hacked or could even be owned by malicious people that are gathering the usernames and passwords of users.

- Contoso Video has the username and password of the target account, which results in unlimited control over what the service can potentially do on the account (for example, it can read the calendar and emails, write emails, or even delete the account). The least security privilege cannot be granted.

OAuth has solved this problem in various ways:

- A user can delegate a service (in our case, Contoso Video) to call another service (in our example, Google Calendar) on their behalf, without directly requiring a username and password

- A user can delegate a service to perform only a subset of actions; in our example, User B can delegate Contoso Video *to read the calendar only* and not perform any further action:

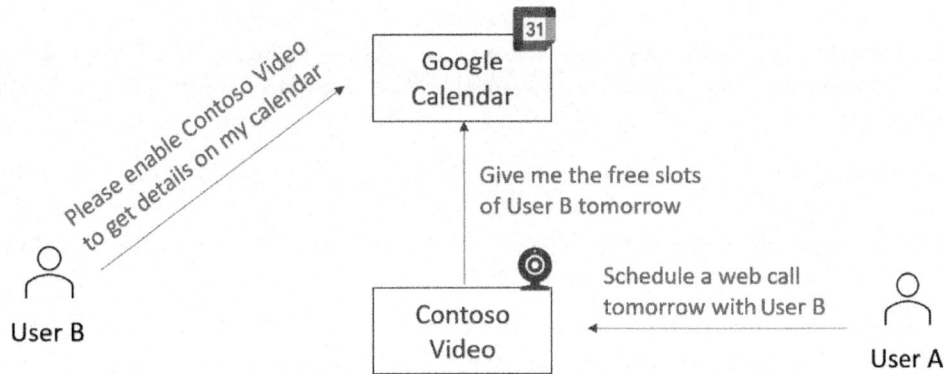

Figure 1.4 – Contoso Video user flow example

For those who are already familiar with OAuth, you should already be aware of how Contoso Video can get calendar details without knowing the password of User B and how this magic works. Further details on how this flow works can be found in *Chapter 4, Authentication Flows*, where this magic will be explained with technical details.

Before moving to the next step, it's important to understand, as will be outlined in the rest of this book, that the OAuth 2.0 protocol is generic and does not differ in enterprise and consumer markets from a technical perspective. The general concepts, flows, and protocol behavior are the same because they are based on the very same **Request for Comment** (**RFC6749**). What changes is the adopted IdP, which is the owner of the identities, and is, most importantly, one of the core topics of this book: how IdPs implement the OAuth specs and what the advantages and pitfalls of this are.

In enterprises, the concept is quite different as companies will manage digital identities and need to handle the IdP.

The upcoming chapters will describe the considerations the owner of IdP (enterprises) needs to take care of.

Digital identities – the duties of an enterprise

As anticipated in the *Digital transformation – the impact on the market* section, before the cloud era, tech giants dealt with technology within their own data centers. Identity management is not new for enterprises; historically, IdPs such as Active Directory or SiteMinder worked inside the network perimeter of enterprises with protocols such as Kerberos and NTLM.

Having an identity directory in the enterprise is paramount to managing users, computers, and enterprise assets in general that belong to the organization and configuring access to the company's assets. The evolution of identity in the consumer and in the enterprise led to most IdPs supporting OAuth, and they typically work as SaaS outside the network perimeter of the enterprise (that is, they are exposed to the internet, not the intranet). This has several benefits because users can now log in to the enterprise's services even outside the intranet and the VPN, improving the company's productivity. This also brings security implications into play, which will be covered in detail in *Chapter 5, Exploring Identity Patterns*.

What companies tend to underestimate is that cloud IdPs nowadays take advantage of the OAuth protocol, which is very different from the previous protocols as it takes into account new concepts such as delegation across different services, app registration within the enterprise, and new authentication flows, which, in turn, can impact the way enterprises develop services and APIs.

In an enterprise, user information, identity, and access are managed by the company, which deals with the life cycle of the digital identities of its employees (at a minimum, some companies even host external identities as vendors and/or contractors in their IdP). Companies typically have processes to onboard the employee's digital identity when hired (provisioning). The identity is then used to enable the user to access the company's tools, services, and websites and, finally, when the user leaves the company, there is a process to delete/disable (deprovision) the user's digital identity to prevent unwanted access to company resources.

From our experience in enterprises, we can certainly state that the concept of the user-centric approach is not yet widely adopted. IT departments and project teams are not able to collaborate efficiently with each other while working on projects/apps because they are not organized properly. Sometimes, different teams inside the organization use different IdPs, which makes the user-centric approach complicated. As a result, it often results in a very bad practice of managing user identity consistently. This outlines the importance of an organization having a clear strategy in this domain. As we are going to see in the rest of this book, it's important to develop a strategy not only to ease the life of the users but also to handle everything that requires authentication, including service-to-service authentication.

If a bad strategy or no strategy is in place, then some applications are even developed without any IdP. When no IdP is used in an application, then the user management feature is usually developed within the application itself with further effort, using independent and custom-developed logic, which is a model that was followed in the past (before 2000) when IdPs didn't exist at all. When this happens, users need to use a different set of credentials according to the application they need to log in to. This scenario is also known as the **distributed identity problem** and was common in the early 2000s. The following diagram shows the distributed identity problem:

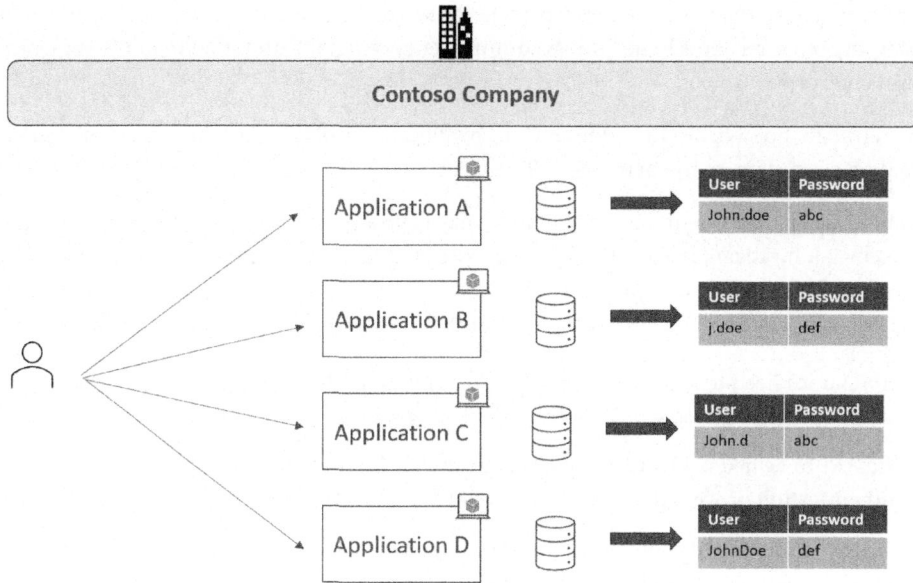

Figure 1.5 – Distributed identity problem example

The consequence of such a model is having less productivity for the following reasons:

- Users need to remember different sets of credentials
- More lines of code have to be written for an application to handle the authentication logic, typically offloaded to an IdP, which results in increased maintenance and more time to market to develop a single application
- User information is not centralized, which might result in users wasting time enriching their profiling information for each application
- Identity needs to be managed by custom implementations, which may lead to security issues

These are the typical scenarios and the duties an enterprise needs to accomplish to manage its digital identities. If we look deeper, there are important implications for an architect to consider, as we will discuss in the upcoming section.

The challenges when defining an identity strategy

Every software architect, during the design phase of an application, should carefully take care of the concept of digital identity first.

Authentication and authorization are usually the very first tasks an application needs to perform before triggering any other business logic. This is common to every application that requires authentication within an enterprise.

When architects are working on demand to develop an application without taking care of the surrounding ecosystem, many items could be neglected.

For example, an application under development may have a subset of requirements that can be easily addressed by taking advantage of API logic that's already present within the company's portfolio. This simplifies the development complexity of the current application and represents a good practice to increase the company's efficiency overall. This kind of scenario has many salient points, as follows:

- Companies need to have a well-known portfolio of APIs with good descriptions that can be evaluated before starting any application development

- The API to be taken advantage of needs to already be registered on an IdP with a well-known authentication process that can be consulted by the architects

- The API should be designed to take advantage of the OAuth scope's capabilities to enhance security within the company (scope is an OAuth spec that will be explored further in *Chapter 3, OAuth 2.0 and OIDC*)

- The API may be designed to accept requests from two possible actors:

  - The application that calls it.

  - The user who is currently logged in to our application. As such, our application needs to call the API on behalf of the user (the concept of delegation will be explained in *Chapter 4, Authentication Flows*).

You don't have to understand what these points mean in depth at this stage. Each of them will be covered in this book; what is important is to have a high-level understanding of the implications that an application design has on a wider ecosystem.

Another example is that an IdP may already have the user information the application needs to acquire. This may have an impact on the user interface and the business logic that needs to be developed.

Another important point to consider is the audience that is supposed to adopt the application under development. An enterprise application can be developed for the customers of the company, for the internal employees, for third-party companies, for a partner, or a combination of them all. This can affect the choice of IdP for the application before the development and for every scenario. It is advisable to identify the options architects can choose from in advance. Not pondering all the IdP options in advance can lead to anarchy or bad architecture, such as having multiple IdPs for the same audiences and purposes. In other words, don't provide clear IdP options to handle digital identities for specific audiences; it will lead to chaos, which is what many companies are suffering from today.

It is also important to spend a few words on anonymous web applications as they are usually still part of a company's application assets.

Anonymous web applications are available to every user without any awareness of who the caller is from an application standpoint. Anonymous web applications were very common in Web 1.0 when the internet was based on static websites with little or no server-side logic. Anonymous web applications, by definition, do not require any user authentication. The scope of an anonymous web application was usually to showcase a product or a service to the end users and, in many cases, was handled with poor or no server-side logic. This is because the page that was served to the client was typically the same for every request.

If you are thinking that anonymous web applications do not need to consider authentication and authorization during the design phase, it's important to note that this is wrong. Anonymous web applications do not require any *user* authentication but can still interact with APIs and with the company's assets and, as such, they may need to have their own identity within the enterprise in the same way as authenticated applications. This concept will become clear in the rest of this book when we describe OAuth flows and application registration in *Chapter 5, Exploring Identity Patterns*.

In the upcoming sections, we are going to tackle this topic more deeply from a technical perspective. We are going to introduce the most relevant identity protocols and technologies adopted within enterprises to lay the groundwork for the rest of this book and to present OAuth 2.0 in *Chapter 3, OAuth 2.0 and OIDC*.

Single sign-on (SSO)

When we talk about authentication, it is practically impossible to not talk about SSO. Everybody has found themselves stuck with different definitions of SSO, but how can we define it and understand in detail exactly what this term means and implies? SSO is an authentication capability that allows a user to not insert their credentials every time they need to access an application. SSO should not be confused with saving your credentials within a web browser when prompted to do so when logging in to a web application through a web form. SSO is more subtle and involves the interaction of different actors that contribute to preventing the user from being asked for their credentials when moving from one application to another.

To make SSO work, a user should provide an application with *proof of authentication*, which certifies that the user has already been through an authentication flow. The application, on the other hand, should *trust* this proof of authentication, which should contain enough information to make the application decide whether user authentication can be skipped entirely.

How is it possible to achieve this? This is where the federated authentication protocols lend a hand; they will be discussed in greater detail in the following chapters.

For now, it is important to understand that to implement SSO, the following components should usually be involved:

- **A common authentication server**: For different applications to trust the same user's proof of authentication, a common authentication server must be put in place. Applications must not manage user credentials directly, but they have to delegate authentication to an external server.

- **A common language and message format**: Messages between applications and the format of the proof of authentication should be standardized to make integration and interoperation among applications easy to implement. This is usually the job that's done by authentication protocols, which will be discussed later in this chapter.

Very often, there is a common authentication server (also known as an IdP), which takes more than one authentication protocol and can create a proof of authentication that's suitable for every trusting application, regardless of the language (protocol) required by each of them.

Let's examine an example. We are going to mention several protocols that will be discussed in detail in the following chapters. For now, the only important thing to know is that each protocol has a way of formatting exchanged messages and proof of authentication.

There is a user who needs to access two applications that trust a common authentication server. This authentication server can either store and manage the user's credentials directly or delegate credential validation to an external system. In this example, let's assume that the user's credentials are directly managed by the authentication server. The user tries to access the first application, but since they don't already have proof of authentication, they are forced to go to the authentication server first to obtain it. Once it is obtained, they can return to the first application with their proof of authentication and get authorized to access it. Now, let's suppose that the user would like to access the second application. The user cannot generally use the proof they already have for the second application and therefore they need to go to the authentication server again to obtain proof of authentication that is valid for it too. This time, the authentication server does not require the user to insert their credentials again because they have already done so, and therefore it just issues new proof of authentication for the second application. This happens because the authentication server, during the user's first successful authentication attempt, established a session with the user, meaning that it saved a state representing the interactions that the user had with it. The user can therefore access the second application without re-entering their credentials: they SSOed into it. A couple of things are worth noting here:

- Each application could potentially use a different authentication protocol with the authentication server

- The authentication server is how SSO happens; it is in charge of recognizing a user's identity by looking at the session information the user established with it during the authentication process

SSO has greatly simplified the UX during the interaction with different applications by reducing the user prompts for credentials. This behavior has several implications, though, some beneficial and others detrimental. On the positive side, the less a user is asked for their credentials, the less they are susceptible to phishing attacks (which require the user to insert their credentials on a malicious login page). The user may wonder why they need to insert their username and password again and why SSO is not working as expected. On the negative side, having one set of credentials means that if they are compromised (or if the proof of authentication is stolen), then an attacker may get access to multiple applications since they all rely on the same set of credentials or trust the stolen proof of authentication. Using MFA and advanced security capabilities prevents most attacks related to SSO scenarios.

LDAP and Kerberos

When most applications used to have user databases/repositories, an effort was made by several companies to create standard ways to centralize user information and details in common places. For the users, this would have meant not needing to remember passwords to access each application anymore.

In the 1980s, telecommunication companies introduced the concept of **directory services** into IT. A directory service was a central place where all the entities that made up a network were represented and given a name. Directory services were introduced as an **Open System Interconnection** (**OSI**) initiative to find common network standards to enable interoperability among different software vendors. This made a standard necessary, and this is one of the reasons why the **x.500** directory service came into the world and subsequently the **Lightweight Directory Access Protocol** (**LDAP**) as the means to authenticate a user and allow them to access the objects within a directory. The term *lightweight* in LDAP was introduced to highlight how it differed from the former DAP protocol: LDAP was based on the TCP/IP protocol stack, which highly simplified the access to x.500 directories.

LDAP was great at centralizing information and making it available to end users and applications. However, it wasn't that great at making collaboration between different directories easy. Having a single directory with all the network users and objects is not easy to achieve, even within the same company. Different business units and areas might have different needs in terms of security and segregation, and they very often do not want to risk that a user without the proper authorization may access restricted and sensitive assets. Luckily, the **Massachusetts Institute of Technology** (**MIT**) developed and published the **Kerberos v5** protocol in 1993 to protect network services through authentication and authorization of users and applications (versions 1 to 3 were internal to MIT, and version 4 was published in the 1980s).

As an authentication protocol, Kerberos introduced several new innovative concepts:

- **SSO**: The Kerberos Foundation is about *ticket exchange*. Successful authentication for either a user or a computer (which is a separate entity) will issue proof of this authentication by an **authentication server** in the form of a *ticket*. The authentication server component that oversees the issuing of tickets is known as the **ticket-granting server** (**TGS**). An authenticated entity can therefore use this ticket to prove they are who they claim to be and, consequently, request authorization from other entities who trust the same Kerberos authentication server. This process involves other tickets being issued by the TGS – generally, one for each service an entity requests access to. Once, for instance, a user has been authenticated and receives their ticket from the TGS, they can then access different services without being required to insert their credentials each time. They can use their ticket to SSO into other services, so long as the ticket has not expired (in that case, the user must re-enter their credentials).

- **Realms and cross-realm authentication**: Kerberos also introduced the important concept of **realms**. A **realm** is a domain where a Kerberos authentication server is allowed and has the authority to authenticate a user, a service, or a computer. When it comes to a complex organization with different business areas and independent administration requirements, then it is very likely that more than one realm should be put in place. What is the difference from LDAP, then? Kerberos introduced the concept of **cross-realm authentication**, where a TGS in a realm trusts tickets issued by the TGS in another realm by creating a sort of trust relationship between Kerberos realms. This quite simple concept enabled new use cases that were impossible to achieve before, such as the highly sought-after collaboration between different business unit realms within the same company.

It is worth mentioning that, at the beginning of the new millennium, Microsoft introduced both LDAP and Kerberos as standard authentication protocols in one of its iconic products, Active Directory. Active Directory has been, and it is still today, the foundation of authentication and authorization for most enterprises. But nowadays, its success is also the main IT professionals' pain in the neck when it comes to shifting that paradigm (which was great in the early 2000s) to a more modern authentication approach.

Everybody remembers that the end of the 1990s was also famous for the advent of a revolution in the IT world. We are talking about the rise of the *global internet*, known as Web 1.0 – that is, commercial use of the internet on a global scale. This important transition brought with it a higher demand for collaboration between companies where businesses had to interact with other businesses more and more, expanding their horizons on a global scale to avoid being cut off from the great innovation that could overwhelm them in the blink of an eye.

In that era, Kerberos and LDAP could not enable this new type of collaboration; their capabilities were not suitable for making users, services, and computers interact when such services were managed by different legal entities.

The reason why Kerberos wasn't ideal to be used over the public internet wasn't related to the security of the protocol but rather to its authentication model, which didn't easily fit the needs of most public internet applications due to its complexity. Try to imagine the distribution of the keys required by the protocol to all the machines used by end users to access a website. LDAP, on the other hand, would need to import the users of our company into all the LDAP directories of those external organizations that publish a website that we would like to get access to. The larger the number of organizations involved, the greater the complexity of making collaboration work.

It was time for a different way to manage authentication; it was time to introduce the concept of federation.

Federation of identities

IT departments had always been characterized by an inclination toward centralization. This is easy to understand: having a centralized IT system makes it simpler to manage, secure, audit, and maintain, but on the other hand, it lacks flexibility and extensibility, and it is certainly hard, if not impossible sometimes, to share and use it outside the company's boundaries.

Businesses usually don't care about how difficult it could be to maintain and manage an IT system; they mainly care about its features and how they can harness them for their profit. Businesses need software to be flexible and extensible, an enabler and a catalyst for new opportunities to make people more productive and, in the end, transform a process into profit.

Let's narrow down this very broad problem to the scope of identity management in the global internet era. Businesses demanded more collaboration with their partners in order not to be overtaken by their competitors. People outside an organization had to have access to the internal applications and assets of another company, they had to share critical information more collaboratively, and the internet was the natural candidate to start this new way of working. IT departments knew that, but they didn't have the right tools to securely enable this new way of thinking and working without increasing the complexity of existing identity management systems based on traditional authentication protocols such as Kerberos and LDAP.

The tendency for centralization was causing too much friction in business-to-business collaboration, integration, and automation, resulting in high costs of identity management and reduced efficiency. Identity management needed a new model that could solve all these problems, and the answer was the concept of **federation**. Federation is based on *trust*. A company trusts that the identities that are managed by another company are reliable because we trust that we and the other company value the relationship that we have. After all, it creates a benefit, most likely profit, for both us and them. Generally speaking, trust is usually based on shared experience: you usually trust other organizations or people because you have a historical and established relationship with them or because other organizations or entities (that you trust) recognize that they are trustworthy.

The *federated* identity model innovates by delivering flexibility into business-to-business collaboration scenarios and by reducing the overall identity management costs.

Within this model, each company manages its own set of identities. Usually, this means managing the life cycles of both personal data and accounts, including the associated credentials of the company's employees and, sometimes, a subset of their external collaborators. The latter scenario is common when the external company we collaborate with does not have an identity system, making federation practically impossible. Therefore, it is more convenient to create and manage an identity representing those external users directly in our identity system. Managing users outside of their organization will likely introduce security and liability risks. With the introduction of protocols such as SAML, WS-Federation, OAuth 2.0, and **OpenID Connect** (**OIDC**), this problem has been solved with a very elegant solution that will be discussed later in this chapter.

Through federation, companies can pursue business integration goals that best align with their business model. IT departments, on the other hand, do not have to create, manage, and centralize external identities within their authentication solutions. This allows them to avoid all those scenarios that may put them at risk of reputation damage or regulatory liability if any identity management action releases or uses information in ways that conflict with individual privacy rights.

A federated identity model has different goals/traits:

- Reduce the cost of identity management because external identity management is delegated to a trusted external company
- Do not bind or impose the use of a specific implementation on the companies that would like to start collaborating
- Leverage open standards to enable secure and reliable collaboration for businesses and individuals

From a technical perspective, a federated identity model comprises several components that build the foundation to enable identity interactions with companies beyond their IT boundaries. It's important to know that federation technologies highly rely on web technologies such as the HTTP protocol (especially the `Redirect` directive).

It is worth mentioning that federation across enterprises is a topic that's historically associated with the SAML protocol. More information on SAML will be provided later.

Federation terminology

Let's dive into the definition of some important terms and components around federation that are common to most authentication protocols:

- **Federation**: In identity management, as stated earlier, federation is a trust relationship between two companies that would like to start a beneficial collaboration and access the services and the assets published by the other party with their credentials. Therefore, it is a trust contract that two or more companies have established that typically includes authentication and may also include authorization.
- **IdP**: An IdP is an entity that provides authentication (and sometimes authorization) to end users. It usually stores information about users' accounts and credentials, but it is sometimes used to proxy authentication to external user stores by means of other authentication protocols, which might be different from the ones used by the applications directly federated with the IdP. An example of an IdP is **Active Directory Federation Services (ADFS)**, which allows federation to other IdPs through the use of federated protocols such as SAML and WS-Federation. ADFS keeps account credentials in an Active Directory Domain Services infrastructure, making the interoperability between modern and legacy protocols (Kerberos and LDAP) possible.

- **Security Token Service (STS)**: An STS is a web service that issues security tokens, and it is usually part of an IdP. An STS makes assertions about users and delivers them to trusting parties by means of a security token.

- **Claim**: A claim is the technical name for the user assertions made by the STS (for example, name, surname, username, and so on).

- **Security token**: A security token is a collection of claims. Claims in a token are organized in a shared format that depends on the authentication protocol used, such as SAML tokens for the SAML and WS-Federation protocols and JWT tokens for the OAuth 2.0 and OIDC protocols.

- **Signed security token**: A signed security token is a security token that is cryptographically signed by the STS.

- **Service provider** (*relying party*): A service provider is an entity, such as an application, that trusts and relies on the assertions (tokens) issued by a specific IdP.

- **Federation metadata**: The federation metadata is a publicly available document that defines the technical details to establish trust with the IdP that publishes it.

- **Home realm discovery (HRD)**: This is the process that identifies a user's IdP.

Federation example

Let's try to apply the concepts explained in the previous section to an example.

Scenario: There are two companies, Contoso and Fabrikam.

Contoso has its own IdP, *ContosoIdP*, and one web application (the *service provider*) where important marketing documents are published.

This marketing portal has already been federated with ContosoIdP. This means that user authentication has been delegated to ContosoIdP; in other words, the marketing portal trusts ContosoIdP and accepts *signed security tokens* containing users' assertions issued by ContosoIdP.

Fabrikam has just its own IdP, *FabrikamIdP*, which authenticates Fabrikam users.

Goal: Contoso and Fabrikam started a business collaboration, and Contoso would like to grant Fabrikam's users access to their marketing portal.

Solution: Contoso and Fabrikam establish a federation between their IdPs. This federation has a direction, meaning that ContosoIdP will *trust* tokens issued by FabrikamIdP but not vice versa.

The way federation occurs in practice depends on which protocol is being used. Most commercial identity and service provider implementations provide automation tools and user interfaces where it is possible to load the federation metadata document (used within the SAML and WS-Federation protocols) of the resource we would like to federate with in the form of an HTTP **Unified Resource Locator (URL)**. Each IdP and application publishes such a document by exposing a publicly available internet endpoint that can be fetched through the HTTP protocol. This document is automatically parsed to extract the information needed to establish the federation, such as public certificates, claim definitions, unique identifiers, and other endpoints.

The following figure shows a typical user authentication flow involving two IdPs:

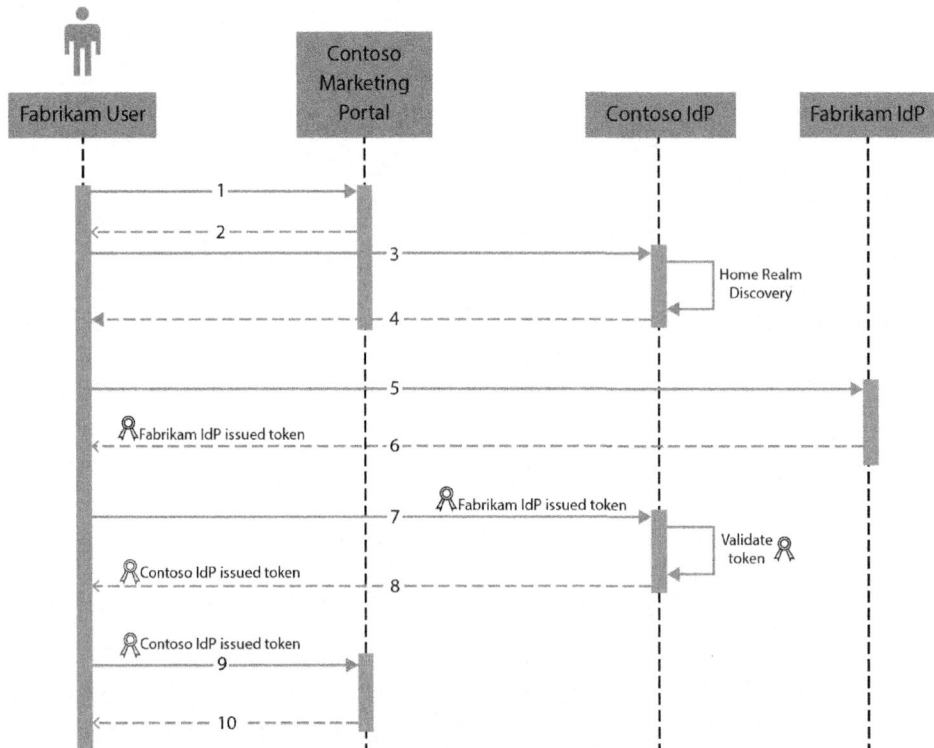

Figure 1.6 – User authentication flow with two IdPs

Once the federation between Contoso and Fabrikam is in place, then a Fabrikam user can initiate an authentication flow to access Contoso's marketing portal. The flow is described as follows:

1. A Fabrikam user accesses the URL of the marketing portal from their browser.

2. The marketing portal checks whether the user is authenticated; if not, it redirects (HTTP 302) them to ContosoIdP.

3. ContosoIdP asks for a user's proof of authentication, which typically translates into asking for the user's username first. ContosoIdP checks whether it can authenticate the user associated with the typed username (that is, whether the user belongs to the Contoso *realm*) or whether it needs to delegate authentication to FabrikamIdP. This process is called HRD.

4. ContosoIdP understands that the user is from Fabrikam and it redirects them to FabrikamIdP.

5. The user inserts their credentials into the FabrikamIdP login page, which validates them and authenticates the user.

6. Upon successful authentication, FabrikamIdP issues a *signed security token* and redirects the user back to ContosoIdP.

7. ContosoIdP validates the signed security token signature and reads the claims within it.

8. ContosoIdP issues a new signed security token and redirects the user back to the marketing portal (the service provider).

9. The user browser sends the *signed security token* to the marketing portal, which validates its signature and reads the claims within it.

10. If the user is authorized, access is granted to the marketing portal.

This example provides several important insights into how a federation and its components work and interact with each other. It is worth noting the following:

- The marketing portal (the service provider) is not aware of the existence of FabrikamIdP, it just trusts tokens issued by ContosoIdP.

- ContosoIdP will always issue a token signed with the certificate/key published in its metadata. It does not relay the token received by FabrikamIdP because service providers federated with ContosoIdP won't trust the signature of this token.

Cookies and tokens

Some of you may be wondering why we haven't mentioned the concept of *cookies* in this discussion. **Cookies** and **tokens** are different entities and must not be confused with each other, even though they are very often found together. A *cookie* (also known as an *internet cookie*, *web cookie*, or *browser cookie*) is a web application artifact used by web browsers to store information about a user's session. It is typically created by web servers when users visit their hosted websites. In other words, a cookie is a way of creating a stateful interaction between the user and a website. A token, on the other hand, is a block of structured data (for example, issuer ID, claims, audience, and so on) strictly related to an authentication protocol, which can usually be embedded within a cookie by the applications themselves.

In the following sections, we will have a closer look at real-world federation implementations – the WS-Federation and SAML protocols.

WS-Federation

Everybody remembers **Simple Object Access Protocol** (**SOAP**). SOAP was one of the very first protocols whose goal was to standardize communication messages for web services among computers in a network. SOAP uses **eXtensible Markup Language** (**XML**) as its message format and leverages protocols such as HTTP for its communication layer because of its great utilization among the most common operating systems, such as Windows, Linux, and macOS.

WS-Federation is part of the **WS-Security** framework (published by OASIS), which is an extension of SOAP created to standardize the *security* of web services in terms of the confidentiality and integrity of their messages. WS-Federation's purpose is to unify the way different *realms* (which could be different companies or different units within the same company) manage identities and authentication by creating a common way of exchanging user information among their web services.

We know federation is based on trust, but how can we establish trust between two web services? WS-Federation introduced the concept of federation metadata to solve this problem. The **federation metadata** is an XML file published by a web service to share all the information needed to establish a trust relationship with the realm that the web service belongs to. The web service could be either an IdP or a service provider, and the information in the metadata differs according to which role the web service has:

- In an IdP, the typical information within the federation metadata file includes claims definitions, the IdP identifiers and endpoints, and the public keys of the certificates used to sign and encrypt the responses and the tokens issued by the IdP's STS (defined in the WS-Trust specification, also part of the WS-Security framework)

- In a service provider, the typical information includes the service provider identifiers and endpoints and the public keys of the certificates used to sign and encrypt the requests to the IdP's STS

Once a federation has been established and the parties have exchanged the information, users belonging to the realm where the IdP is located can start using web services provided by the realm where the service provider is.

There are two ways (or *profiles*, as defined within the protocol specification) to implement an authentication flow: the **WS-Federation Passive Requestor Profile** and the **WS-Federation Active Requestor Profile**, which will be briefly described next.

WS-Federation Passive Requestor Profile

A web browser, the *Passive Requestor Profile*, tries to access the web service resource that requires the requestor to be authenticated. If the requestor hasn't already obtained proof of authentication, then it is redirected to its identity provider's STS where, after successful authentication, it will obtain a security token. This security token will be redirected to the web service resource, which will decide whether to authorize access based on the information included in the token.

This flow is a typical *service-provider-initiated flow*, where the passive requestor tries to access the service provider directly. A slightly different flow, called the *identity-provider-initiated flow*, starts with a web browser (the passive requestor) accessing the IdP first but specifies in the request the web service resource (the service provider) it would like to be redirected to after successful authentication.

WS-Federation Active Requestor Profile

WS-Federation added the *Active Requestor Profile* to support all those clients that behave as active requestors. An active requestor (which could be a native application running on Windows or Linux), unlike a web browser (a passive requestor), which passively follows the redirections provided by the web service resources it would like to access, collects the information needed for the authentication first (typically, the username and the password of a user) and then it sends them directly to the identity provider's STS to obtain a security token that can later be used to get access to the web service resource (the service provider) if the user is authorized. The IdP usually exposes a dedicated HTTP endpoint to enable this flow.

In the next section, we will focus on another important authentication protocol: SAML.

Security Assertion Markup Language (SAML)

The OASIS **Security Services Technical Committee** (**SSTC**), in 2001, had the very ambitious goal of defining an XML framework that could be used for exchanging authentication and authorization information. WS-Federation only partially achieved this as SAML also adopted the XML format for the request and response messages, unofficially signing the death warrant for the declining SOAP specification.

The SAML protocol came out of the joint efforts of several companies that were part of this committee as a passive and claim-based authentication protocol for federated identities.

The SAML specification defines three roles:

- The *principal* (typically, this is a user, also known as the *subject*)
- The *IdP*
- The *service provider*

In a typical SAML use case, the principal requests a service from the service provider. The service provider usually redirects a user accessing it from a web browser to the IdP to obtain an authentication assertion (a signed security token). Based on the assertions included in the token, the service provider can decide whether to authorize the security principal that completed the authentication flow or simply block the access because the requested permissions cannot be requested.

Before issuing the signed security token to the service provider, the IdP may require the user to prove their identity, usually by asking for a username and a password.

Here is an example of an extract from a signed SAML response token:

```
<?xml version="1.0" encoding="utf-16"?>
[..]
    <Issuer
```

```
xmlns="urn:oasis:names:tc:SAML:2.0:assertion">http://sts.
katsuton.com/adfs/services/trust</Issuer>
    <samlp:Status>
        <samlp:StatusCode
Value="urn:oasis:names:tc:SAML:2.0:status:Success" />
    </samlp:Status>
[..]
        <ds:Signature xmlns:ds="http://www.w3.org/2000/09/
xmldsig#">
[..]
            <ds:SignatureMethod Algorithm="http://www.
w3.org/2001/04/xmldsig-more#rsa-sha256" />
[..]
    <ds:SignatureValue>OUPJpFsnUODCK2h7T5SYMVhlWDnCBT6Qy
T9CcVnrjcWUPZTAaz2FNGEpPPhb/P9kW23cw5D1+fjhtAQurN/
Du9uYfdkGtXcTPfcOOVfuzgQT1d75HmYnbAtTvhsOrS8gvGCY6o
Jk3wsqNar3hrqLHDFxsszY41lZvOe2/
Qax1SMpHeglQSbu6WOFe3sPdSiLY8rnWBE5QubS85N1E+HNvjHqXS7Luwr
RDNK0InMM+LdPZw1YdOGUikgTbyIFKMR/
eXR5UqbVrvmwv58XxT9C5p7FYPu3eKjWLD2aGjCnJufFNfHiVGYrB8OU1FN1E/
2sLNXnSuMyNnQJ5iWCQWP3vQ==</ds:SignatureValue>
[..]
        </ds:Signature>
<Subject>
<NameID Format="urn:oasis:names:tc:SAML:2.0:nameid-
format:persistent">fabarca@katsuton.com</NameID>
</Subject>
[..]
        <Conditions NotBefore="2021-06-28T09:26:39.720Z"
NotOnOrAfter="2021-06-28T09:27:39.720Z">
            <AudienceRestriction>
    <Audience>urn:microsoft:adfs:claimsxray</Audience>
            </AudienceRestriction>
        </Conditions>
        <AttributeStatement>
            <Attribute
Name="http://schemas.xmlsoap.org/ws/2005/05/identity/claims/
name">
```

```
      <AttributeValue>kadmin</AttributeValue>
          </Attribute>
          </AttributeStatement>
[..]
</samlp:Response>
```

Let's discuss the main pieces of information within the token:

- **Issuer**: This is the identifier of the IdP that issued the token.

- **Status code**: The status code of the whole authentication process. If anything other than success is returned, then the receiving party (typically, the service provider) has to raise an error.

- **Signature method**: The signature algorithm that's used to sign the token.

- **Signature**: The signature of the token. The signature can be calculated for the entire response or just for the assertions within the token: it must be agreed upon upfront between the parties involved.

- **Validity**: The time window when the token is considered valid. Once the token has expired, the user must return to the IdP and ask for another token.

- **NameId**: The SAML token's part that uniquely identifies the user. It can contain the user's username in different formats (for example, `userprincipalname` format), which are usually specified in the `Format` attribute.

- **Audience**: The party the token has been issued for. An application (service provider) must control whether the token it receives has been issued for itself and not for another application by checking the `Audience` field.

- **Attributes** (*claims*): A list of assertions regarding the authenticated user needed by the service provider to authorize access and implement its business logic.

Most of the information provided here can be found in different types of tokens, such as JWTs in the OAuth 2.0 and OIDC protocols. To avoid confusion, please note that SAML is both the name of the token format and the protocol. WS-Federation uses SAML tokens within its authentication flows.

SAML does not specify which method of authentication must be used by the IdP. This is a key point: SAML was created to rely on existing authentication protocols. It naturally integrates with them as its source of authentication. Kerberos, LDAP, and Active Directory can still be used as SAML sources of authentication while leaving the SAML protocol with the task of federating with the identities of external companies.

Summary

This chapter covered both technical and non-technical topics. In the first few sections of this chapter, we were provided with an overview of the current market landscape, where identities are used, and the differences between the markets. We also discussed how the evolution of identity protocols has enabled a simplification of the UX and an improvement in user engagement in the services that delegate the authentication logic to external IdPs. This chapter also drilled down to showcase the technical landscape of the identities around today, the most common protocols, and a specific emphasis on SSO, which is widely adopted in the enterprise market.

In the next chapter, we will provide a historical overview of cloud identity and its evolution in enterprises, why it is needed, and the difference between cloud and hybrid identities. We will also provide an overview of the future of identity technologies.

2
The Cloud Era and Identity

This chapter will discuss the current technology landscape. It will provide a basic idea about the trends, the evolution of technology, and the typical challenges of identity management and governance at this moment in time. Knowing the current technology landscape promotes interoperability because then, organizations can easily collaborate by using common standards and enterprise architects are equipped with the means to design modern, secure, and reliable applications.

This chapter is focused on preparing you to better understand the technical details that will be provided in the upcoming sections.

In this chapter, we'll cover the following topics:

- The cloud era
- Identity in the cloud era
- The challenges of identity
- The cloud identity
- A hybrid identity
- The future of identity

The cloud era

The cloud is boosting productivity and changing the components and tools used in application architectures, which, in turn, are *affecting the way software is designed*.

As a matter of fact, according to Gartner's research, the total cloud market will reach something around 600,000,000,000 (billion) USD of overall revenue before 2023 with a double-digit percentage increase year by year.

As outlined in the previous chapter, user requirements are evolving, growing, and changing, and as a consequence, the technology paradigms, standards, and patterns are following the user requirements and evolving in parallel. In this chapter, we are going to have a detailed look at the impact market change has had on technology and software development, specifically identity.

We'll start by viewing the present-day technology from a high-level point of view, regardless of the specific identity. If we think about IT a few years ago, there was the concept of a system administrator or infrastructure consultant and software developer or dev consultant. This distinction exists today as well but the line between them is getting more blurred every day. That is because, until a few years ago, companies used to have their own data center and needed system administrators to ensure the infrastructure worked properly; in the same way, they needed software developers to ensure the software was developed and that it worked. The cloud has developed and is changing our understanding of concepts.

Infrastructure is considered to be a commodity and not something companies need to administer anymore. System administrators are gradually pivoting their skills to support their companies in different and more efficient ways. Today, an infrastructure consultant is the one who takes care of either the Kubernetes cluster being properly configured or an infrastructure-as-code pipeline working correctly, rather than focusing on server configuration as happened in an on-premises environment. In the DevOps world, the system administrator works closely with software developers and their job roles merge at multiple junctures. If we think about it, an infrastructure-as-code pipeline is similar to a pipeline that follows the same principles of code development.

The following is a graph that is going to show how the most famous on-premises technology had been superseded by many cloud providers, according to Google's search engine trends:

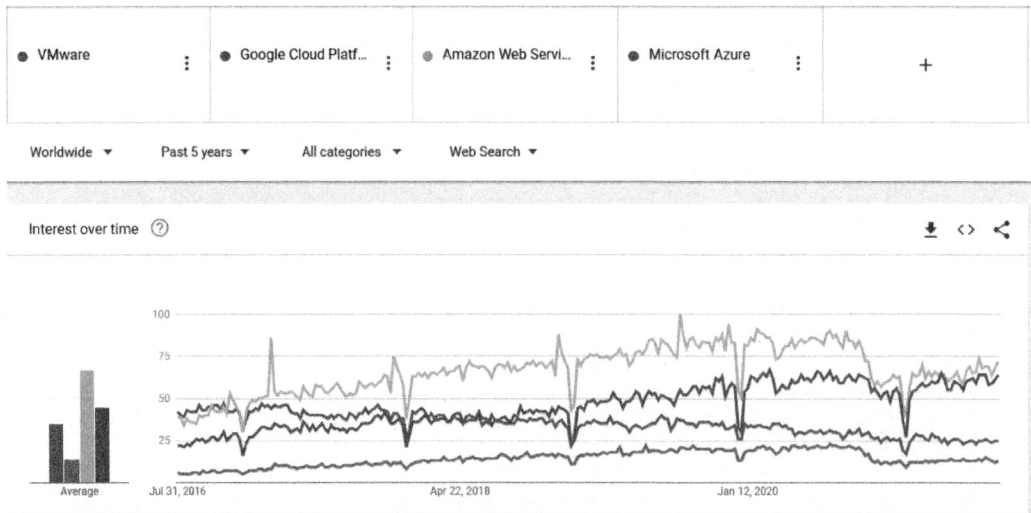

Figure 2.1 – Evolution of cloud trends over time versus the most famous
on-premises virtualization according to Google trends

Let's have a look at the implications and how identity fits into the picture.

Living in a cloud era doesn't mean simply offloading some IT complexities to the cloud providers. Living in a cloud era is about the uptime of services and whether these services are accessible every time (ideally) and everywhere from heterogeneous devices.

Living in a cloud era also means that more services are exposed to the internet and, hence, more accessible. Additionally, it also means there is a user-centric approach where the ease of service adoption and productivity capabilities for an employee or a customer using the service is one of the most crucial aspects to consider because it is indirectly connected with monetization. All of this has a direct implication for security and identity, which are two highly coupled factors in the cloud era.

It is not possible to understand the impact of the cloud on identity if we don't try to understand how security paradigms change in the cloud first.

In the pre-cloud era, we worked for different institutions such as banks, public administration, and commercial companies that used to have a very weak security posture in their internal network. They used to pay attention to and invest in enforcing the network perimeter with firewalls and making the system inaccessible from the outside. This made them feel safe. The fact, however, was that to ensure passwords were strong and best security practices were adopted, a constant inspection of the internal perimeter, in addition to process revision, was required, and the standards that needed to be followed were pretty expensive. That's why many companies only focused their investments on firewalls, reverse proxies, and web application firewalls to prevent access from the outside. This has been the security approach of many companies in the pre-cloud era – a strong perimeter nobody could get past and usually very weak security defense within the company. We can compare it to a medieval city with very high and protected walls but with no weaponry or protection inside, where, if an attacker had entered, they could have killed everyone.

However, this practice wasn't actually recommended, even in the past. The common suggestion was to have good security on the inside too and always work under the assumption that an attacker has already entered (a defense-in-depth approach). The reality, however, for most enterprises that we visited was different. We worked for several banks and government entities that had very simple passwords, which a hacker would have guessed in a couple of attempts. Despite our recommendations to enforce internal security processes, it never happened and wasn't seriously perceived as a priority. We went back to these companies a few months ago and found that the company had finally migrated to the cloud and all our previous pieces of advice had finally been implemented.

Let's have a look at the rationale behind this – why the cloud has been a driver to adopt an in-depth defense strategy within companies rather than just at the boundary.

Cloud services, especially **Platform-as-a-Service (PaaS)** ones, are created to be accessible through the public internet. Despite cloud providers providing a mechanism to insert PaaS into private networks, placing them in a network is usually expensive, and cloud services, in general, don't have a network. The idea is to be able to develop a service quickly and make it easily available for internal users and consumers. This is where identity comes into play, as it is turning out to be one of the most important security measures to ensure services are not improperly accessed.

To get an idea of how the multi-factor authentication (which will be discussed in greater detail in later chapters) security measure trend has evolved over the last 5 years, refer to the graph, which outlines the trend according to Google (source: `https://trends.google.com`):

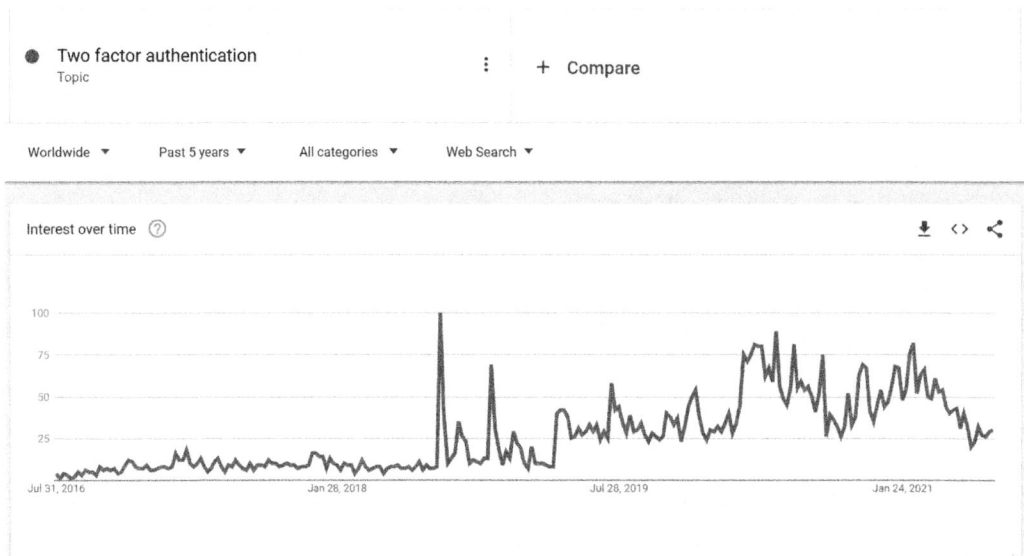

Figure 2.2 – The search trends for two-factor authentication on Google in the last 5 years

With the cloud, a stronger security mechanism is required for identity verification. This doesn't mean that two-factor authentication is new. As a matter of fact, it existed even before the cloud era, and many providers made it available for on-premises installation. It's just that it was not a priority for companies because of their security boundaries. That's the reason why identity management is the foundation of modern security.

Zero-trust security principles are now widely adopted by many companies from different markets. This makes them more confident to embrace cloud technology, reduce time to market, become more agile, and reduce security exposure.

The cloud didn't just pivot priorities in terms of security principles; it enabled a new protocol to be used in an open ecosystem (the internet) rather than in an internal enterprise accessible with VPN only (an intranet).

Figure 2.3 shows the trend comparison in the last 5 years, according to Google Trends, between an authentication protocol commonly used on-premises (Kerberos) with OAuth, which is a protocol commonly used on the public internet today that implements a delegation framework that authorizes applications to act on behalf of a user:

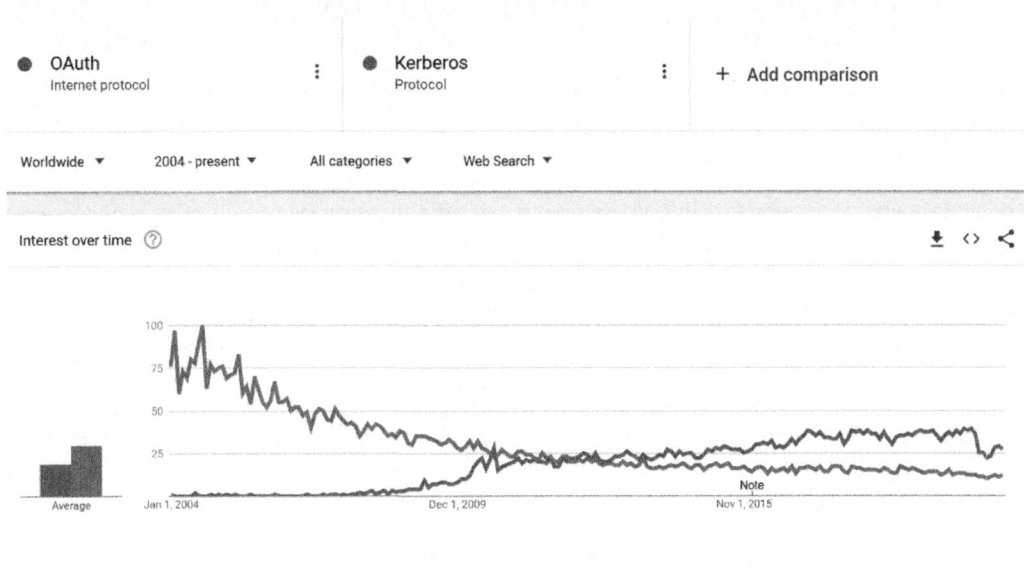

Figure 2.3 – Trend comparison between a historical enterprise protocol (Kerberos) versus OAuth

Another important implication of the cloud is that architectural design paradigms have changed – today, there is the concept of microservices applications, which are usually applications designed with independent components and an independent life cycle. Having these components decoupled means they can be built and deployed independently and can even be written in different programming languages, as they are usually interconnected through the HTTP protocol. They can also be developed by different independent software companies.

Gaining this kind of component granularity in a cloud solution will enable better scaling (each component can scale independently to the others) and control (developers do not need to know about the whole complexity of the application; they just need to know the contracts between components and about the single component they are developing). This means that every time an independent portion of the application needs to communicate with another independent block, authentication takes place, which, in turn, has an impact on identity. To seamlessly integrate microservices, a common identity system should be used to reduce complexity while increasing interoperability and trust between the different components of the application.

Another architectural trend is to distribute application components across different hosting platforms without letting developers worry about where their code is actually running, also known as a serverless application. This pattern is very similar to microservices. In microservices, the services often communicate through a public channel and not within an internal network, protected from external access. In times such as these, when a service communicates with another on a public channel, identity management is even more important from a security perspective because it is sometimes the only security mechanism in place. This can help us understand why reliable authentication is paramount for these kinds of architectures.

It is paramount for an enterprise to implement a clear identity governance strategy and, most importantly, adapt itself to a very fast-moving world, where protocols are evolving continuously, to guarantee further reliability and improve security principles.

Designing a next-generation identity system requires specific attention from enterprise architects who want to take advantage of cloud capabilities. Too often, different OAuth **Identity Providers (IdPs)**, or even custom ones, are used by developers of the same enterprise without clear guidelines or criteria for which one to use and why. Other times, we can find situations where a single enterprise adopts one IdP to authenticate on a specific API and another IdP for a different one. This creates chaos and challenges whenever an application needs to take advantage of both.

That's the reason why identity services and, as a consequence, authentication mechanisms need to be carefully designed in advance so that developers can take advantage of decisions taken by an architect with the full picture in mind.

Now that we have an idea about the importance of identity in the cloud era, it is time to take a closer look at what is out there and what pillars an enterprise needs to take into account to be cloud-ready and prepared for the future.

Identity in the cloud era

Nowadays, there are plenty of standards, protocols, and practices related to identity. Some of them have been outlined in the previous chapter and are *must-know* concepts for an identity expert. Regardless, these concepts can get very complicated.

Just to give a brief idea of what we are talking about, the following is a list (but not an exhaustive report) of the available standards at the time of writing. It is important to note that some of the standards or protocols we have mentioned are still in draft (under development) at the time of writing:

- **Passwordless:**
  - **World Wide Web Consortium (W3C):**
    - WebAuthn
  - FIDO:
    - **Client to Authenticator Protocol (CTAP)**

- **Authentication/authorization:**

  - OpenID Foundation:

    - OpenID Connect

    - **Continuous Access Evaluation Protocol (CAEP)**

    - Shared Signals and Events

    - FastFed

    - OpenID Connect Federation (`https://openid.net/specs/openid-connect-federation-1_0.html`)

  - IETF:

    - OAuth

    - **System for Cross-Domain Identity Management (SCIM)**

    - **Grant Negotiation and Authorization Protocol (GNAP)**

- **Decentralized identity:**

  - DIF:

    - Presentation Exchange

    - Sidetree and ION

    - Zero-knowledge proof protocol (`https://www.blockchain-council.org/blockchain/zero-knowledge-proof-protocol/`)

    - Well-known **Decentralized Identities (DID)** configuration

    - Credential Manifest

  - IETF:

    - JSONPath

  - W3C:

    - **Decentralized Identifiers (DID-core)** (`https://www.w3.org/TR/did-core/`)

  - OpenID Foundation:

    - Self-issued OpenID provider

  - ISO

- Overview of existing **Distributed Ledger Technology (DLT)** systems for identity management
- Overview of trust anchors for DLT-based identity management

- Cards and security devices for personal identification:

  - Personal identification – ISO-compliant driving license

- Information security, cybersecurity, and privacy protection:

  - ISO:

    - 27560: Privacy technologies – Consent record information structure
    - 24760-2: A framework for identity management
    - 29115: Entity authentication assurance framework
    - 27554: Application of ISO 31000 for identity management-related risk

We have assisted a small number of enterprises that had applications with custom authentication protocols that didn't follow any standard in their portfolio. This prevented smooth interoperability between the two authentication systems, which, for instance, would have been integrated if they had used a standard federation protocol instead. This is, of course, a bad practice, as we're going to understand in the rest of this section.

We are living in an era where not only identity but also technology, in general, represents a core asset of almost every company in the world. Cloud solutions need to be reliable and scalable and, as such, standardization matters. Moreover, we are living in a cloud era where laptops, mobile devices, and sensors need to be to be authenticated and authorized seamlessly to the systems regardless of where they are in terms of physical location. If a company wants to provide these capabilities and be properly prepared in the cloud era, these are the points that need to be taken care of, which are true for identity as well:

- Standardization
- Portability
- Reliability
- Security
- Agility

We will try to understand why they are so important in the upcoming sections.

The pillars of a cloud company

Standardization is a core concept in IT, which is not only valid for identities but also forms the core principles for most things concerned with IT.

As we go through this section, we'll see that the five core pillars of a cloud company are centered around the concept of standardization. Standardization is a necessary condition for all the other pillars to exist.

The following diagram will report the core pillars required by a company that wants to embrace the cloud. Standardization is the central one and all the other pillars are based around it:

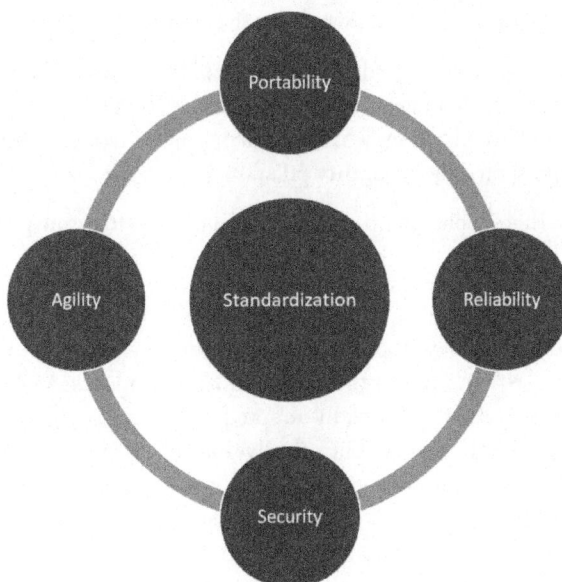

Figure 2.4 – The pillars of a cloud company

According to `igi-global.com`, this concept is defined as follows:

> *Formulation, publication, and implementation of guidelines, rules, methods, procedures and specifications for common and repeated use, aimed at achieving optimum degree of order or uniformity in given context, discipline, or field; standards are most frequently developed on international level; there exist national standardization bodies cooperating with international bodies; standards can be either legally binding or de facto standards followed by informal convention or voluntary standards.*

`(https://www.igi-global.com/dictionary/interoperability-medical-devices-information-systems/28157)`

This definition is true for enabling interoperability not only across different companies that need to adopt a common standard but also within a single company to ensure they adopt something that is well-proven and maintained by a group of experts.

Setting standards and rules that are universal for all companies across the board is important for a number of reasons, such as the following:

- **Portability**: Something can be portable to another platform if that platform follows the same standards.

- **Reliability**: Adopting standards that are well-tested and enterprise-ready provides more assurance and reliability of the overall solution wherever the standard is adopted.

- **Security**: If something is a standard, it often implies that it's adopted widely and so is proven to be reliable and secure. Standardization often ensures that specs can be followed at scale by replicating the standard adoption, which, in turn, is a concept connected to the capability to be agile and is represented by the **agility** pillar.

- **Interoperability**: This enables companies or manufacturers to create products that can interact with each other.

To understand the concept better, let's suppose there's a company that developed its own authentication and authorization protocol for its own applications and defined it as a standard protocol to be adopted inside the company. Can we then say that they are following standards? Well, not really. A standard is supposed to be widely discussed and broadly adopted to become truly advantageous for its users. Just establishing a new standard developed by ourselves for our company does not guarantee that it is reliable and secure. Standards can indeed enhance reliability and security. In these instances, the employees or a restricted circle of people within the company who developed the standard cannot be asked to prove the reliability and security of the standard. In other words, this protocol would not be a standard outside of the company. Moreover, the company needs to maintain and invest effort, time, and money to keep the standard up to date in the cloud world, which evolves faster than ever. This is something that a company may want to avoid. Just as an example, let's talk about the security aspect. A hacker may exploit our standard protocol in a way that the small group of people who developed it didn't think about. A vulnerability exploit would require much more effort on a protocol adopted worldwide, where security exploits are usually published and fixed. The previous example is perfectly in line with *security by obscurity* and *security by design*, as system security should not depend on the secrecy of the implementation of its component. The same example can be extended to the reliability of a protocol. Generally speaking, something is more reliable if it is widely adopted and proven.

This is how the adoption of international or de facto standards that are widely adopted makes a positive difference in multiple ways. Contrary to the early days of IT, it is very rare nowadays to come across a company that wants to develop its own standards.

Agility and portability are other important factors to take into account. Since these terms are strictly connected, we are going to cover them together. *Agility* is the ability of a company to create efficiency with a low time to market. *Portability* is the capability of a company to move from one platform to another with zero or very little effort. Following a standard can enable a company to adopt a standard on multiple platforms and, as a consequence, move across cloud environments easily, rather than developing code or creating ad hoc customization. Let's suppose our application adopts a standard authentication protocol; the company can decide years later to move to a different IdP or cloud vendor that has adopted the very same standard without hassle. This is also important since most companies want to avoid vendor lock-in and also be free to choose any vendor without technical restrictions. This is an example of agility enabled by embracing standardization.

Let's take a look at the top challenges concerning identity.

The challenges of identity

When we think about the definition of a new specification, a new standard, or a new protocol in the identity area, we may imagine a lot of experts having multiple meetings to look for an optimal solution and define the perfect standard. What we tend to underestimate is that these experts cannot invent a new protocol without taking into account several technical constraints and the technical limitation of the market. In other words, their output is usually a trade-off. They need to consider how the browsers work, how HTTP works, what the behaviors of the browser on specific HTTP returning code are, and how the standard they are going to define usually sits on top of this. They cannot just invent what they believe is a perfect protocol from scratch.

This is because the history of IT and, more specifically, the internet clearly shows that de facto standards are much harder to bypass – we cannot force a model if this model requires a change in technology that is not yet implemented. In the early days of the internet, there was an attempt to force the adoption of the OSI stack. This didn't work because TCP/IP was widely used at the time and that's what became a standard.

We cannot, for instance, define a standard that implies behaviors a browser does not yet implement and force it. Likely, it will not work. Suppose we try to access an application we are not yet authenticated against and we want to prevent our username and password from being exposed to the application. We need a way for the user not to be prompted again for their credentials. One of the few ways to ensure the user is authenticated without submitting the password directly to the application is to take advantage of the HTTP status code 302. The related browser behavior is going to take the user to a different page and take advantage of another redirection to take the user back to the original application once they have provided their credentials to the IdP. This behavior will be better explained later in the book when we cover the technical aspects of OAuth flows.

It's important to keep in mind that a spec represents a trade-off between the possibilities offered by the current technology standards and the objective of this spec. In the case of OAuth, we're talking about a trade-off between the best grade of reliability and security for authentication and the features offered by the technologies, such as browsers and HTTP.

Another thing to consider when defining a new protocol is who is going to consume it. OAuth, for example, is a general-purpose protocol that is supposed to be consumed by both internet and enterprise users (see also the *Digital transformation – the impact on the market* section in *Chapter 1, Walkthrough of Digital Identity in the Enterprise*), unlike many other protocols, such as Kerberos, which are more enterprise-oriented. Making the protocol usable for both markets is another degree of complexity that makes the challenge for the authors even bigger. When creating the OAuth specification, just to give you an example, over the course of 22 revisions of the standard, the web and enterprise contributors continued to disagree on fundamental issues. The only way to resolve the disagreements and continue making progress was to pull out the conflicting issues and put them into their own drafts, leaving holes in the spec that were called *extensible*. All of this may create ambiguity and complexity during the definition of a standard, which, as you may understand, is not an easy job at all.

One thing that is worth noting is that at the moment of writing, there are some trends driven by important internet players (such as Google, Microsoft, and Apple) that may change certain behavior of browsers. There is a common wish to prevent third-party cookies from being used and the main browser makers are finding alternative ways to achieve a similar goal. This topic is out of the scope of this book; for further information, we recommend watching this interesting video that covers the topic in depth: `https://www.youtube.com/watch?v=1g2uQfP1Q3U&t=138s`. What we want to highlight here is that browsing is evolving as well, and as a consequence, the constraints are changing and new opportunities for even more effective, emergent protocols approach.

Once a spec becomes available, the next step is to understand the degree of adoption, and OAuth is one of, if not the, best trends in the area of identity.

In any case, regardless of the protocol that needs to be adopted, when we are focusing on the enterprise, one of the most important things is to define standards to be adopted and followed even within the company. When a company creates new applications that need to interact with each other or, as outlined in the *The cloud era* section, even parts of the application that interact with each other, this requires defining a common model, as a model is important for avoiding anarchy and keeping a good governance model. This is where the enterprise architect comes into the picture. They need to dictate what standards the company intends to adopt for each possible case, and they need to define guidelines. Let's look at an example of why an enterprise architect must do this by contextualizing what is happening right now in the enterprise area.

Nowadays, companies are focusing on software development to support the business, rather than on infrastructure to support software development, and as a consequence, the skills required in IT are pivoting as well.

During our experiences, we noticed that, often, software development is outsourced to external companies, which are focused mainly on mere delivery. These external companies usually don't focus on important aspects such as identity management and security. Their goal is to achieve the most with the minimum effort to increase the margin, or in other words, the dollars they are going to gain from a specific engagement. According to our experience, in these circumstances, it is likely that an external company will strictly follow only the basic requirements in the contracts and not always the best practices. This scenario is where a good enterprise architect of the company comes into play – they need to provide requirements that include quality, security, and extensibility of the solution. For example, suppose an external company or vendor has been contracted by your company for the development of an API. This API can be written in many different ways, but in order to take advantage of OAuth protocol capabilities, which will be outlined later in the book when we cover the technical part, it may be important for this API to handle different scopes. As a matter of fact, a consumer may be interested in only reading specific content and, as such, requires an **access token** that only has the read scope, which implicitly means that they are not allowed to write, in order to follow the least-privilege principle and best practice. If the API in question is not developed to handle a scenario such as this, it may not be possible to take full advantage of the OAuth protocol, which suggests the usage of scopes in the token instead.

The concept is broad, and what we've discussed is just the current context we have. You may have already read about some examples of other challenges in the chapter. There are challenges to defining an identity strategy, such as API reusability, so we are not going to focus further on that. We assume that at this point, you have a high-level idea of why having an identity strategy is important.

The cloud identity

In identity, standards are a serious thing. According to the Business Dictionary (`https://businessdictionary.info/`), a standard is defined as a "*formulation, publication and implementation of guidelines, rules, and specification for common and repeated use, aimed at achieving the optimum degree of order or uniformity in a given context, discipline, or field.*" This sentence encompasses brilliantly why standardization is so important – by adopting standards and protocols commonly agreed upon by a vast community of people, enterprises are enabled to make choices without having an active participation in the realization of the model that needs to be developed.

In the previous chapter, we talked about the cloud being a hugely transformational phenomenon that has greatly impacted our lives by making a plethora of services available to people in all parts of the world, all thanks to the distributed nature of cloud services.

Up-and-coming companies were provided with a series of ready-to-use tools that allowed them to start their journey to make a profit quickly (whatever that journey was) by using cloud-native services. New companies didn't have the burden of managing and modernizing an existing IT infrastructure, which was likely to have been used by companies long before the cloud became the most common means of providing services to end users and organizations.

New companies started building their IT infrastructure from scratch (the so-called *greenfield* scenario) so they could pick up the best technology for their needs from a great number of available cloud services, including those needed to manage their identity assets and everything related to the authentication and authorization of their users. We may now have a good understanding of the importance of having a good identity strategy (this topic will be discussed in greater detail later in this chapter) – cloud services have simplified the adoption and implementation curve of information technologies. However, greater caution should be used when choosing the best service to accommodate your company's identity needs because that means putting your most valuable asset in the hands of another company, which must be implicitly trusted and thoroughly scrutinized.

Nowadays, several actors provide authentication and identity services as PaaS or **Software as a Service (SaaS)**. The most famous are Microsoft Azure **Active Directory (AD)**, Google Identity, Amazon Cognito, and Okta.

Each of the preceding cloud IdPs has built its own implementation of the web authentication protocols described in the previous chapter by making different technical choices and, at the same time, agreeing on others, such as the adoption of the same token format (JSON Web Token) for OAuth and OpenID Connect protocols. Creating this kind of convention is fundamental for interoperability and healthy competition, where the real key differentiators between one technology and another are the additional features on top of the mere authentication and authorization capabilities defined in the protocol RFCs.

This does not mean that an enterprise architect should ignore how a protocol works just because another organization has already implemented and provided it as a commodity. On the contrary, deeper protocol knowledge and understanding highly simplifies and accelerates the adoption of cloud services because the architect can focus on and harness the real differentiators that a particular service provides as compared to its competitors.

Without diving into the details and the features of a specific cloud IdP (*Chapter 8, Real-World Identity Provider – A Zoom-In on Azure Active Directory*, is dedicated to Azure AD), let's try to focus on the different types of identities that a cloud IdP can usually manage. As a matter of fact, an enterprise architect should understand the importance of and the difference between managing **cloud-only identities** and **hybrid identities**. Let's focus on the former now.

A cloud identity directly originates in the cloud and seldom has an on-premises counterpart. As discussed previously, it is unlikely that a newly born company will have the hardware to host its servers. The best way of reducing the *go-to-market* curve in these particular and common scenarios is to purchase IT services directly from external organizations that provide them as SaaS either through a licensing or consumption model (no upfront costs, just **Operating Expenses (OPEX)**).

Imagine you are the IT administrator of an emerging start-up and you need to quickly start managing different IT assets of the new company. You will likely be asked at the very beginning to find a solution that allows the management of users and identities. As the passionate IT administrator that you are, you will likely start developing a solution by yourself at first, but once you understand the effort and the time needed to accomplish this endeavor, you will likely shift your ideas into using an existing end-to-end solution that provides a faster and more convenient way to start with (for those who are still interested in creating their own solution, there are several GitHub repositories that may help you with that, such as `https://github.com/IdentityServer/IdentityServer4`, now turned into a commercial solution).

Now, let's say that you select the best cloud IdP that fits your requirements – for example, Azure AD. You then start creating all the identities one by one for the people that need an account to access your company's assets. In the beginning, everything looks fine and you are proud of the great job you've done so far. As your company grows, you will, however, likely need to have some automation in place and delegate different business unit accounts and identities of your soon-to-be enterprise organization to different people and different tools. How can you handle this complexity?

Before answering this question, first, we need to distinguish between the concept of identities and user accounts (or simply users or accounts). Identity is a broader term that encompasses the whole life cycle and information regarding a person or employee within a company. This information may include the employee's salary, family contacts, and contract duration, and, theoretically, all these pieces of information may live independently from the existence of a user account. Typically, the information around a person is stored in a **Human Capital Management** (**HCM**) system and it may span different tools and systems within a company.

A user account, on the other hand, can be defined as the security principal associated with a specific identity. A security principal is an entity usually used within an authentication system that can be assigned to one or more roles or permissions for other entities defined within the same authentication system. A user account is comprised of user credentials (typically, a username and a password), which, together with the account's roles and permissions, are bound to a specific authentication system or IdP. Ideally, a unique IdP should be used to manage all user accounts in one company.

How do identities and user accounts relate to each other? Systems containing information about identities are usually the source of authority for the user accounts associated with them. This means that each identity might have one or more user accounts associated with it, although the best-case scenario is when each identity has only one user account.

If you've paid attention, it must be clear now that the problem we are talking about is user provisioning. The user provisioning process is basically the activity that relates identities and user accounts by automating the creation of accounts based on the information of the corresponding identity. A separate user provisioning tool can be used for this goal, which basically interacts with both the system where identities are stored (such as an HCM system) and the IdP (such as Azure AD) to synchronize the information from the former to the latter based on some business logic, such as *assign the administrator role to all those identities that have a job role in the IT department*. The Azure AD user provisioning tool is shown in the following screenshot:

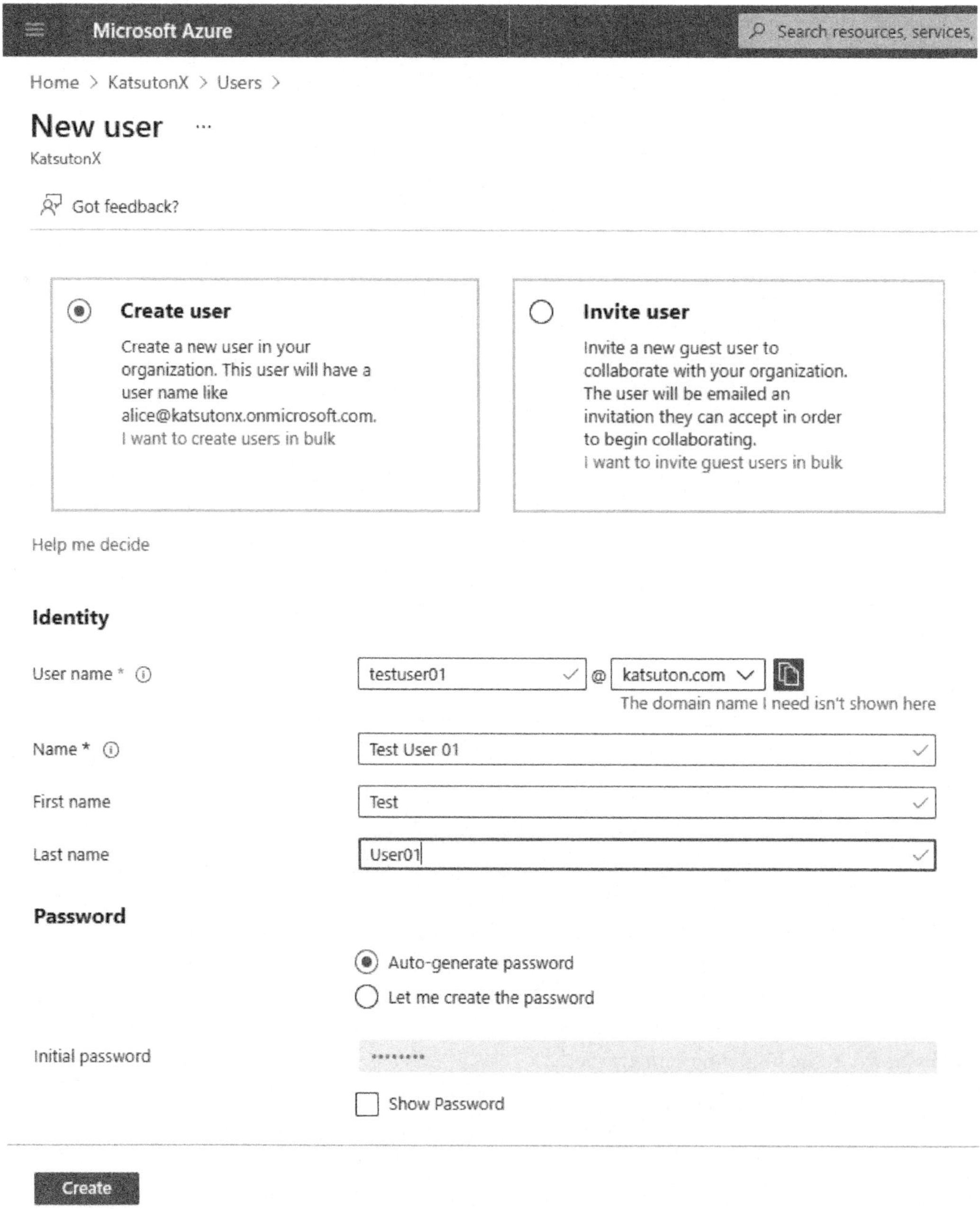

Figure 2.5 – Azure AD user creation example

The Google user provisioning tool is shown in the following screenshot:

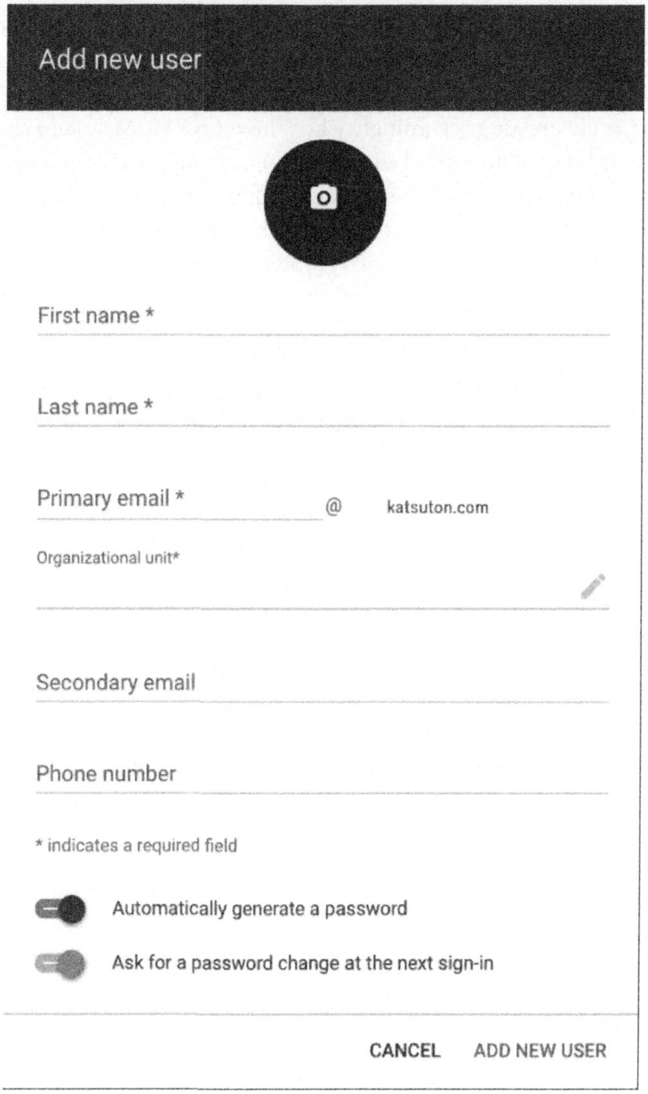

Figure 2.6 – Google user creation example

Using an external tool to manage user provision introduces complexity that an IT administrator has to add to the increasing number of tools that they use every day. If you think about this thoroughly, only the identity system (HCM system) and the IdPs are the systems strictly needed to enable an authentication process based on the user's information; the user provisioning tool is just a commodity that interconnects them through some business logic.

Is there a way to get rid of a custom rule to reduce complexity by automating this provisioning? The answer is yes, and the solution is the SCIM protocol. SCIM is an open standard protocol for automating the exchange of user identity information between identity systems and IT systems (such as an IdP). SCIM ensures that the identities of employees added to an HCM system are automatically created in an IdP so that user attributes and their profiles are synchronized between the two systems and are also automatically updated accordingly when the source HCM system changes the status or the role of a user. SCIM has standardized the way a user can be provisioned between two systems by defining common endpoints such as /Users and /Groups. It uses common **Representational State Transfer** (**REST**) HTTP verbs to create, update, and delete objects and it defines a schema for frequently used attributes, such as the name of a group and the username, first name, last name, and email address of a user.

To get rid of a manual provisioning tool (which can still be used for complex scenarios involving more than two identity systems), the SCIM protocol must be implemented directly using the aforementioned HCM and identity system – the former, as a source of the information, should use the SCIM endpoints published by the identity system.

Luckily, most HCM and identity systems nowadays implement the SCIM protocol and enable integrated scenarios where an automated process is put in place so that the following occurs:

- A relationship is established between the identity in the HCM system and the user account in the IdP

- An automated process is triggered every time a user account needs an update because the corresponding identity has been created, modified, or deleted

- The proper administrative delegation has been set up correctly

The last point mentioned in this list is key to the success of the overall solution enabled by the SCIM protocol. Our main goal was to reduce complexity. How have we accomplished that? Business managers were already used to managing internal and external users under their business unit with an HCM system. A business manager is therefore the owner of the knowledge that provides insights about which resources a particular user is allowed to access, but they have no proficiency (and should not have that) in how an IT system or IdP works. This is where an IT administrator comes into the picture, who knows the technology very well but has no clue about what a user should actually have access to.

By enabling an automated process that integrates an HCM system with an identity system, SCIM highly reduces the complexity of managing user identity and an account's life cycle by freeing the business managers from knowing how the underlying technologies work, and the IT administrators from knowing a user's roles and permissions upfront. Once both actors agree on this automated process, they can continue doing their daily job within the scope of this new delegation and segregation of duties and tools.

Once a user account has been successfully created on an IdP, they can start accessing all the applications that trust this IdP using **Single Sign-On** (**SSO**). As seen in the previous chapter, when an application federates (trusts) an IdP, it means that it trusts the tokens (proof of authentication) that the IdP issues by checking its signature.

Typically, not all user accounts stored in the IdP (which could be very high in number) must be granted access to a particular application (even if sometimes this may happen) and therefore, the application has to find a way to authorize an authenticated user whose token has been correctly issued by the IdP. Authorization logic can be implemented either directly within the application or in the IdP.

In the case of the former, the application has to build a list of authorized users belonging to a particular IdP. This is usually done by importing CSV files or by manually maintaining a list of users together with their roles and permissions within the application's local database. This is an error-prone approach that could lead to unsustainable and complex management of user accounts in the long term. The application team also cannot promptly react to the change in the status of a user in the IdP that may change their permissions within the application. When authorization is entirely delegated to the federated application, the IT administrators have limited control over the users' access policies.

In the latter case, it's the IT administrator that decides on and implements the authorization policies for the users stored in the IdP in order to allow or prevent them from accessing a specific application. Administrators, however, do not know whether or not a user requires access to an application – a business manager does.

This is where SCIM comes to the rescue (again). We already discussed earlier that SCIM can facilitate and automate the user provisioning process from an HCM system to an identity system. Well, SCIM can also be (and in fact, is) used to provision users from an identity system to applications. This is the most common approach used for modern SaaS applications that federate with most of the publicly available IdPs, such as Azure AD. With this approach, an IT administrator can (again) agree with the business manager upon a specific business logic that can automatically provision, de-provision, or update a user in a SaaS application with specific attributes or roles (for example, all the users that have the marketing department attribute can access the marketing portal). Of course, for the (SaaS) application to support this flow, it must implement and publish a SCIM endpoint.

How does all of this apply to external cloud identities as well? It is very common for an organization to collaborate with an external partner who may need access to an application offered by that company. External partner identities are likely stored in an external IdP that is not directly managed by us. How does user provisioning work in this case? There is no universal recipe for this scenario since it strictly depends on the implementation of the specific IdP, but generally speaking, the following considerations should apply:

- A federation between one company's IdP and the external one can be put in place.

- External users can be created and represented within one company's IdP as references or placeholders that contain a sort of link to the user in the external IdP that effectively stores user credentials. Having this representation allows you to define authorization policies directly in the application's IdP.

- If an external user's placeholder is not created, then the final applications will likely have to implement authorization policies within the application logic by making decisions only on information (claims) received within the proof of authentication (tokens) coming from the external IdP and relayed by the local IdP.

When it comes to all the applications that an organization offers to their customers, it is common to allow and configure an application to federate with several external IdPs, such as social IdPs, including Facebook, Google, and Microsoft, in order to let the user choose the account they prefer to log in with. This area is intended for consumers, not for the enterprise. For enterprise applications that target **Business-to-Business (B2B)** collaboration, controls are more strictly secured because the information managed by the applications is likely confidential. Access must, therefore, be granted only to the authorized company's employees or external collaborators. This is one of the most common reasons why enterprises that manage both customers and B2B applications have different and separate IdPs – their need to have a more diligent security posture justifies greater management complexity.

To summarize, managing cloud identities can be complex, but most of this complexity is simplified today by modern cloud technologies (such as **Identity-as-a-Service (IDaaS)** solutions) that reduce the time to market of an enterprise identity solution considerably. IDaaS solutions can orchestrate all the aspects of user provisioning, authentication, authorization, and interaction with external IDaaS providers thanks to the standard protocols that most vendors implement today.

In the next chapter, we will extend the concept of cloud identities by explaining how their interaction and interoperability with on-premises legacy identity systems are a requirement for many enterprises. Next, we will understand what hybrid identities are.

A hybrid identity

As already touched on in the previous chapter, before the advent of the public internet and cloud technologies that gradually decentralized the services accessed by an organization outside of the organization's perimeter, it was sufficient to provide users with an authentication model that granted access to internal assets. Information technology efforts were mainly focused on keeping the perimeter secure and preventing malicious users from breaching security defenses and, consequently, accessing sensitive assets within the organization's internal network.

Let's imagine the typical workday of an employee, Alice, in the early 2000s. Alice is a part of the engineering team of a big manufacturing company and she needs to use several services to fulfill her role and responsibilities. Alice turns on her **Personal Computer (PC)** first thing in the morning and logs into the operating system. She then starts her mail client to access her emails. Next, she starts the AutoCAD software, saves project files to a network file share, and finally, checks the internal human resources portal to check the travel policy so that she can safely book her flight for a business trip the month after.

Let's analyze the different types of authentications involved in the aforementioned flow and which technologies were likely involved at that time:

- **Operating system login**: Windows was the most common operating system for corporate client computers that were used by users such as Alice. With Windows 2000 and Windows XP, log-in authentication started using AD as the user repository. As already seen in the previous chapter, NTLM and Kerberos protocols were used for this purpose. Within, an authentication server, called a **Domain Controller,** was implemented the **Key Distribution Center** role, which allowed Kerberos tickets to be issued to clients. This enabled SSO to other services that belonged to the same Kerberos realm (also known as a domain) of AD.

- **Email client login**: If Alice was lucky enough, the authentication within the email client (which would likely have been Outlook or Lotus Notes) was integrated with AD as well; if this was the case, then Alice would have seamlessly single signed-on to the client, which used Alice's proof of authentication in the background to access the mail server (for example, Exchange Server).

- **Network file share login**: Depending on the operating system, network file shares were usually accessed through two different protocols – **Service Message Block** (**SMB**) for Windows and **Network File System** (**NFS**) for Linux. Both can be integrated with Kerberos; the former supports NTLM and the latter supports UNIX authentication.

- **Human resources portal login**: Web portals were the most flexible services in terms of user authentication technologies. You could find many different implementations – Kerberos or NTLM (Windows) authentication on **Internet Information Services** (**IIS**) web servers, local databases, and LDAP against a directory service, to mention just a few.

It becomes evident that the complexity of identity systems before the explosion of the public internet wasn't negligible. For large enterprises, the transition to modern identity technologies was not straightforward because of the friction of the existing identity solutions they were already using. Technically speaking, it was not feasible to just get rid of the existing systems and fully embrace the new technologies because users still had to use those legacy systems to access the applications that strongly relied on them.

Another important aspect to mention is that organizations were reluctant to move their users' information outside the safe perimeter that they had built over the years. Security, in fact, was changing too. It was slowly shifting to a new paradigm that didn't value the frontline defenses that were used at that time anymore but put the users (and therefore the identities) at the center instead. Users were starting to access applications hosted outside their company's boundaries and, very often, the user was doing that from their personal device outside their company's network (for example, from their home or a public place such as a hotel). With the shift in trends and use cases that technology had to follow quickly, there were still those sticking to their perimeter and firewall model who didn't believe that something was really changing, were just too lazy to roll up their sleeves, or, in some cases, simply didn't have enough money (in terms of investments) to accommodate these changes.

It is not rare that identity and security travel on the same or parallel rails. One change to either of the two will inevitably affect the other one.

So, what about the brave and reckless people that took the leap of faith into changing their security and identity model instead? It wasn't easy at the beginning. Well, it's not that easy even today; otherwise, we would have not written this book!

Going back to the brave people, it was hard, because business users wanted to do the following:

- Seamlessly access the new technologies wherever they were hosted
- Continue to access the applications they were already using
- Have just one set of credentials to access all the applications
- Use SSO whenever possible

It was reasonable to a certain extent. This is where hybrid identities enter the picture. Hybrid identity is just a fancy term to describe identities that have a presence in more than one place. Today, hybrid identities are identities that have a presence both on-premises and in the cloud. The on-premises identity and the cloud twin should have a clear link that allows you to treat them as a single entity. This is needed if we would like to ensure the first two requirements mentioned previously are met. Keeping a single set of credentials and enabling SSO, on the other hand, can again be accomplished using federation between a cloud IdP and the on-premises one using SAML, WS-Federation, or OpenID Connect.

Wait a minute – why should we federate a cloud IdP with our on-premises one instead of federating cloud applications directly? The reason is that it is just more convenient to do so. Each time a new cloud application is added to a company's portfolio, that application has to be federated with the on-premises IdP. Federating directly with the cloud IdP instead requires establishing the federation just once and all the cloud applications will benefit. Even third-party applications that already have a native integration with that cloud IdP can automatically leverage on-premises identities. This is, of course, just the natural outcome of the industry trends in how cloud IdPs have been designed. Consider Azure AD from Microsoft as an example. All Microsoft first-party applications, such as Azure, Office 365 (Microsoft 365), and Dynamics, are natively set up with Azure AD and cannot be set up on IdPs other than Azure AD (although it is possible to establish a federation between Azure AD and a third-party IdP). This is also true for other cloud services, such as Google Workspace and Google Identity, and, in general, this translates to having a single choice when it comes to harnessing these services with an organization's existing users – federating commercial cloud IdPs with on-premises ones.

This solution allows us to concentrate identity management and governance into IdPs, which simplifies the task of provisioning users to cloud applications using SCIM in these implementations.

In most cases, this translates to choosing just a single cloud IdP in order to minimize the effort of contemporarily managing multiple identity systems at once. No matter the choice taken, the solution should be comprehensive of all the capabilities needed to manage identities regardless of their source of authority. Azure AD, for instance, allows you to manage both on-premises and cloud identities by providing a single pane of glass for hybrid identity management. Let's talk about how this works by showing you a real-world example involving Alice again.

Alice's company has started using Microsoft's first-party cloud services, such as Microsoft 365 and Azure, and therefore, they now have an Azure AD tenant that manages authentication and authorization to these services. Azure AD allows you to create local cloud users, but Alice's company would like to let their existing users who just have on-premises accounts use these services with their existing credentials and SSO. We need a way to synchronize these users to Azure AD and this is easily done with native tools, such as Azure AD Connect in this case, which takes accounts from on-premises AD environments and provisions them to Azure AD, which will therefore be aware of their existence and consequently enable their management. This is not a new concept. For years, enterprises were used to synchronizing on-premises identities among different identity systems. The cloud IdP is likely just another edge node within their existing user provisioning processes.

With the advance of the decades and the prevalent role of cloud technologies, the weight of an identity management strategy shifted more and more toward cloud IdPs. A cloud IdP very often needs to *write back* some information on the on-premises identity systems and manage the authorizations and access controls that once were done on-premises. This is needed to enable the transition to a full cloud identity model, which, nowadays, is believed to be the natural evolution of current on-premises solutions. On-premises solutions will most likely never disappear completely because of the nature of some workloads that will be kept on-premises for compliance with local regulatory requirements. Many workloads also have to be close to the edge for performance reasons (such as software that manages plants in a manufacturer). This is why hybrid identities are and will remain important now and in the future.

So, hybrid identities are just an extension of existing on-premises identities, a way to interconnect an on-premises user with its cloud counterpart. Now is an exciting time to work with identities. While most enterprises still struggle a bit to keep up with this new way of governing identities in a hybrid world, a new perspective is coming to light, thanks to the huge developments around blockchain technologies. Let's try to understand what the concept of **Decentralized Identities** (**DID**) is and why this is important for the future of identity management in an enterprise.

The future of identity

Cloud, hybrid, and federated identities have been around for years and still many enterprises are struggling to fully harness their full potential. We hope that after reading this book, you will be one of those people that successfully survived the design and implementation stage of a good identity strategy in their organization.

However, technology is never static; it's an ongoing stream of change that constantly veers toward the next breakthrough that will radically change our lives, so you may wonder what the next big thing for identity is.

First, let's understand the factors that contribute to the need to have a different way of managing identities and the credentials associated with them. We already know that credentials are part of our daily lives. We are not just referring to digital credentials but to credentials as a broader concept, such as the government ID that your state has issued to you or the degree you received from your university. You normally use these credentials to benefit from and access specific services in the physical world that are only enabled because you have these credentials (for example, the proof of being a citizen of a state grants you the right to vote during elections). As a matter of fact, it is difficult to express things such as educational qualifications, healthcare data, and other kinds of verified machine-readable personal information on the web, which makes it difficult to benefit from the same commodities we usually benefit from in the real, physical world.

The joint efforts of several organizations contributed to developing different standards to support this view under the W3C umbrella:

- **W3C DIDs**

  DIDs are a new type of identity that uses a common trusted ledger (blockchain) as a secure store to share users' information among the different actors involved in the authentication process

- **W3C Verifiable Credentials Data Model 1.0**

  Verifiable credentials describe the processes and protocols that all the parties involved in an authentication flow must adhere to in order to verify that the credentials (DIDs) used by the security principal are trustworthy and reliable

Together, these two standards have the potential to shape a new way of managing identities at scale so that it resembles how we use our credentials in the physical world today. Let's see what they are, why we need them, and how they work.

Individuals (and organizations) use globally unique identifiers in a wide variety of contexts. The vast majority of these globally unique identifiers are not under the control of the individuals in question. They are issued by external authorities (for example, Facebook or Google) that control their whole life cycle without letting individuals such as you and me choose which context they can be used for. Moreover, these identifiers are tightly connected to the life of the organization that issued them, which means they can cease to exist if these organizations want them to. These identifiers are also often subject to identity theft, which leads to their improper use to the detriment of their real owner.

DIDs are a new type of identifier designed to enable individuals and organizations to generate globally unique identities. These new identifiers enable individuals and organizations to prove they own them by authenticating through cryptographic proof (e.g., digital signatures).

The DID specification does not require any particular technology or cryptography to implement the life cycle, including the creation of a DID. For example, implementers can create DIDs based on accounts registered in federated or centralized identity management systems, allowing almost all types of existing identity systems to support DIDs. This is fundamental to creating interoperability between the current centralized, federated systems and the DIDs. You can find an example of the structure of a DID in the following figure:

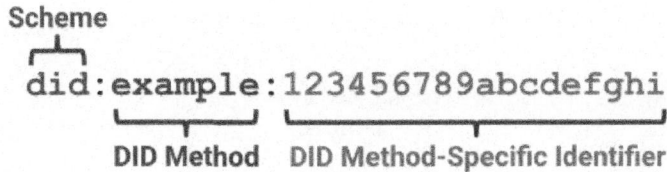

Figure 2.7 – An example of DID

A **verifiable credential**, on the other hand, is a way to digitally replace the information included within its physical counterpart. The addition of technologies, such as digital signatures, makes verifiable credentials more trustworthy.

While it is true that many verifiable credentials do use DIDs in the technical implementation of the specification, verifiable credentials and DIDs are not strictly interdependent.

A verifiable credential involves the interaction of the following actors or entities:

- **Holder**: An entity (typically an individual) that owns one or more verifiable credentials and generates verifiable presentations. A typical holder could be a student of a university, a citizen of a city, or an employee of a company.

- **Issuer**: An entity that issues claims about one or more subjects (see the following definition) and generates a verifiable credential from these claims. An issuer sends the verifiable credential to a holder that will use these credentials against a verifier as authentication proof. Examples of issuers include corporations, universities, governments, and individuals.

- **Subject**: This is the entity for whom the claims have been issued within the verifiable credential.

- **Verifier**: An entity that receives and processes one or more verifiable credentials. Examples of a verifier include employers and websites.

- **Verifiable data registry**: An entity (typically an information system) that is in charge of the creation and verification of identifiers, keys, and other relevant data, such as verifiable credential schemas, revocation registries, and issuer public keys. It is the decentralized repository containing verifiable information regarding issuers, holders, and verifiers, which is typically implemented through a distributed ledger.

The relationship between these entities is represented in the following figure:

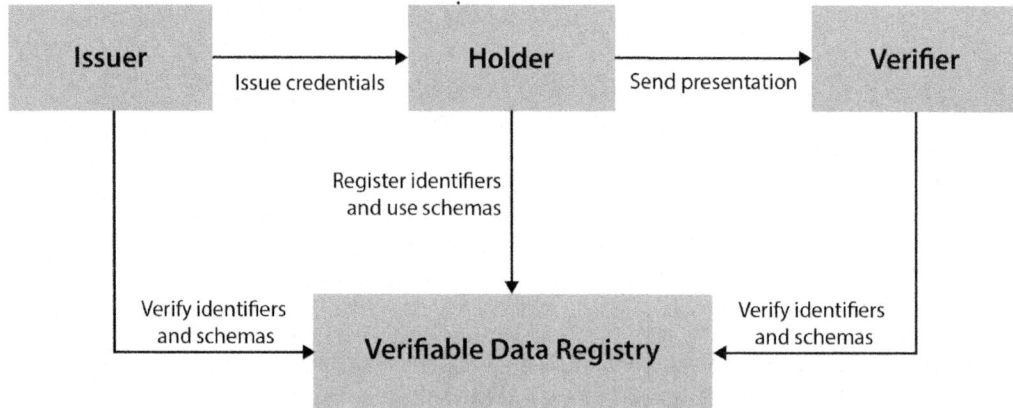

Figure 2.8 – Verifiable credentials example

DIDs and verifiable credentials are promising, and they have great potential to really change how we see and think about digital identities. Some vendors are starting to implement these standards and offer them as a service (for example, Azure AD). Maybe it's too early to say whether they will be the new de facto standard for managing credentials in the future but we can surely say that today, they are the closest representation of the physical credentials we exchange and use every day to prove that we are who we say we are.

Summary

In this chapter, we explored the differences between cloud and hybrid identities, why they are important for an enterprise, and how they relate to each other. Synchronization protocols such as SCIM help an organization keep its different identity systems under control and allow them to seamlessly integrate legacy and modern identities. This chapter also provided an overview of the current state of technology, and we outlined the points that affect protocol creation, as well as the important pillars an enterprise-grade design needs to take into account. This helped us to not only understand what it is today but also the trends and the possible implications of the next-generation protocols that will be based on technology aspects not yet adopted. A great example of what we can expect in the future is represented by third-party cookie removal by browsers, which, in turn, will likely contribute to evolving protocols and standards.

With these concepts in mind, we are ready to take things a step further, contextualize them a little more in the present, and review the specs on the most used protocol that is adopted in the business world in the next chapter – OAuth.

Part 2: OAuth Implementation and Patterns

This part will gradually guide the reader from the basic concepts of OAuth (OAuth flows) to the complex advanced patterns of an application composed of multiple APIs, which need a coherent authentication mechanism with an IDP – or even multiple IDPs.

This section contains the following chapters:

- *Chapter 3, OAuth 2.0 and OIDC*
- *Chapter 4, Authentication Flows*
- *Chapter 5, Exploring Identity Patterns*

3
OAuth 2.0 and OIDC

This chapter is going to get you started on the technical journey to understand the advanced concepts that will be covered in the following chapters.

In this chapter, we are going to learn about the basics of the most used authentication protocol for cloud applications, which is OAuth 2.0, and we are going to appreciate why OAuth 2.0 has become the de facto standard in web authentication.

This chapter will also introduce you to **OpenID Connect** (**OIDC**).

OIDC extends the OAuth 2.0 protocol by introducing new flows, reusing some existing ones, and making the user, not the application, the center of these flows.

In this chapter, we will go through and learn all about the basics of OAuth 2.0 and OIDC, their similarities and differences, where they can be used and why, and what the actors that participate in authentication and/or authorization flows are.

This chapter will not analyze the flows of these protocols in depth; those will be covered in the next chapter. We are going to provide some technical background information that will be needed to better understand the upcoming chapters of the book.

In this chapter, we are going to cover the following topics:

- OAuth and OIDC basic concepts
- How OAuth and OIDC work together
- How the protocols are implemented in the real world
- Technical background

OAuth and OIDC basic concepts

The basic architecture of applications that are composed of multiple tiers separating the presentation from the business logic and data, with the business logic exposed through a set of services, has largely gone unchanged for the last decade.

However, the environment in which these applications are expected to operate has completely changed in this same timeframe. Today, you cannot just offer a simple browser-based website; you need to also support IoT devices (such as presentation screens, smart devices, sensors, and electrical appliances) and mobile clients, and these mobile clients must be supported across a broad range of devices, mostly based on iOS, Android, or Windows.

In today's landscape, users expect applications and services to interoperate – to be able to be used together. For example, users expect to be able to post the latest purchase they have made from Amazon or ASOS to their Facebook wall or share a photograph on Instagram from the camera application on their mobile phone. These requirements have also brought the need to manage user consent for sharing information.

Over the course of the last decade, we have already seen the movement to extract identity management logic out of applications and enable users to authenticate to applications from external identity providers and utilize claims-based authentication. Historically, we have seen WS-Federation and SAML fulfilling this requirement. These protocols have been covered in *Chapter 1, Walkthrough of Digital Identity in the Enterprise*. There is also an undeniable trend of retail websites (among others) today offering authentication through external identities.

With the growth of mobile clients, the widespread adoption of REST-based web APIs, and the need to support user consent on resources across these APIs, the industry has come together and agreed on OAuth as the delegated protocol for securing web APIs, with the latest evolution, OAuth 2.0, supported by Google, Microsoft, Facebook, and PayPal.

It's important to know that OAuth 2.0 is intended to be an authorization protocol, not an authentication protocol. As you may also be aware, authentication is the process of determining whether someone or something is, in fact, who or what it says it is, whereas authorization is mainly the process of checking what privilege the user has to access a specific domain or application.

It's important to note that **OIDC** is intended to be used for authentication and **OAuth** is the protocol to be used for authorization. This is the reason why OAuth and OIDC complement each other and why, in technical literature, they are often found mentioned together.

How OAuth and OIDC work together

Despite OAuth being commonly used together with OIDC to cover both authentication and authorization requirements, it is not mandatory for them to be used together. Just to provide an example, OAuth can be used for authorization even in contexts where another protocol (for example, the SAML protocol, described in the *Security Assertion Markup Language* section in *Chapter 1, Walkthrough of Digital Identity in the Enterprise*) is used for authentication. As a matter of fact, the specification of OAuth does not include OIDC, which can be seen as an optional layer to add.

Let's use a concrete example to better understand the usage of the OAuth protocol without any authentication flow. OAuth is the protocol that is used by Facebook when a user needs to access a third-party application (for example, Spotify) with their Facebook account. In this context, the user is usually already logged in to the Facebook platform and they are just prompted to grant privilege to the third-party application to use information stored in the Facebook account so that the third-party application can acquire this information when the user enables Facebook to release it to the third party. The granting of this privilege is done through the OAuth protocol and it can happen without any explicit authentication. Once the third-party application grabs the access token (the concept of the access token will be covered in detail in the next chapter) from the Facebook identity provider, it can allow the user to register or authenticate with whatever protocol the third-party application wants to implement, which is completely independent of the OAuth Facebook authorization flow described previously.

The previous flow outlines a scenario where OIDC is not involved.

The following screenshot shows the login prompt presented by Spotify. The blue **LOG IN WITH FACEBOOK** button triggers the OAuth flow, which is supposed to provide Spotify with the authorization to access the user's Facebook data. It also allows the user to log in with their username and password and not just with Facebook:

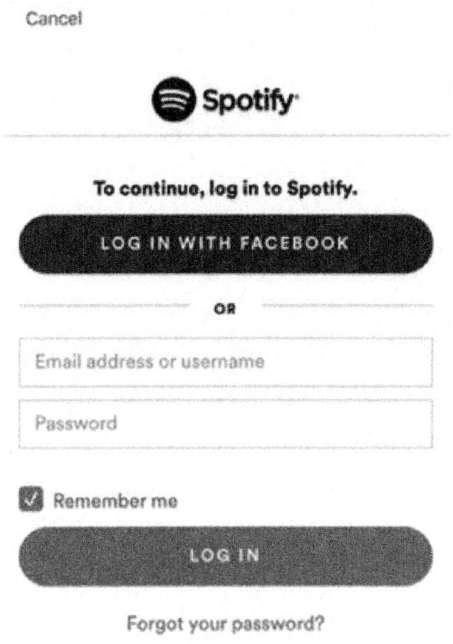

Figure 3.1 – Sample of OAuth login

In the next chapter, we will also provide examples of flows focused on authentication rather than authorization as the one we've just presented was; as a consequence, these flows will have OIDC as the main actor, rather than OAuth.

To best appreciate the differences between the OAuth and OIDC protocols, it is important to reference how they are defined in the original specs (`https://openid.net/connect/`):

The OpenID Connect specification is a simple identity layer on top of the OAuth 2.0 protocol. It allows Clients to verify the identity of the End-User based on the authentication performed by an Authorization Server, as well as to obtain basic profile information about the End-User in an interoperable and REST-like manner.

Technically speaking, OIDC is built on the OAuth 2.0 protocol. OIDC uses an additional **JSON Web Token (JWT)**: the ID token. This is to create standards for areas where OAuth 2.0 leaves ambiguity (for example, scopes and endpoint discovery).

How the protocols are implemented in the real world

It is important to note that both OAuth 2.0 and OIDC are standards supported by a number of services, including Azure Active Directory, OWIN and Katana, NetIQ Access Manager, Google Authentication, and PingFederate, just to mention a few.

Generally speaking, as they are the de facto standard, a developer who wants to implement an OAuth/OIDC flow for their application doesn't necessarily need to know the specification in depth and apply custom code to their solution. Client libraries, generally grouped into frameworks, that implement these protocols can be found in the most widely adopted programming languages to ease the development of an application that implements these standards.

The following is a non-exhaustive list of technologies that enable developers to take advantage of either commercial or non-commercial libraries to implement authentication/authorization through OIDC/OAuth:

- ActionScript
- C
- ColdFusion
- Dart
- .NET
- Elixir
- Elm
- Erlang

- Go

- Java

- JavaScript

- Kotlin

- Lua

- Node.js

- Objective-C

- Perl

- PHP

- PowerShell

- Python

- C++

- Ruby

- Rust

- Scala

- Swift

To better understand OAuth, this book will not focus on these libraries but on the protocol specs themselves. For more information about the implementation of these libraries, you can consult the following website: `https://oauth.net/code/`.

Often, when we are approaching OAuth for the very first time, the questions at the forefront of our minds are generally focused on how these protocols fit into the wider picture. The typical questions on a newbie's mind are the following:

- In what kind of solution can I adopt OAuth?

- Can I adopt OAuth for an IoT solution? If so, how can I do it?

- Can I use OAuth for both web applications and single-page applications? What are the differences?

All of these are valid questions and they need to be tackled individually in detail. The current chapter will focus on *what* can be done using OAuth. The next chapter will tackle the OAuth flows and it will tell us more about *how* to perform certain authentications/authorizations using the OAuth/OIDC combination.

The following is a list of the most typical use cases that can help you to understand in which context OAuth can be adopted:

- Single-page apps
- Web apps
- Web APIs
- Mobile apps
- Native apps
- Daemon apps
- Server-side apps

How OAuth or OIDC is adopted and which authentication flow needs to be chosen is dependent on the scenario. Whether it is browser-to-server communication, mobile-to-API communication, or server-to-server communication, each of them is going to have a different flow. The flow can also be different for the same scenario but with a different implementation; for example, within browser-to-server communication, a single-page application typically has a different OAuth flow than a multi-page application (we will discuss this in more detail in later chapters). This requires careful attention to the application design. It is important to identify what our context is before moving forward and choosing the proper flow to implement. The wrong flow may expose the application we are designing to unwanted security risks.

OAuth flows will be discussed in depth in *Chapter 4, Authentication Flows*.

For further information about which authentication flow to use in a specific scenario, it is recommended to use the external Microsoft documentation as a reference: `https://docs.microsoft.com/en-us/azure/active-directory/develop/authentication-flows-app-scenarios`. This article provides a full picture of which OAuth flow to apply to a specific context.

This chapter provides a high-level picture of the main use cases for OAuth; you can appreciate them in depth once you are familiar with the flows discussed in upcoming chapters.

Technical background

Before diving deep into flows, it's important to understand some basic concepts regarding the actors that participate in the authorization or authentication process. If you are familiar with other protocols, you will appreciate that the concept is not so different.

Let's start with the basics by trying to understand what the actors, devices, and servers involved in an OAuth 2.0/OIDC flow are and what their role during the authentication and authorization process is.

These are the main parties involved in nearly all protocol exchanges. The following diagram summarizes all of them:

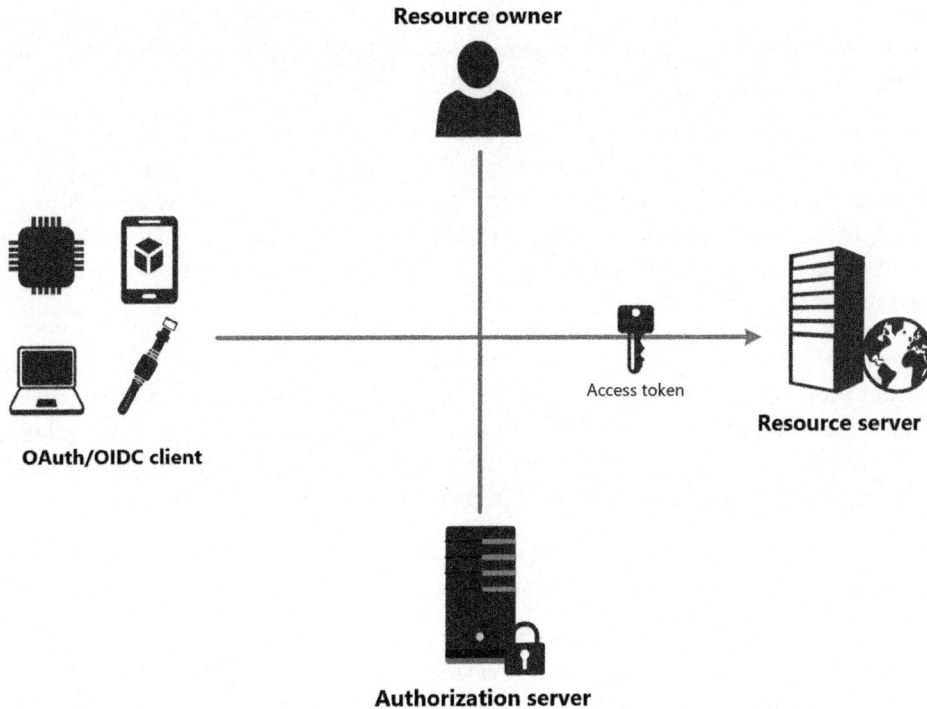

Figure 3.2 – OAuth/OIDC parties

The preceding diagram shows the typical parties involved in authorization/authentication flows. The following are descriptions of each of the roles reported in the diagram:

- **Resource owner**: This is the entity that allows access to the final resource (the resource server). If this entity is a human, then it is also called an end user.

- **OAuth/OIDC client**: This is the means by which the resource owner accesses the resource server. A client can be any device: an IoT sensor, a smartphone, a desktop, or a server. Technically speaking, regardless of the device that implements the flow, usually, there is a major distinction between a native client and a web client.

- **Resource server**: This is the entity that hosts the resource that needs to be accessed by the client. Access to this server must be protected properly by checking the validity of the client requests' access tokens.

  In other words, we can connect the dots with the OAuth/OIDC client and say that in a context when the OAuth/OIDC is passive (that is, authentication is carried out by a web client and not by a native client), the resource server is the entity that sends HTTP responses as redirects to take the user to the authorization server. This enables this component to drive the behavior of the OAuth/OIDC client.

- **Access token**: The access token is released by the authorization server upon successful authorization/authentication. More information about access tokens will be provided later in this section.

- **Authorization server**: Finally, the authorization server is the entity that issues the tokens. It publishes the endpoints of the protocols that the clients need to use to implement the authentication flows and receive the access tokens. The authorization server typically has a configuration stored somewhere either in their filesystem or an external database that contains all the applications (clients) allowed to invoke their endpoints and the resource servers from which these applications are allowed to ask for a token.

A web client typically behaves passively. In other words, the web client does not directly implement the authentication/authorization logic; rather, the flow is driven from the server and not from the client. This means the server sends an HTTP status code (that is, a 302 redirect) to drive the behavior of the client and redirect it to the identity provider to require the user to log in. This logic is not even known by the client, which passively executes the instruction received on the server side.

Indeed, a native client explicitly implements authentication flow logic and does not need the server to tell it what it has to do or where it has to go by using a redirection, which is typical of OAuth flows adopted out of the native client context.

As you will probably already know, generally speaking, in all contexts where user interaction is not possible (for example, an IoT device), a native client should be considered and a non-passive flow should be implemented. On the other hand, in all contexts where the user can explicitly log in to the web client, this is generally adopted.

To summarize, the OAuth/OIDC client is the entity that receives the protocol's final tokens (the access token and ID token), stores them, and uses them to access resource server-provided services if authorized.

To understand the concepts discussed in the previous list better, let's see how the actors mentioned so far are used in a sample application design.

We are going to describe a sample that covers the most typical application design, which implements web client authentication.

The resource server is the server where the application is implemented. Web applications are implemented on top of application servers such as Apache, NGINX, or IIS. The application server can be on a virtual machine, a PaaS service such as Azure Web Apps, or AWS Elastic Beanstalk, just to mention a few of the most used cloud services. For the sake of understanding, it is important to know that the resource server is where developers deploy their code, which will then be consumed by the browser. During development, the developer chooses to delegate the authentication to an external entity, which is the **authorization server**. As a consequence, we can expect the application not to store information such as passwords because the whole authentication (OIDC) or authorization (OAuth) process will be delegated to the authorization server. As we are going to learn in the next chapter, when an **OAuth/**

OIDC client accesses an application that is exposed through a resource server, the **resource owner** will never make their credentials visible to the resource server. This is because the resource server will just redirect the OAuth/OIDC client to the authorization server, and only in this location is the resource owner supposed to insert their credentials.

It's important to remember that what we described so far is consistent with the web client authentication.

An authorization server that is implemented by major identity providers nowadays enables both authorization and authentication. As a consequence, they tend to follow both the OIDC and the OAuth specs.

Reporting the full list of specs for each protocol is out of the scope of this book; however, it is important to mention the well-known endpoint. The well-known endpoint is usually a suffix that can be added to the authorization server URL to obtain public information about it.

As an example, in Azure Active Directory, which is the Microsoft identity provider that follows the OAuth 2.0 and OIDC specification, it is possible to add the `.well-known/openid-configuration` suffix to the authorization server URL to obtain information about the logged entity. More information about the OAuth 2.0/OIDC authorization server metadata can be found in the OAuth 2.0 specification, under *Obtaining Authorization Server Metadata* at the following URL: `https://datatracker.ietf.org/doc/html/rfc8414`.

According to the **Request for Comment** (**RFC**) and in order to be compliant with its standards, an authorization server must provide an endpoint to enable public entities, including the resource servers, to obtain information about it. This is particularly important to enable the resource server to get access to the public keys required to validate JWTs signed by the authorization server with the related private keys.

To enable a resource server to delegate the authentication to an authorization server, the resource server needs to be registered against the application server.

In other words, the authorization server needs to be aware of all the applications that can perform authentication against it. A registered application will obtain a pair of strings from the authorization server: the client ID and client secret. This is necessary because this pair of strings will then be used by the resource server whenever an authentication or authorization activity needs to be performed against the authorization server. This pair of strings is supposed to be confidential and, as a consequence, be used by the resource server as proof of an already-performed registration. This can happen because, for every authorization/authentication request, the authorization server will double-check whether the pair of strings matches with the one released to the resource server during the registration phase.

Application identity details are registered in the authorization server, which typically retains the following information:

- **Application ID**: This is a string that uniquely identifies a client application within the authorization server.

- **Client secret**: This is a secret, password, or certificate that is used in some OAuth flows to authenticate a client application so that it can retrieve an access token from the authorization server.

- **Redirect URIs**: These are the URIs specific to the application to which the issued tokens are sent.

- **Allowed scopes**: These are allowed scopes that a client application can request for a specific resource server. For instance, a client application may only be allowed to request the *read* scope for a specific REST API protected by the authorization server.

OAuth uses the following types of tokens (which are issued by the authorization server):

- **Access tokens**: Access tokens are basically credentials used to access protected resources (resource servers). An access token is, according to the public definition (`https://datatracker.ietf.org/doc/html/rfc6749`), *"a string representing an authorization issued to the client. The string is usually opaque to the client. Tokens represent specific scopes and durations of access, granted by the resource owner, and enforced by the resource server and authorization server."* Typically, access tokens are issued in a specific format called a JWT, which is a JSON file made of three parts: the header, the body, and the signature. The body contains the claims for the application or the user for which the token has been issued. The following is an example of a JWT:

```
{
  "typ": "JWT",
  "alg": "RS256",
  "kid": "JRX9C2vPdG2-3YDi14buhEVvO_O9bFwzz-pMBxtDh18"
}.{
  "exp": 1633425451,
  "nbf": 1633421851,
  "ver": "1.0",
  "iss": "https://myauthzserver.issuer.com/",
  "sub": "application_or_user_unique_id",
  "aud": "audience_unique_id",
  "acr": "signin",
  "nonce": "defaultNonce",
  "iat": 1633421851,
  "auth_time": 1633421851,
  "name": "unknown"
}.[Signature]
```

The most important claims are as follows:

- `aud`: The audience or the entity (resource server) the token is intended for

- `iss`: The unique ID of the authorization server that issued the token

- `exp`: The expiration of the token; the timeframe for which the token is considered valid

- `sub`: The subject of the token; the entity the token has been issued for (an application)

- **Refresh tokens**: Refresh tokens are credentials used to obtain a new access token when it becomes invalid without involving the user in the process. They typically have an expiration time far greater than an access token, they are opaque to the client, and they are intended for use only with the authorization server. They are never sent to the resource server.

OIDC introduces a new type of token:

- **ID token**: An ID token is basically an access token for users. It's the SAML token counterpart used for user authentication that contains the user's claims needed by either the client OIDC or the resource server to establish a user's identity.

Both the OAuth and OIDC protocols utilize two authorization server endpoints (HTTP endpoints) within their flows:

- **Authorization endpoint**: This is used by the resource owner who interactively obtains (by typing in their username and password) an authorization grant after successful verification of the resource owner's identity by the authorization server.

- **Token endpoint**: This is used by the client to obtain an access token, an ID token, or both (depending on the specific flow used).

- **User info endpoint**: This is an authenticated endpoint that is used by an application to retrieve additional information (claims) about a user that has already been authenticated. To access this endpoint, an application must use an access token that is typically issued by the authorization server during the user's authentication.

Last but not least, let's understand the different types of client applications that can be encountered in the different flows:

- **Web applications**: A passive web application hosted on a web server and accessed through a browser

- **Native applications**: An application that typically does not use a web browser and is installed on the resource owner's device (for example, a mobile application)

Moreover, web and native applications can be of two different types:

- **Public clients**: Client applications that are not trusted because they are installed on a resource owner's device

- **Confidential (private) clients**: Client applications hosted on a secure server and accessed remotely by a user agent (for example, a web browser)

Each HTTP request against one of the authorization server endpoints contains specific headers (or query string parameters) that the protocols describe within their specifications. The most important are described as follows:

- `response_type`: This parameter is used by an application during the initial authentication request to specify which piece of information it would like to receive in the response returned by the authorization server

- `grant_type`: This is used to specify which OAuth 2.0 or OIDC flow must be used

- `client_id`: An ID for the application that has been registered in the authorization server

- `redirect_uri`: The URL, registered in the authorization server, to which the token should be issued

- `client_secret`: A secret (password) assigned to an application and used by a confidential client to authenticate the application's identity

- `scope`: A set of space-separated strings that specify the information (claims) and the audience (resource server) that should be issued within the security token

- `username`: The username of a user, specified only when using the **Resource Owner Password Credentials (ROPC)** flow

- `password`: The password of a user, specified only when using the ROPC flow

Knowing how OAuth 2.0 and OIDC work in the background might seem like something that is done just to satisfy a technical appetite (if any), but this is far from the truth; knowing the protocols can really make a difference during the design phase of an application. As a matter of fact, the interoperability of an application with other applications in the same enterprise or applications developed by external teams strongly depends on the authentication and authorization strategy that has been chosen for your application. Choosing the right OAuth 2.0 or OIDC flow can really make the difference in the user experience since single sign-on can only be achieved if specific authentication flows are selected, and the possibility to strengthen the overall identity security and surface attack area depends on these choices too (we will see how those flows work later in the book).

Summary

In this chapter, we reviewed the analogies and differences across OAuth and OIDC. We understood OAuth and OIDC to be authorization and authentication protocols, respectively. These protocols share the same flows and logic.

OIDC is defined as an authentication protocol that runs on top of OAuth. This is because the flows adopted are the same.

We also familiarized ourselves with the terminology needed to understand the OAuth 2.0/OIDC flows that we will cover in depth in the next chapter, and the patterns that will be discussed in a later chapter.

This chapter provided the basis to understand these protocols and their related flows better. In the next chapter, we are going to view how these concepts are implemented and look at OAuth flows in much more detail.

4

Authentication Flows

We know that **OpenID Connect** (**OIDC**) extends the OAuth 2.0 protocol by introducing new flows, reusing some of the existing ones, and by placing the user, not the application, at the center of such flows. In this chapter, we will go through OAuth 2.0 and OIDC basics, learn about their flows, similarities, and differences, and where they can be used and why.

The chapter covers the following main topics:

- The authorization code grant flow
- The authorization code grant flow with Proof Key for Code Exchange
- The implicit grant flow
- The client credentials grant flow
- The **Resource Owner Password Credentials** (**ROPC**) grant flow
- The **On-Behalf-Of** (**OBO**) flow
- Hybrid flows

Here's a list of the flows and their support:

Protocol /Flow	Authorization Code Grant	Implicit	Client Credentials	Resource Owner Password Credentials	On-Behalf-Of	Hybrid
OAuth 2.0	YES	YES	YES	YES	YES	YES
OIDC	YES	YES	NO	NO	NO	YES

Figure 4.1 – OIDC/OAuth 2.0 flow support summary

The authorization code grant flow

The authorization code grant flow is used by a client application to obtain both an access token (or an ID token for OIDC) and a refresh token, and it is even more secure when used with *confidential* clients. Because this is a redirection-based flow, the client must be able to connect with the resource owner's user agent (usually a web browser) and receive inbound requests from the authorization server (via redirection).

The flow is described in the following diagram:

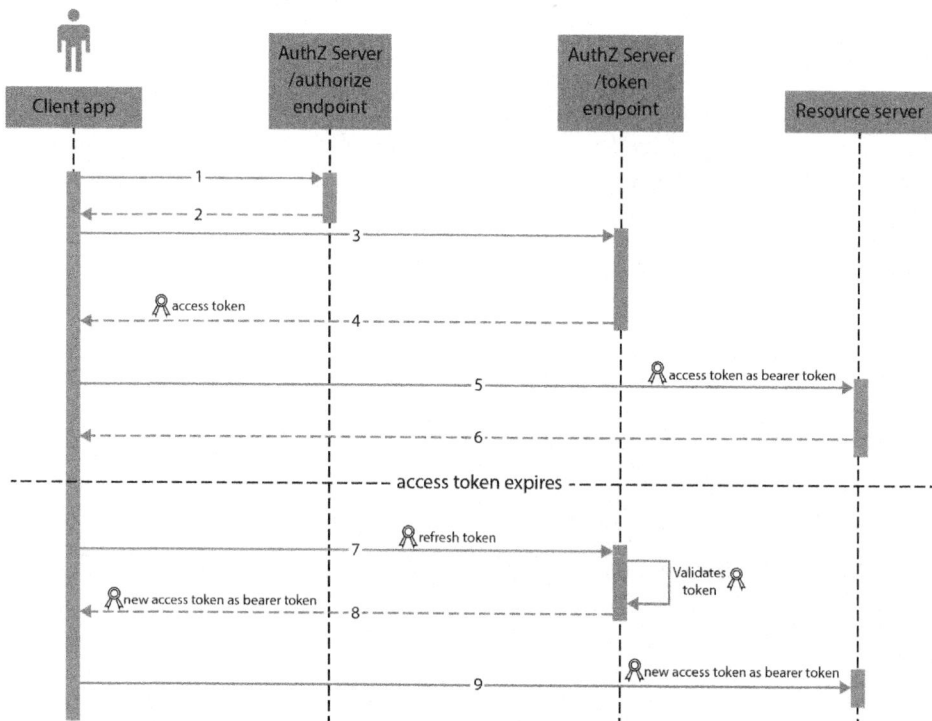

Figure 4.2 – Authorization code grant flow

The diagram is explained in detail in the following list. Each item reports the specific interaction that occurs at the numbered point in the diagram:

1. The client application requests an **authorization code** (authorization grant proof) from the /authorize endpoint of the authorization (AuthZ) server. This is what a request looks like:

    ```
    GET /authorize?
    response_type=code
    &client_id=s6BhdRkqt3
    ```

```
&redirect_uri=https%3A%2F%2Fclient.example.org%2Fcb
&scope=openid%20resource_server_id
&nonce=n-0S6_WzA2Mj
&state=af0ifjsldkj HTTP/1.1
Host: autzserver.example.com
```

2. The resource owner grants the authorization to the client application, typically by inserting their credentials. The authorization server returns an authorization code to the client application.

3. The client application (a public client specifically, since a confidential client must specify the `client_secret` parameter too) requests an access token from the `/token` endpoint by sending the authorization code received in the previous step. This is what a request looks like:

```
POST /token HTTP/1.1
Host: authzserver.example.com
Content-Type: application/x-www-form-urlencoded
Authorization: Basic czZCaGRSa3F0MzpnWDFmQmF0M2JW

grant_type=authorization_code&code=Splx10BeZQQYbYS6WxSbIA
    &redirect_uri=https%3A%2F%2Fclient.example.org%2Fcb
```

4. The authorization server verifies the permission code and sends an access token and a refresh token (if one is required) to the client application.

5. The client application sends the access token as a bearer token within an HTTP request to the resource server to retrieve some data from it.

6. The resource server validates the access token by looking at the signature, the issuer, the audience, and the expiration and sends back the requested data.

7. After some time, the access token expires and a new one is requested by the client application by sending the previously obtained refresh token to the authorization server.

8. The authorization server validates the refresh token and issues a new access token to the client application.

9. The client application sends the new access token as a bearer token within an HTTP request to the resource server to retrieve some data from it.

The authorization code grant flow is the most widely used flow among web applications that natively support redirections when accessed through a web browser. During *step 3*, the authorization server might require a *secret* from the client application if it is configured as a *confidential* client. The authorization code grant flow and its better variation, **Proof Key for Code Exchange** (**PKCE**), are the most secure flows that OAuth and OIDC offer, since the access token is never exposed to the resource owner's user agent. PKCE is explicitly designed for **Single-Page Applications (SPAs)**, as it does not allow us to store any secret on client machines that are considered *untrusted*.

The authorization code grant flow with PKCE

PKCE is a more secure variation of the authorization code grant flow that was mainly introduced for SPAs. It was introduced to mitigate the authorization code interception attack, which aims to steal the authorization code from a legitimate application in order to obtain an access token.

Let's see how this flow works:

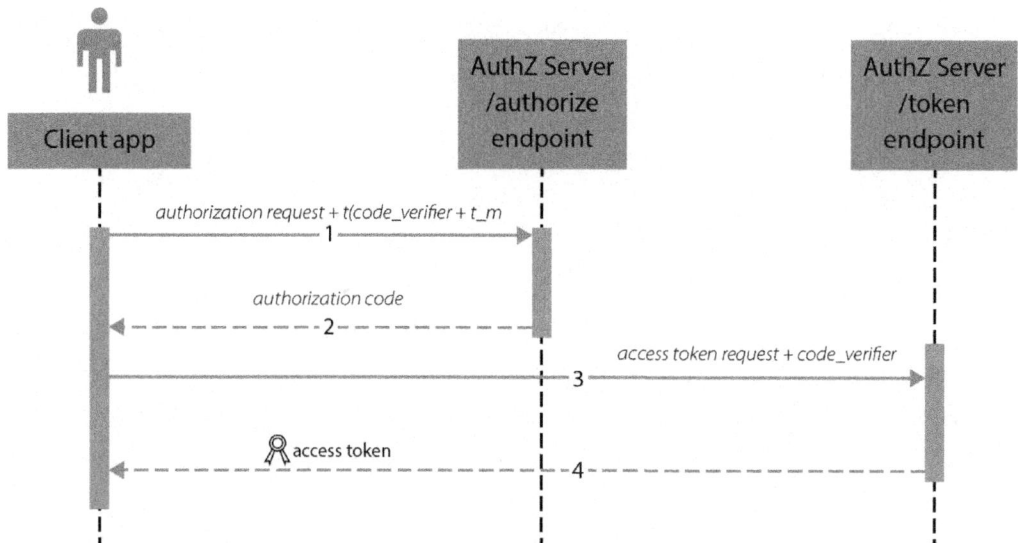

Figure 4.3 – PKCE

The flow is explained in detail as follows:

1. The client application requests an authorization code (authorization grant proof) from the /authorize endpoint of the authorization (AuthZ) server. Before sending the request, the client application generates a secret named code_verifier; it transforms it with a transformation named t_m and attaches the following to the authorization request:

    *   t(code_verifier): The transformed secret
    *   t_m: The transformation function

2. The authorization server stores the transformed secret, t(code_verifier), and the transformation function, t_m, and returns an authorization code to the client application.

3. The client application then requests an access token from the `/token` endpoint by sending the authorization code received in the previous step together with the secret it generated in *step 1*, `code_verifier` (not transformed).

4. The authorization code is validated by the authorization server, applies the `t_m` transformation to the `code_verifier` secret received in *step 3*, and compares this value with the `t(code_verifier)` value received in *step 1*. If the values are not equal, then access is denied and the authorization server does not issue an access token to the client application.

The PKCE flow should always be the preferred choice of an enterprise architect when designing the authentication flow of an application because it prevents the storage of an application's secrets within browsers and clients.

The implicit grant flow

The implicit grant flow is used to obtain an access token (or an ID token for OIDC) and is optimized for SPA public clients. Such clients typically run in a web browser, using a client-side scripting language such as JavaScript. This flow does not issue a refresh token, and the interaction between the client and the authorization server is done through the `/authorize` endpoint only.

The flow is described in the following diagram:

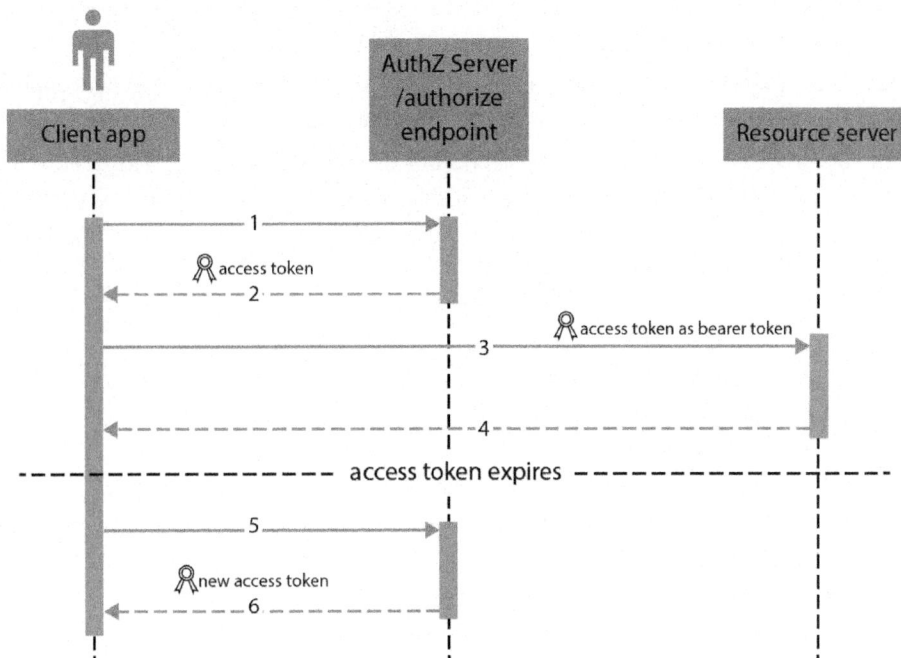

Figure 4.4 – Implicit grant flow

The diagram is explained in detail as follows:

1. An access token is requested by the client application; this is achieved by accessing the /authorize endpoint on the authorization (AuthZ) server. This is what a request looks like:

```
GET /authorize?
response_type=token     (or id_token)
&client_id=s6BhdRkqt3
&redirect_uri=https%3A%2F%2Fclient.example.org%2Fcb
&scope=openid%20resource_server_id
&nonce=n-0S6_WzA2Mj
&state=af0ifjsldkj HTTP/1.1
Host: autzserver.example.com
```

2. The resource owner grants the authorization to the client application, typically by inserting their credentials; an access token is returned by the authorization server to the client application within the redirection URI fragment.

3. The client application sends the access token as a bearer token within an HTTP request to the resource server to retrieve some data from it.

4. The resource server validates the access token by looking at the signature, the issuer, the audience, and the expiration and sends back the requested data.

5. After some time, the access token expires and a new one is requested by the client application, which sends a new access token request in the background.

6. The authorization server validates the application session and issues a new access token to the client application within the redirection URI fragment.

The implicit grant flow is the flow that's used most often by SPAs, but, unfortunately, it is also one of the least secure flows that OAuth/OIDC provides. The access token, as a matter of fact, is received directly by the web browser, making it more susceptible to misuse by malicious applications hosted within the resource owner's device. The implicit grant flow will be removed from **OAuth 2.1** specification.

The client credentials grant flow

The client credentials grant is a flow that must be used only by confidential clients, and it enables non-interactive application authentication. This makes sense because embedding the application credentials in a public client (such as a mobile application) exposes them to malicious users, making the whole purpose of keeping such credentials safe and secure in vain.

The flow is described in the following diagram:

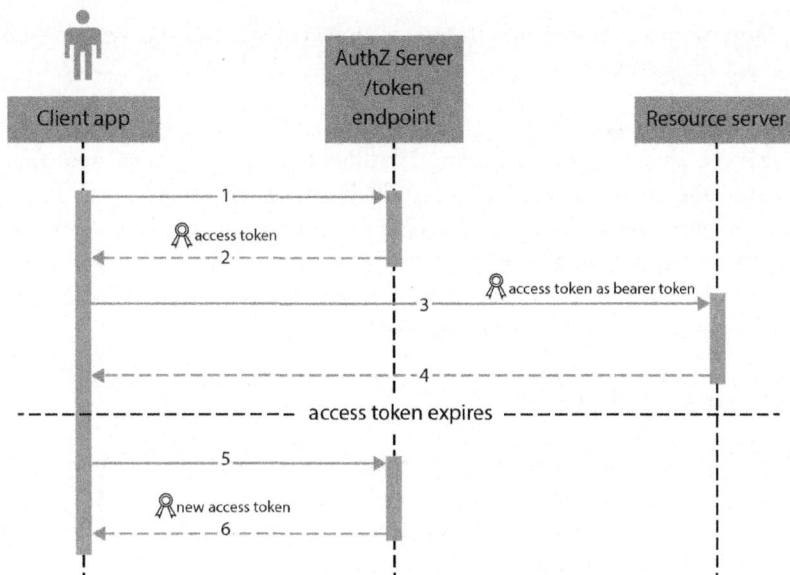

Figure 4.5 – Client credentials grant flow

The diagram is explained in detail as follows:

1. The client application requests an access token directly from the /token endpoint of the authorization (AuthZ) server by providing its previously configured credentials (such as client_id and a secret or certificate). This is what a request looks like:

    ```
    GET /token?
    grant_type=client_credentials
    &client_id=s6BhdRkqt3
    &scope=resource_server_id
    &client_secret=uayaskiR$£QDcfa
    Host: authzserver.example.com
    ```

2. The authorization server validates the client application's credentials and then returns an access token to the client application.

3. The client application sends the access token as a bearer token within an HTTP request to the resource server to retrieve some data from it.

4. The resource server validates the access token by looking at the signature, the issuer, the audience, and the expiration and sends back the requested data.

5.   After some time, the access token expires and a new one is requested by the client application, which sends a new access token request in the background.

6.   The authorization server validates the application credentials and issues a new access token to the client application.

An application must have its own credentials, which it uses to obtain an access token from the authorization server. This flow is very common in those scenarios where an application needs to authenticate and get the authorization to call an external API that trusts the same authorization server, without user intervention. The OAuth RFC specifies that a confidential client can use a password (*secret*) to authenticate against the authorization server in order to obtain the access token, but it also states that other HTTP authentication schemes are possible, and as a matter of fact, it is very common to find solutions that also use a *certificate* to accomplish this goal.

The ROPC grant flow

The ROPC flow moves the resource owner's credential management into the client application. The resource owner is prompted directly by the client application, which usually has a form where the user can insert their credentials. For this reason, ROPC is not a recommended flow because it trusts that the client application will not misuse a user's credentials.

The flow is described in the following diagram:

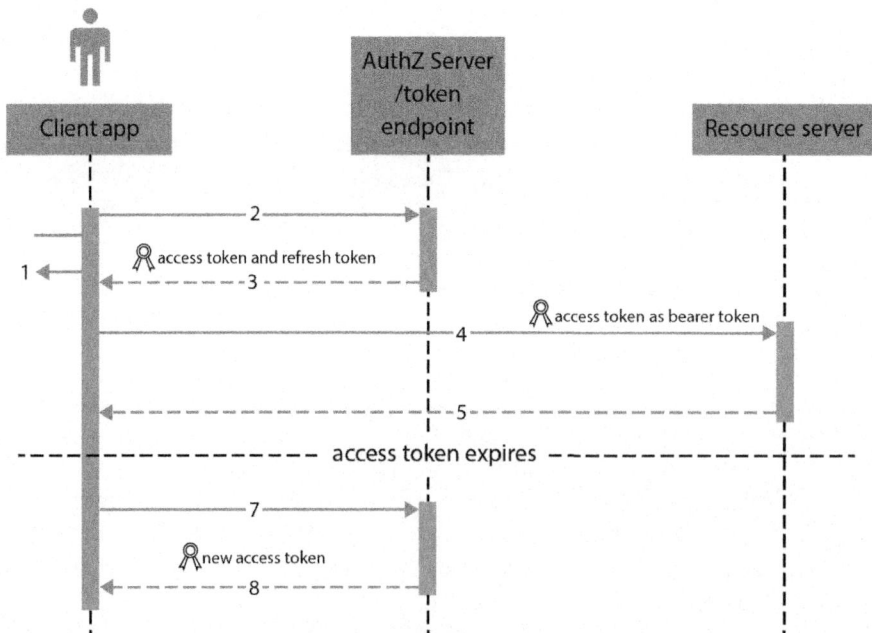

Figure 4.6 – ROPC grant flow

The diagram is explained in detail as follows:

1. The resource owner directly inserts their credentials within the client application.

2. The client application requests an access token directly to the /token endpoint of the authorization (AuthZ) server by sending the credentials the resource owner provided in the previous step. This is what a request looks like:

```
POST /token?
grant_type=PASSWORD
&client_id=s6BhdRkqt3
&scope=resource_server_id%20offline_access
&username=userid1
&password=84ru2hkajhf
Host: authzserver.example.com
```

3. The authorization server validates the client application's credentials and then returns an access token to the client application. Optionally, the authorization server can also return a refresh token.

4. The client application sends the access token as a *bearer token* within an HTTP request to the resource server to retrieve some data from it.

5. The resource server validates the access token by looking at the signature, the issuer, the audience, and the expiration and sends back the requested data.

6. After some time, the access token expires and a new one is requested by the client application, which sends a new access token request in the background using the refresh token acquired in *step 2*.

7. The authorization server issues a new access token upon the validation of the refresh token to the client application.

ROPC is very often used within native applications – for example, first-party mobile apps such as the Facebook app – but, generally speaking, a more secure flow such as the authorization code grant flow should be used instead. The ROPC flow will be removed from the OAuth 2.1 specification.

The OBO flow

The OBO flow (which is not part of standard OAuth 2.0 (IETF) but is specific to Microsoft Azure Active Directory implementation) is used to allow a resource server to call another resource server in the background without any user interaction. This is useful when there are two resource servers, usually managed by different parties, that trust the same authorization server and contribute to the logic of a single application, and need to be used in the background seamlessly. To allow a resource server to use the OBO flow, the authorization server must be properly configured.

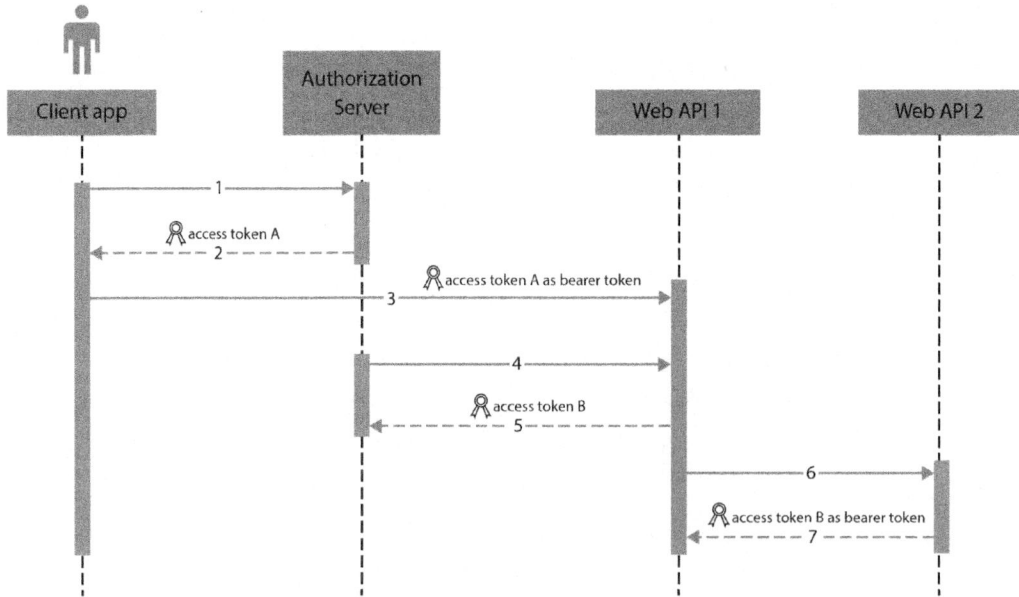

Figure 4.7 – OBO flow

The diagram is explained in detail as follows:

1. The client application requests an access token to the authorization server using the authorization code grant flow or another authentication flow, as described in the previous paragraphs.

2. The authorization server validates the request and issues an access token to the client application.

3. The client application sends the access token as a bearer token within an HTTP request to the resource server (Web API 1) to retrieve some data from it.

4. At some point in time, Web API 1 authenticates against the authorization server to obtain an access token for Web API 2 on behalf of the user. When authenticating against the authorization server, Web API 1 sends the access token received by the client application, a client ID, and a secret.

5. The authorization server issues another access token for Web API 1 to be used with Web API 2.

6. Web API 1 sends access token B as a bearer token within an HTTP request to Web API 2 to retrieve some data from it.

7. Web API 2 validates the access token by looking at the signature, the issuer, the audience, and the expiration and sends back the requested data.

In *Chapter 5*, *Exploring Identity Patterns*, we will see more use cases regarding this flow, which is used in specific scenarios.

Hybrid flows

Hybrid flows (part of the OIDC specification) mix authorization code grant and implicit flows together, enabling the issuing of access tokens and ID tokens at different phases compared to when those flows are used alone.

During the first call to the `/authorize` endpoint of the authorization server, a client application can specify the following values for the `response_type` parameter, making the authorization server behave differently:

- `code token`: When specified in the HTTP request, an access token and an authorization code must be included in a successful response

- `code id_token`: When specified in the HTTP request, an authorization code and an ID token must be included in a successful response

- `id_token token`: When specified in the HTTP request, an ID token and an access token must be included in a successful response

- `code id_token token`: When specified in the HTTP request, an access token and an ID token must be included in a successful response

The following code snippet shows a client application request using a hybrid flow:

```
GET /authorize?
response_type=id_token%20token
&client_id=s6BhdRkqt3
&redirect_uri=https%3A%2F%2Fclient.example.org%2Fcb
&state=bfansly HTTP/1.1
Host: authzserver.example.com
```

It is important to note that due to its similarities with the authorization code grant flow, the hybrid flow needs to be considered for confidential clients. This is because both the client and the secret of the application need to be sent.

Consequently, the hybrid flow is not recommended for public clients, such as browsers.

Summary

In this chapter, we have gone through the authorization and authentication flows provided by OAuth 2.0 and OIDC protocols. We described their usage and their main objectives in terms of the best scenarios where they can be used.

In the next chapter, we will get a broader view of how these flows can be used to solve specific problems by providing a set of recipes, or **patterns**, that can be used in particular scenarios that are usually encountered when working in an enterprise.

5

Exploring Identity Patterns

In this chapter, we will finally put into practice the knowledge that we acquired throughout the book before now. We now know how the **OpenID Connect** (**OIDC**) and OAuth 2.0 protocols work and, most importantly, what authentication flows they enable.

Understanding the right scenario for an authentication flow is a key aspect for an enterprise architect during the design of an application: the **patterns** described in this chapter can be used as a quick reference to guide the decision-making process around the authentication and authorization of an application.

To make a parallel with the programming world, these patterns can be applied to authentication in the same way that today, we, as programmers, design and write the code of a modern cloud application architecture by leveraging software design patterns (e.g. Ambassador, retry, sidecar, etc.).

This chapter will give you the tools (or *patterns*) to choose the best authentication design for an application, which can be harnessed side by side with software design patterns to engineer all the aspects of an application before it is effectively deployed into a production environment.

We will cover the following topics in this chapter:

- Understanding the basic terminology
- Web applications
- Native applications
- SPAs

Understanding the basic terminology

Before diving into each pattern, we will present you with some terminology that will be used throughout the following presentation of different patterns. Then, we're going to review the patterns recommended for different application styles:

- **Application identity**

    As we'll see later, there are different kinds of applications that exist. It's important to grasp the concept of application identity though before expanding to examine the different types of applications that can be encountered.

    Application identity is a concept that is tightly coupled with the OIDC and OAuth 2.0 authentication protocols. When interacting with an identity provider, an application must have and use an identity that the identity provider knows, an identity that an administrator has previously registered as part of the application configuration. Typically, an OIDC or OAuth 2.0 flow requires two application identities to be registered: a client and a server application identity.

    The client application may require an ID token to authenticate the user or an access token to be authorized to call a particular server application. In this scenario, the server applications are also named resources or resource servers and, typically, they are in the form of web (REST) APIs when related to complex enterprise applications.

- **Single-page applications (SPAs)**

    SPAs do not typically involve a web server in the backend to host static content (a web server may be used to host the API on which the SPA will rely). Static files such as JavaScript, CSS, and HTML are retrieved from a publicly available location and all the application logic is typically handled by JavaScript running in the browser, which interacts with the API on the server side to tune the page accordingly. A SPA, as a matter of fact, even if it is very complex, interacts with APIs to send and retrieve data and most of the time, this interaction requires some kind of authorization artifact (obtained once the SPA is authenticated) that in OIDC/OAuth 2.0, we know takes the shape of an access token.

- **Native application**

    A native application is very similar to a SPA if we just look at the core functionality: it is an application that needs to interact with (typically REST) APIs to accomplish a task or business feature. The main difference with SPAs is that a native application is not browser-based and therefore, it does not run within the context of a browser, rather running directly as an application of the operating system where it is installed. A native application can be a Win32 or Store app in Windows, or an app retrieved from an app store and then installed on a mobile operating system, such as iOS or Android.

- **Web (REST) API**

  By web API, we mean a RESTful API that understands HTTP and is published on a network to provide some sort of functionality to consumer applications. A web API usually needs a form of authentication in order to be successfully used by a caller application – there are different methods used by enterprises for web API authentication, including the client and server certificates used in a mutual authentication scenario, but the focus of this book will be on OAuth 2.0 protected APIs.

- **Service**

  By service, we mean an application that can operate without any user intervention. A service could be a background task, a job that can act according to an external trigger (an event or an HTTP request trigger), or a schedule (for example, a job that runs each day at 2:00 a.m.). During task execution, a service may need to interact with external components that may be another service or a web API. Within these two scenarios, it is common to have an authentication flow happening in the background that cannot depend on a user providing authorization for the service to perform a specific task because it would make the automation of that task impossible. As per the web APIs, different authentication methods can be used here (including certificates), but we will focus on the ones leveraging the OAuth 2.0 protocol.

- **User agent**

  A user agent is a commodity software that acts on behalf of the user by translating the user's intentions (or user inputs) into actions in the context of an application. For multi-page applications and SPAs, the user agent is typically a web browser. The web browser handles the application code and translates it into a human-readable format, ready to accept any user input. Why is the concept of a user agent important to us? This is easy to explain – the user agent acts as the bearer of the client application's identity. As already said, for multi-page applications and SPAs, the user agent is the web browser, whereas, in the case of native applications, it corresponds to the native application itself (because it carries out user actions on behalf of the user).

We will now use this terminology to present the different design patterns throughout this chapter. We will go through the different application types that are typically encountered in an enterprise (using the aforementioned terminology) and understand which patterns are best applied to design their authentication flows, along with examining their relationships with the application identities registered with the identity provider.

We will assume that a single identity provider exists in the following sections unless explicitly stated otherwise.

Web applications

In this section, we refer to a web application as a multi-page application to distinguish it from the SPA discussed later in this chapter.

When we use the term multi-page application, we refer to the traditional web application backed by a web server. A user accesses a multi-page application through a web browser (see the previous definition of user agent), which interacts with the web server by exchanging and requesting data – the web server typically responds to browser requests (HTTP requests) by computing a new page and sending it back to the browser for user visualization and further interaction.

We can think of a typical web application as a set of layers. The set of layers is defined according to the framework used – for example, **Model-View-Controller** (**MVC**), **Model-View-Adapter** (**MVA**), or **Presentation-Abstraction-Control** (**PAC**). Regardless of the framework used, we can increase the level of abstraction (without going into detail) and think of a web application as something built on top of two main components: business logic, which represents the core implementation of the web application itself, and the interceptor, which is the layer triggered in every request to "intercept" the request up front, before it hits any business logic:

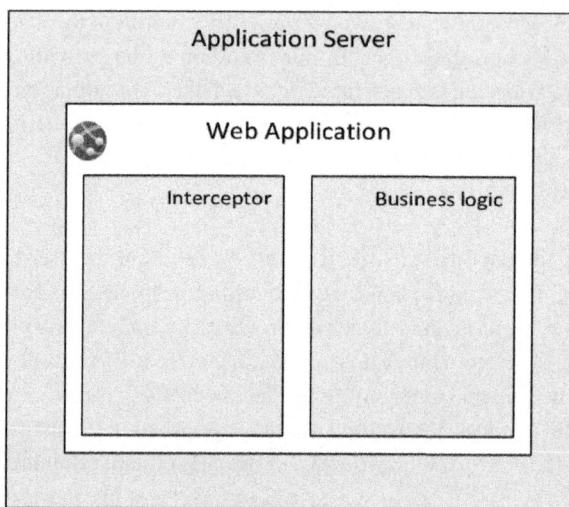

Figure 5.1 – Web application layers

The business logic is usually implemented using frameworks such as MVC, which is the most common framework adopted by most technologies (such as .NET, Java frameworks, Ruby on Rails, etc.). Regardless of the technology, the interceptor layer is the first piece of logic to be executed and validates whether the request can be directly served (and as such, triggers the implemented business logic), whether it should be refused, or whether it requires authentication. In certain technologies, the interceptor layer logic is implemented in the middleware, but the concept is still the same – no business logic can run if the request is not evaluated by the interceptor layer first. We can surmise here that one of the most important duties of this kind of layer is to validate whether the user is already authenticated and as such, the request can be moved on to the business logic or sent to the identity provider for authentication.

Traditional web applications (written using common web development frameworks such as .NET, Spring, or Laravel) hosted on a web server usually provide a consistent user experience without relying on external services (that is, external web APIs).

When external dependencies are not present, then it is likely that an access token is not needed, but for the application to completely achieve its business logic, it is sufficient to extract the information (claims) that comes with the ID token.

An example of an application without external dependencies could be the typical "monolith" application hosted on a server and usually replicated on a wider set of servers for availability and load-handling purposes.

The multi-page application presented in this section differs from a SPA because, in the multi-page application, the business logic is responsible for returning the view (HTML and CSS) to the browser according to the request and the business logic. The view is served according to server-side operations, unlike a SPA, where the view is typically performed on the client side according to the API response, which is typically JSON.

User authentication only pattern

In the case of multi-page applications, we recommend using a pattern named **user authentication only**, described in greater detail later in this section.

Before going into the authentication logic, it is important to recap how the logic of the application is supposed to be implemented to run the authentication flow:

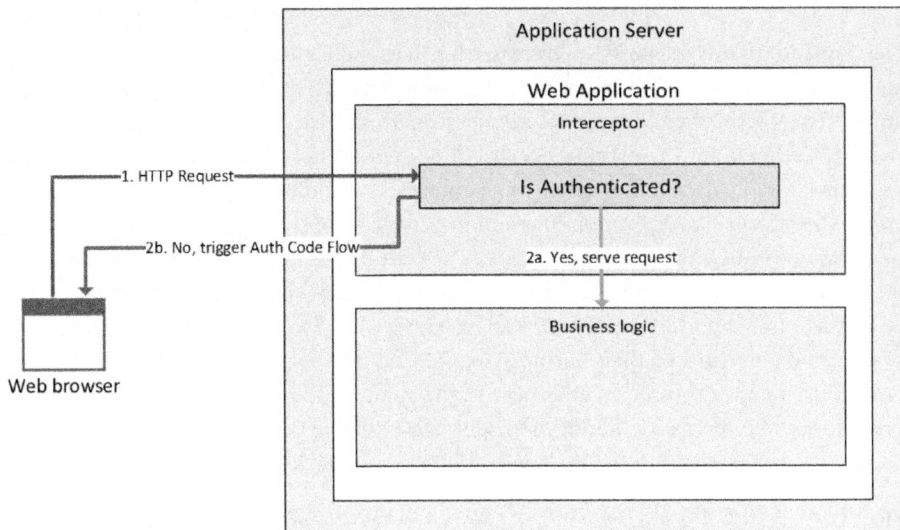

Figure 5.2 – Sample application logic for an AuthZ code grant flow

The *interceptor layer* of the application determines whether or not the user is already authenticated and thus whether authentication needs to be triggered.

How the application determines this depends on the implementation of the interceptor layer itself. The most typical approach is to take advantage of cookies – whenever the user is authenticated the first time, the application will release a cookie that will then be used for any subsequent HTTP request as proof of authentication already having been performed.

Let's now get familiar with some of the important concepts related to the user authentication-only pattern:

- **Scenario**:

  - **Application type**: Multi-page web application hosted on a single web server. By *web server*, we mean a generic hosting platform that is auto-consistent and does not need to communicate with other external services, which could be other web servers or a hosting platform that publishes a service through a REST API.

  - **External dependencies**: None.

  - **User agent**: In this scenario, the user agent is a *web browser* that renders *HTML* pages and interacts with the web server by translating the user's actions into HTTP requests. The web server typically responds to the web browser by either sending back data or new HTML pages to render.

- **Recommended pattern**: User authentication only.

- **Protocol/flow**: **Open ID Connect (OIDC)** with the Authorization Code Grant flow (with PKCE if possible).

- **Description**: In this scenario, we have just a single application. This application requires user authentication before the user can access and interact with it. Once a user shows their proof of authentication, the application does not need anything else to function properly – we say that the application is auto-consistent because it does not rely on external services to implement its business logic. A typical example in an enterprise could be an informative web portal such as an *intranet* portal. A common interaction between a user and an intranet portal is the user navigating through the different pages of the portal to find relevant information about, for instance, internal corporate policies, the latest news, or upcoming events. To accomplish all these tasks, the intranet portal usually just needs to know who the principal (user) is and some pieces of information regarding their business area, country, and so on, to provide a user experience tailored to the specific user. In other words, the application needs the user to authenticate and provide some information about themselves to enhance the overall experience for the end users – we can agree that what the application needs here is an *ID token*.

- **Technical details**: We already know we are focusing on a single multi-page application with no external dependencies, whose user agent is a web browser. Now, the question is what the steps required to configure the application with the suggested authentication protocol and flow are. In this chapter, we won't focus on a specific identity provider but will provide generally applicable configuration steps that are common to most publicly available identity providers that implement the OIDC and OAuth 2.0 protocols.

The Authorization Code Grant flow (see *Chapter 4, Authentication Flows*) typically requires registering two application identities in the identity provider – one for the application requesting authorization and one for the resource that the requesting application seeks to access.

In our scenario, however, there are no external dependencies, which means there is no resource our application needs to access. In other words, we could say that, in this case, the client application and the server application (resource) are the same entity.

With that in mind, it is easy to work out the number of application identities we need to register in the identity provider – just one, representing our multi-page web application. When we have just one application and the only requirement is to authenticate the user, then the OIDC protocol should be used.

Now that we have explained in greater detail why we need certain artifacts, we can show them more clearly with an example. Our example is comprised of the following:

- An end user named `User1` who accesses the application
- A multi-page web application named `WebApp1`
- The `WebApp1` reply URL is `https://webapp1.example.com/auth`
- A web server named `WebServer1` that hosts `WebApp1`
- An identity provider named `Idp1`, in charge of authenticating the end user
- The `Idp1` URL is `https://idp1.example.com`
- An identifier for `WebApp1`, registered by an administrator in `Idp1`, as `WebApp1-Id`
- A client secret configured for `WebApp1-Id` in `Idp1`, called `WebApp1-Secret`

The Authorization Code Grant flow implementation then follows the standard process as presented in the previous chapter's *Authorization Code Grant flow* section. It is important to note the following two points:

- The `WebApp1` application is considered a *confidential client* because it runs on a web server (`WebServer1`, which is typically deployed within a protected corporate network) and not directly in the `User1` web browser like a SPA – the browser, as a matter of fact, interacts with the server to implement the business logic of the application and therefore, the *ID token* never flows through the browser, which only sees the *authorization code*. This code is sent to `WebServer1`, which retrieves the ID token by contacting `Idp1` directly and providing `WebApp1-Secret`.

- Since there is only one application identity (WebApp1-Id) registered in Idp1, the *scope* parameter of the authorization request that WebApp1 sends to Idp1 (through the web browser) cannot include any specific *resource identifier*, but can use common OIDC-only scopes such as OpenID, profile, and so on.

The flow with the details of the requests is explained as follows (for the sake of simplicity, we are not considering the PKCE variation of the AuthZ Code Grant flow, which would indeed be the preferred choice):

1. WebApp1 (through the web browser of User1) requests an authorization code to the /authorize endpoint of Idp1. This is what the request looks like:

```
GET /authorize?
response_type=code
&client_id=WebApp1-Id
&redirect_uri=https%3A%2F%2Fwebapp1.example.com%2Fauth
&scope=openid%20profile
&nonce=n-0S6_WzA2Mj
&state=af0ifjsldkj HTTP/1.1
Host: idp1.example.com
```

2. User1 grants authorization to WebApp1 by inserting its credentials in the Idp1 login page. Idp1 returns an authorization code to the WebApp1 reply URL.

3. WebApp1 (in the background) requests an access token from the /token endpoint by sending the authorization code received in the previous step. This is what the request looks like:

```
POST /token HTTP/1.1
Host: idp1.example.com
Content-Type: application/x-www-form-urlencoded
Authorization: Basic WebApp1-Secret

grant_type=authorization_code&code=SplxlOBeZQQYbYS6WxSbIA
    &redirect_uri=https%3A%2F%2Fwebapp1.example.org%2Fauth
```

4. Idp1 validates the authorization code and issues an ID token, an access token, and a refresh token (if requested) to WebApp1.

As you may also have noticed, an access token is issued by Idp1 to WebApp1 even if it is not needed. This happens because the OIDC official specification says to do so.

Once the ID token is received and validated by `WebApp1`, the user is considered authenticated. At this point, several techniques can be put in place to store the `User1` information for later requests to avoid `User1` being prompted for authentication a second time within the token validity timeframe. These techniques are out of the scope of this book, but to name just one, a web application usually stores session information (including information retrieved from the ID token) within an application cookie.

What is important though is how the authentication and single sign-on are handled by `WebApp1` and `Idp1`. Typically, what happens is the following:

1. An application cookie of the same validity period as the ID token, which has a short duration (usually 1 hour), is issued to the web browser by `WebApp1`. Within the cookie validity period, the user is not prompted for authentication.

2. Once the ID token (and therefore the cookie) expires, `WebApp1` may use its refresh token to obtain a new ID token from `Idp1`.

3. If `WebApp1` has no refresh token or the refresh token has expired, then the user is redirected back to the identity provider to get a new ID token (in the Authorization Code Grant flow). If `Idp1` issued a cookie during the first successful authentication attempt with the web browser, then it can be used to avoid prompting the user for authentication a second time, providing the cookie hasn't expired.

In the next two sections, we will see why other OIDC flows are generally discouraged for this scenario.

Additional considerations

OIDC and OAuth 2.0 provide different flows that could be used in the multi-page application scenario we described previously: we are talking about the implicit flow and the resource owner password credentials grant flow.

Although they may be used for very specific use cases, their usage is generally discouraged because of the security concerns (for more info on this, refer to the *Security considerations* section in the next chapter) that have been raised by the authentication community since the protocols were officially released. If you're interested, more details can be found on the **Internet Engineering Task Force (IETF)** website.

Here follows a list of exploits that can be further reviewed online, highlighting why OAuth flows should be avoided:

- **Insufficient redirect Uniform Resource Identifier (URI) validation**

    If the authorization server does not enforce strict validation of the redirect URIs that can be registered for each application, an attacker can redirect the user agent to a bad URI under the attacker's control.

- **Credential leakage via a web browser plugin**

  When the access token is received by a web browser, a malevolent plugin (or browser extension) can steal it and use it within a legitimate application, impersonating the user who initially requested it.

- **Credential leakage via browser history**

  A web browser may save code and access token information within the browser's history, exposing it to other applications running on the user's client.

- **Access token injection**

  Once an access token has been obtained by a malicious user, it can be injected into a legitimate application to impersonate a different user or authorize the application to do something that it is not supposed to be able to do.

Moreover, there is no mechanism in place in the implicit flow that can bind an access token to the specific client that requested it because clients using the implicit flow are public clients. This means they cannot use any form of secrets because these secrets would be available directly in the web browser or native application using them.

Adoption of both the implicit flow and the resource owner password credentials grant is discouraged. The resource owner password credentials grant insecurely exposes the credentials of the resource owner to the client. Even if the user is using a trusted client, this increases the attack surface (credentials can leak from more places than just the authorization server) and users are trained to enter their credentials in places other than the authorization server, which usually makes them more prone to a phishing attack.

These additional considerations are important factors that require consideration from architects at design time. In this section, we explored how OAuth can be used in different ways and how some of these ways are discouraged from a security perspective. When an interactive login is required from a web application using OAuth, it is important to adopt the concept highlighted by the user authentication only pattern and avoid, wherever possible, the implicit flow and the resource owner password credentials grant flow, for the reasons reported previously.

In the next section, we will describe other use cases that differ from the standard user interactive login path.

Native applications

A native application, as already explained, is a non-web application (by non-web application, we mean something that is not supposed to be browser-based, but still uses the REST or SOAP protocols for client-server interaction) written for a specific operating system that runs side by side with other applications on that operating system. Nowadays, native applications run mostly on mobile platforms such as iOS and Android, but it is very common to encounter native applications running on Windows as Win32 and Store applications, among other things.

It's rare to find a native application that does not interact with external APIs to implement its business logic and therefore, it's also common that these applications require an access token to securely communicate with such external services.

As we will appreciate in the rest of this chapter, native applications have many similarities to SPAs. This is because both of them interact with APIs located on the server side and dynamically evolve the UX according to the API responses, which, in turn, are affected by the user behavior.

From a design point of view, native applications do not usually differ so much from SPAs, and as such, the authentication and authorization flows are often similar.

Application authorization pattern

The recommended authorization pattern for native applications is the authorization code grant flow discussed in the previous chapter.

From a high level, the flow to authorize a native application against the API it needs to consume looks like the following:

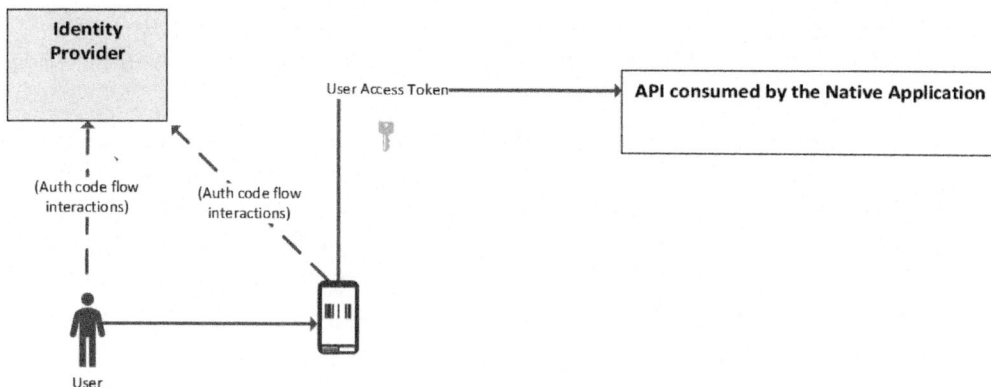

Figure 5.3 – Native app – application authorization pattern

In this scenario, both the OIDC and OAuth 2.0 protocols are needed, and the recommended pattern in this case is named **application authorization**.

As in the previous section, we'll review the scenario details in bullet fashion to see which OAuth flow is suggested for adoption in this scenario, what the user agent is, and a description of the technical details required to fully understand how it is recommended to implement authentication in a native application:

- **Scenario**:

  - **Application type**: A native application directly runs in the context of an operating system. Mobile applications are the most common example of native applications (e.g., the Facebook app or your banking app) – they usually do not store any data locally, except for caching purposes, and instead, are highly reliant on authenticated external APIs in order to retrieve the relevant information needed by the end user.

- **External dependencies**: One or more external APIs registered on the same identity provider as the client application.

- **User agent**: In this scenario, the user agent is the native application itself, which both implements the user interface and manages the interactions with the external REST APIs in the background to exchange the data needed to fulfill the application logic. Modern applications using this approach commonly leverage the JSON format for data exchange – an external REST API receives an HTTP request containing data in its body in JSON format and the API responds with the requested information by embedding it into a JSON document in the HTTP response body.

- **Recommended pattern**: Application authorization.

- **Protocol/flow**: OIDC and OAuth 2.0 with the Authorization Code Grant flow (with PKCE if possible).

- **Description**: A native application requires both an authenticated user and authorization to access the external APIs it depends on. In other words, a native application needs both an ID token and an access token.

  The ID token, once obtained, is usually stored locally in the application and is used to tailor the user experience according to the operations the authenticated user can and cannot do. The access token is also stored locally and it is used as a bearer token in the HTTP requests against the external APIs as proof of authorization for performing a specific task. As part of the Authorization Code Grant flow, a refresh token can also be issued and stored in the application to renew the access token when it expires.

  Since the Authorization Code Grant flow requires that the user inserts their credentials in the authentication form provided by the identity provider, the native application (not being a web browser) will likely leverage an external application provided by the operating system to render the web page containing the aforementioned web login form. This application is usually opened by the native application in an external or pop-up window and it is usually referred to as a web view. This user experience is not optimal because the authentication flow does not happen as a whole within the native application, but it is safer than using alternative approaches that make use of the resource owner password credentials flow, which requires handling user credentials directly in the native application logic.

- **Technical details**: What are the steps required to configure a native application with the suggested authentication protocol or flow? In this chapter, we won't focus on a specific identity provider but will provide generally applicable configuration steps that are common to most publicly available identity providers that implement the OIDC or OAuth 2.0 protocols.

The Authorization Code Grant flow (see *Chapter 4, Authentication Flows*) typically requires defining two application identities in the identity provider – one for the application requesting authorization and one for the resource that the application seeks to access.

Since, in this scenario, we know one or more external dependencies exist, it means that there could be several resources our application needs to access. *In other words, we could also say that in this case, the client application and the server applications (resources) are separate entities.*

For simplicity, we assume that the external API needed by our native application is just one, and therefore the number of application identities we need to register in the identity provider is two – one representing the native application (the client application) and one representing the external API (the server or resource). When we have multiple APIs, it is easy to see that we need to register an application identity for each of them.

Let's now see how this pattern can be put into practice with an example. Our example is comprised of the following:

- An end user named `User1` that accesses the application.
- A native application named `NativeApp1` that represents the `client` application.
- An external web API named `WebAPI1` that represents the `server` application (resource).
- An identity provider named `Idp1` in charge of authenticating the end user.
- The `Idp1` URL is `https://idp1.example.com`.
- An identifier for `NativeApp1` that has been registered by an administrator in `Idp1` as `NativeApp1-Id`.
- An identifier for `WebAPI1` that has been registered by an administrator in `Idp1` as `WebAPI1-Id`.
- One or more scopes (for example, read or write) can be defined for `WebAPI1`. These scopes define what operations can be done when calling the API and are interpreted by `WebAPI1` itself. The scopes must be registered in the configuration of the `WebApp1-Id` application registered in `Idp1` and a client application (in our example, `NativeApp1-Id`) must be explicitly allowed to request such scopes.
- The `NativeApp1` reply URL depends on the schema supported by the specific authentication library used – for instance, when using **Microsoft Authentication Library** (**MSAL**), it could be something like `msalc38ukiaghksg73ldsg://auth`. This URL must be registered in the configuration of the `NativeApp1-Id` application registered in `Idp1`.

The Authorization Code Grant flow implementation then follows the standard process presented in the previous chapter's *Authorization Code Grant flow* section. It is important to note that the scope parameter of the authorization request sent by `NativeApp1` to `Idp1` typically includes the resource identifier of the web API, `WebApp1-Id`, together with the scopes `WebAPI1` offers (read and write, in our example).

The flow with the details of the requests is explained as follows (for the sake of simplicity, we are not considering the PKCE variation of the AuthZ Code Grant flow, which would be the preferred choice here):

1. When a user opens `NativeApp1` on their device, the application requests an authorization code from the `/authorize` endpoint of `Idp1`. This is how the request looks:

    ```
    GET /authorize?
    response_type=code
    &client_id=NativeApp1-Id
    &redirect_uri=msalc38ukiaghksg73ldsg%3A%2F%2Fauth
    &scope=NativeApp1-Id%3Aread%20NativeApp1-Id%3Awrite
    &nonce=n-0S6_WzA2Mj
    &state=af0ifjsldkj HTTP/1.1
    Host: idp1.example.com
    ```

2. `NativeApp1` opens a web view showing the `Idp1` login page.

3. `User1` grants the authorization to `NativeApp1` by inserting their credentials into the `Idp1` login page – `Idp1` returns an authorization code to the `NativeApp1` reply URL.

4. `NativeApp1` (in the background) requests an access token from the `/token` endpoint by sending the authorization code received in the previous step. This is how the request looks:

    ```
    POST /token HTTP/1.1
    Host: idp1.example.com
    Content-Type: application/x-www-form-urlencoded

    grant_type=authorization_code&code=SplxlOBeZQQYbYS6WxSbIA
        &redirect_uri=msalc38ukiaghksg73ldsg%3A%2F%2Fauth
    ```

    Notice that, in this case, a secret is not sent because native applications are not considered confidential clients since they run fully on the user device, which is considered untrustworthy.

5. `Idp1` validates the authorization code and issues an ID token, an access token, and a refresh token (if requested) to `NativeApp1`.

Once the ID token is received and validated by `NativeApp1`, then the user is considered authenticated. At this point, several techniques can be used to store `User1` information for further requests so that `User1` is not prompted for authentication a second time within the token validity timeframe; these techniques are out of the scope of this book. On the other hand, the access token can be used to invoke the operations exposed by `WebAPI1` by sending it as a bearer token within each HTTP request sent to the API.

SPAs

In this section, we are going to look at SPAs. First, we will learn about how they differ from web applications (aka multi-page applications) described in the *Web applications* section of this chapter, allowing us to appreciate the implications of the authentication and authorization mechanisms in question.

A typical SPA is served as static content to the browser. Since the initial static content consisting of HTML, CSS, and JavaScript files is still the same for all users, it is not uncommon to serve this content directly from a cloud storage service, rather than a web server, as covered in the *Web applications* section in this chapter. Determining whether to choose a multi-page application or SPA in line with the application requirements is beyond the scope of this book. For more information, it is recommended to refer to the following link: `https://docs.microsoft.com/en-us/dotnet/architecture/ modern-web-apps-azure/choose-between-traditional-web-and-single- page-apps`.

The reason why many implementations of SPAs take advantage of cloud storage capabilities and do not use an application server to store their content is that, for static content, there is no server-side logic involved, storage is cheaper, and this is typically the most convenient solution. Moreover, offloading the web server from serving static content can enhance performance; more specifically, the API that needs to run server-side logic can focus on computation only and doesn't need to waste compute time on serving static content.

The following is a logical diagram outlining the composition of a typical SPA:

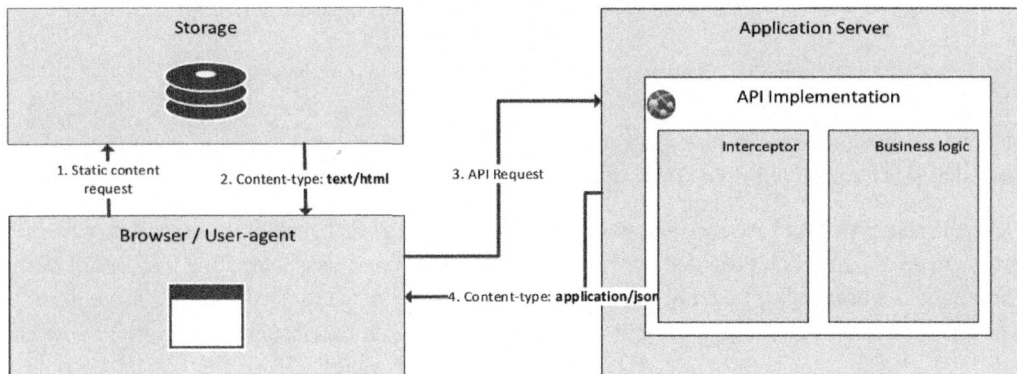

Figure 5.4 – SPA – logical diagram

As shown in the preceding figure, the browser will get the static content without any server-side logic involved. Then, the page will evolve according to the browser's interpretations of the HTTP responses coming from the API as a result of the user's behavior.

Single-page authentication pattern

To better understand this pattern, we need to think of the browser and the user as two different entities.

In this case, in fact, we are going to see an important concept of OAuth that was described in *Chapter 3, OAuth 2.0 and OIDC* – an entity that spends its access token to access the API. This is something we weren't able to appreciate in the *Web applications* section, as it used a pure OIDC flow. In this section, the access token and OAuth concepts are really important for this pattern to work.

The following is a representation of the actors and steps involved:

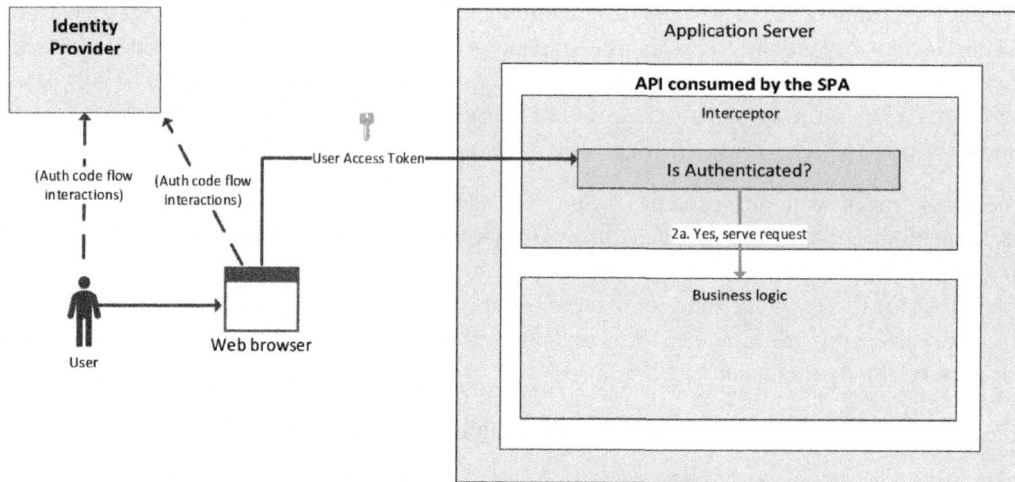

Figure 5.5 – Single-page application pattern – a monolith design

The preceding figure represents a monolith where both the interceptor layer and the business logic layer share the same application server and are developed within the same solution.

Figure 5.5 shows that we have a web browser that accesses the API on behalf of the user. This is possible thanks to an access token provided by the identity provider upon user login. The final result of the operations is a user access token dispatched to the browser and spendable by it until its expiration, which is commonly around an hour (this depends on the default time set in the identity provider).

It's important to note that the user access token is provided upon first accessing the API. Ensuring the user is still authenticated during future interactions between the web browser and the API itself depends on how the API is implemented, and there are multiple ways to achieve this.

Let's start by reviewing the implementations from an application point of view. From this perspective, the typical logic implemented within the interceptor belongs to one of the following categories:

- **Access token-based**

  - Checks the presence of a valid (unexpired) access token upon every request.

  - If the token is not present or has expired, the API will refuse the request by returning an HTTP status 401 (*access token not present*) or 403 (*access token expired*). This can be then interpreted by the *client-side* logic, which triggers the proper action to get the user to request or renew the access token.

- **Cookie-based**

  The access token is evaluated and validated during the first interaction between the user and the application. After that moment, the interceptor releases an application cookie that represents proof of an already verified access token, and at the same time, potential extra information about the session that will be retransmitted by the web browser in the next interaction. Whenever a cookie is created, its lifetime should match the access token expiration time to increase the overall application's security posture: cookies are very often also used to keep a user's session for a much longer time (even days) – it's always a trade-off between security and usability.

The choice between cookie-based or access token-based logic also depends upon the software and infrastructure design. There are circumstances where the access token is more convenient than the traditional cookie approach. Access tokens are usually preferred when the interceptor logic is not developed within the application, as demonstrated in *Figure 5.4*, but rather when it is external to the application, as shown in *Figure 5.5*. Access tokens are generally used by an application when calling a web API that does not require user interaction but does require the caller to be authenticated.

If the application is implemented on microservices or serverless technology, it is common to use an external service to implement the interceptor and not do it in the middleware of the application itself. In other words, the interceptor and the application logic may not be part of the same monolith – the business logic and the interceptor in this design do not share the same application server. They are hosted on two different application servers. This kind of design pattern is gaining momentum in the cloud because cloud-native architectures tend to privilege a decoupled design with independent services to enhance the scalability and reliability of the overall application.

When the interceptor logic is not present in the application code, the business logic lives in independent memory and stack. In these architectures, information between services is exchanged via HTTP; using a shared context variable set by the interceptor and reading by the business logic (as happens in a monolith design) is not an option. The advantage of this design is that developers can focus on the business logic, as the interceptor layer is usually developed in an external component by a different team. The design of this kind of architecture is therefore different from the monolith design presented in *Figure 5.4*. In the picture here, the business logic coexists with the interceptor layer; in a decoupled component design, the architecture will look like the following diagram:

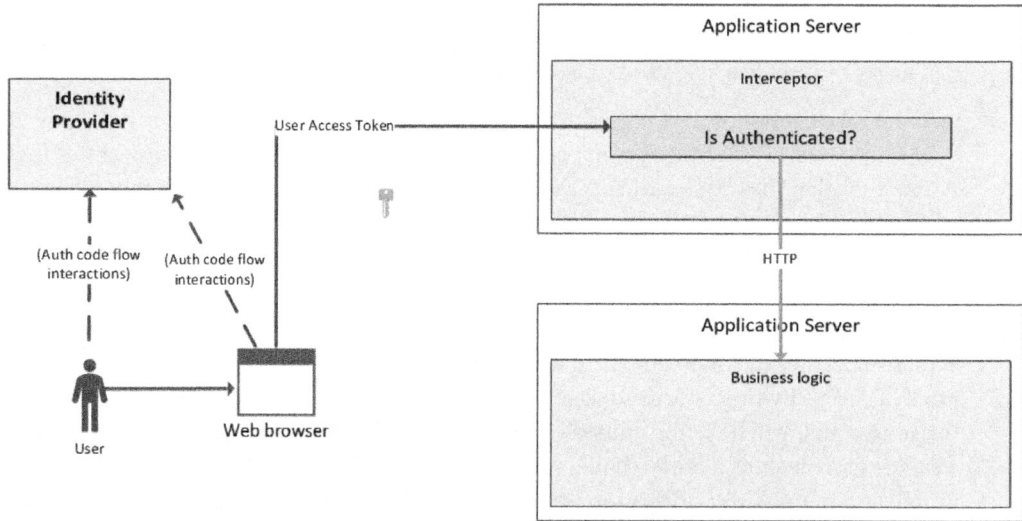

Figure 5.6 – Decoupled architecture

The authentication and authorization concepts are the same in any case if we see the application as a unique entity, regardless of the final design. In both designs, the business logic of the application receives the request from the client only if the request was *approved* by the interceptor layer. It is important to keep in mind that in this latter design, the information about the user needs to be propagated to the business logic via HTTP. This can be done in multiple ways, including adding custom headers to inject the information required by the business logic, or propagating or sending the access token itself again to the business logic, which doesn't need to validate it anymore but can still check the information contained in the token's claims. However, again, the business logic cannot read a context variable set by the interceptor because they are different processes in different servers.

The interceptor role in a decoupled design is tricky: we have a set of different services that need to identify the users once, ideally, like a central brain in a decentralized architecture. In this context, the client needs to deal with multiple APIs and it is recommended to prevent the user from performing multiple authentications. In this kind of design, the role of the interceptor layer can be covered by an infrastructure appliance with the duty of validating the access token before sending the request to the application business logic. The most important cloud providers, such as Amazon Web Services and Microsoft Azure, provide *Layer 7 network appliances* that can implement this logic.

In other circumstances, especially in Kubernetes-based architecture, the interceptor can be a *sidecar* (more information about the sidecar pattern can be found here: `https://docs.microsoft.com/en-us/azure/architecture/patterns/sidecar`) that lives in a dedicated container hosted alongside the application's container. Here, the logical architecture does not change – containers hosted in the same Pod need to exchange information in HTTP, as they were logically hosted in different application servers.

It's time to focus on the authentication logic and inspect the technical details, which as mentioned earlier, do not differ from the monolith or decoupled architectures discussed previously.

Let's review the scenario details in bullet fashion as in the previous sections of this chapter:

- **Scenario**:

  - **Application type**: A SPA that runs in the browser. In this type of application, HTML and JavaScript are only served once, and then the page will dynamically evolve according to the user's input and the API responses.

  - **External dependencies**: One or more external APIs registered on the same identity provider as the client application.

  - **User agent**: In this scenario, the user agent is the browser itself, which both implements the user interface and manages the interactions with the external REST APIs in the background to exchange the data needed to let the client react to the user's input. Modern applications using this approach commonly leverage JSON (`content-type: application/json`) for data exchange. The external REST API receives an HTTP request containing data in its body in JSON format, and the API responds with the requested information by embedding it in a JSON document in the HTTP response body.

- **Recommended pattern**: Single-page authentication pattern.

- **Protocol/flow**: OAuth 2.0 with the Authorization Code Grant flow (PKCE is recommended to enhance security, but for the sake of simplicity, the following flow will be discussed without using PKCE).

- **Description**: As depicted in *Figure 5.4* and *Figure 5.5*, the interactions between the client-side logic and API require an access token to be sent to the API (then, according to the application implementation, a cookie may be released, but this aspect is not relevant, as the first step will not change – as explained previously).

  It is important to note that, optionally, an ID token can be served to the client side as well in case the client-side logic requires the user's information without requiring any interaction with the API. If this is the case, the protocol or flow here needs to also use OIDC, which needs to work together with OAuth in such a way that both the ID token and access token will be released.

  The rest of this description assumes that only the access token is required.

- **Technical details**: As mentioned at the beginning of the chapter, the user agent and the API that the user agent needs to consume are the two distinguished entities. The entity we need to register on the identity provider, then, is the entity that needs to perform the end-to-end authentication process, which is the application that is running within the user agent context and the API, as in the native app.

As outlined in previous sections, the web browser cannot be considered a trusted entity. This means that application registration will use the client ID only and not the secret (the application is considered a public client here).

Not using a secret in the client makes the adoption of the state parameter even more important in contexts where SPAs are used.

The macro steps needed to finalize the operations are the following:

1. The web browser initiates the authorization request.
2. The user approves the request or logs in.
3. The web browser exchanges the authorization code for an access token.
4. The access token is available on the browser and can be used to authenticate the request against the API.

The following table will better outline the four preceding steps with further details and sample HTTP request expected:

Step	Description	Sample code/Sample HTTP request
1.	The static content served to the web browser will propose the option to the user to authorize the application to call the API on their behalf.	`<a href="https://authorization-server.com/authorize?response_type=code &client_id=sampleClient&state=sampleState">Connect Your Account</a>`
2.	The user is taken to the auth server and can log in or approve the OAuth request if already logged in. Once the operation completes, the authorization server will redirect the user to the redirect URI specified in the app registration, along with a code that will be used later by the browser to grab the access token.	`https://contoso.com/cb?code=sampleCode123`

3.	The app makes a POST request to the service's token endpoint in order to exchange the authorization code for an access token.	`POST /oauth/token HTTP/1.1`
		
		`Host: authorization-server.com`
		
		`grant_type=code`
		
		`&code=sampleCode123`
		
		`&redirect_uri=https://contoso.com/cb`
		
		`&client_id=sampleClient`

4.	At this point in time, the SPA has the access token that will be included in the host headers of the calls to be authorized by the API.	`Authorization: Bearer <access_token>`

Table 5.1 – OAuth steps for a SPA (example)

The end-to-end flow just described can be summarized by the following sequence diagram:

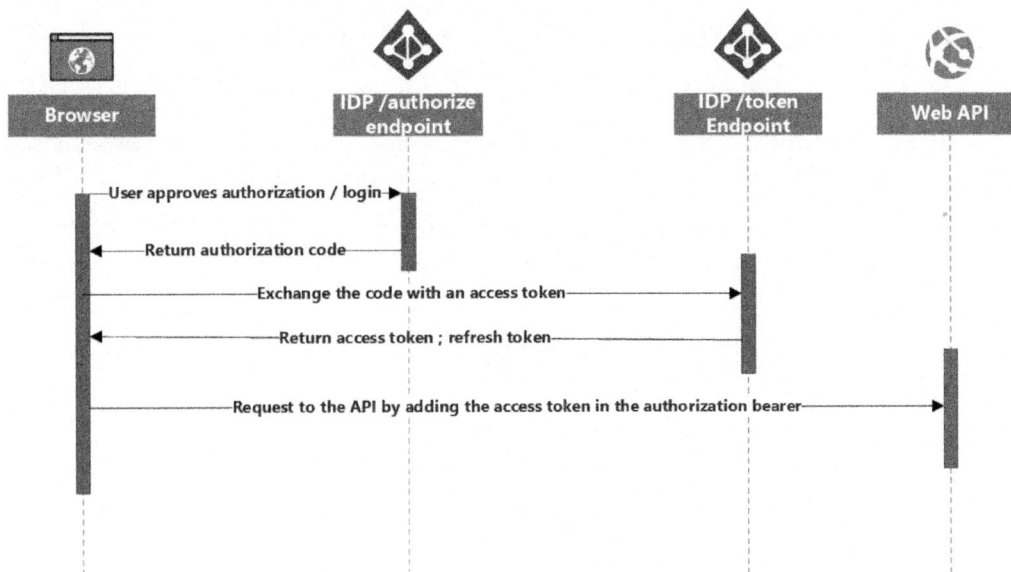

Figure 5.7 – SPA authorization sequence (the Authorization Code Grant flow)

It's important to note, as shown in the preceding diagram, that upon successful validation of the code, the token endpoint returns both the access token and the refresh token.

This is important because as soon as the access token expires, the browser may require a new one without having to repeat all the interactions shown in *Figure 5.5*. In fact, the browser can require a new access token by just submitting the refresh token and the client ID, as detailed in the *Authorization Code Grant flow* section in *Chapter 4, Authentication Flows*.

Another important aspect is that a SPA has to be able to send a POST request to the authorization server in order to leverage the Authorization Code Grant flow. This means that the server must support the relevant CORS headers if the authorization server is on a different domain. If it is not possible to implement CORS headers, the service may choose to use a different flow instead.

Additional considerations

This flow for a SPA should only be followed if, for any reason, the Auth Code Grant flow outlined in the previous chapter is not an option.

Most of the information about the SPA and the interceptor layer and how they are composed has already been covered in previous sections. This section will focus only on the implicit flow, which is discouraged as a primary option for the SPA, but it needs to be evaluated as a secondary option.

The main reasons why the implicit flow should not be adopted are the following:

- The Auth code grant flow is more secure, as there is an extra step for code validation
- The renewal of the token is done by taking advantage of third-party cookies, which will eventually be disabled by the browser and can even break the application experience
- The access token will be provided back in the URL, which exposes sensitive token data further (it will even be present in the address bar and as such, will be part of the history of navigation within the browser)

The implicit flow is simpler than the one proposed in the *Single-page authentication pattern* section previously:

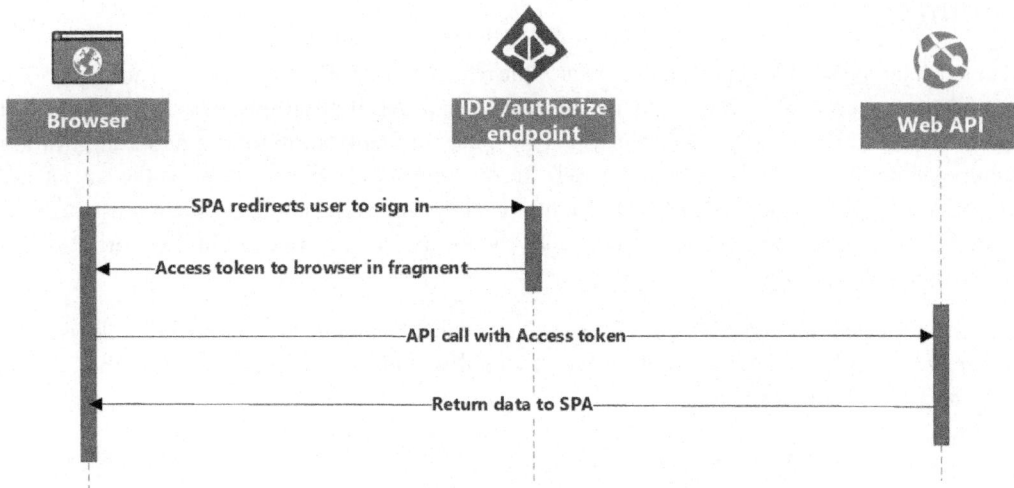

Figure 5.8 – SPA authorization sequence (the implicit flow)

The representation of the flow in *Figure 5.5* highlights that the interaction in the implicit flow scenario is done only on the *Authorize* component of the identity provider and the access token is directly delivered to the browser in fragments. This flow has many security implications, which we will look at in closer detail in the following section.

Security considerations

As reported in the *User authentication only pattern* section, the auth grant code flow is preferable for security reasons.

It's important nonetheless to state that, in general, all the authentication and authorization flows outlined for SPAs are less secure than those for web applications, as described in the *Web applications* section at the beginning of this chapter.

This is because the entity that validates and requests the access token is a client-side component (browser) that needs access to the client ID of the application. This information will, of course, be available to any attacker that downloads the static content and as such, they can attempt to attack the identity provider by using all the information available to them. This is not the case when the token is validated in the backend in a trusted environment where the secrets and client ID can be protected and are not available to an attacker.

Utilizing the `state` parameter and limiting the redirect URL to trustworthy clients is the approach adopted to ensure the security of the Authorization Code Grant without a client secret (as mentioned in the *Web applications* section earlier in this chapter). Since the secret isn't being utilized, the only method to confirm the client's identity is by utilizing a registered redirect URL. The redirect URL must be pre-registered with the OAuth 2.0 service for this reason.

Summary

In this chapter, we had the opportunity to review the recommended ways to implement authentication in different contexts. We covered user authentication in a web application scenario in a dedicated section and then reviewed the differences between user authentication from a native application standpoint and from a SPA standpoint as well. Throughout the chapter, we covered the advantages and disadvantages and the specific OAuth 2.0 flow to adopt according to the given circumstances. As we outlined in the chapter, whenever applicable, the Authorization Code Grant flow with PKCE is the recommended OAuth flow to adopt.

In the next chapter, we're going to describe how these authentication patterns and OAuth flows relate to current IT trends, API proliferation, and service meshes, and, in general, how to match new trends to the concepts of authentication.

Part 3:
Real-World Scenarios

The reader will go through several real-world use case scenarios where the patterns explained in previous chapters will be used to overcome real challenges.

This section contains the following chapters:

6
Trends in API Authentication

The previous chapter introduced you to the authentication and authorization flows available in the OAuth literature; we proposed a mapping between specific applications' architectures and recommended an authentication and authorization flow. When you are looking for guidance on which OAuth flow to adopt, according to a specific need, the previous chapter provides a reference point, but it is important to outline that it is meant to provide guidance and answers bounded to specific needs. It does not help an organization to understand how to create governance and blueprints around authentication, as the concept is way more complicated than individual scenarios produced to address specific requirements.

The aim of this chapter is to report how authentication and authorization map to an API enterprise's landscape and to discuss the implications of authentication and authorization at scale.

It is not possible to tackle this topic without introducing you to the challenges and complexity of API management, as authentication and authorization for APIs are part of this topic.

We will cover the following topics in this chapter:

- The complexity of defining standard guidance
- The vertical API approach
- API landscape complexity
- The application frontend API flow
- The application automation API
- The multiple IdP dilemma
- Defining enterprise standards for identity
- The service mesh and identity management
- Authentication implication in a service mesh
- Common antipatterns

Let's discuss the complexity of defining common cross-organization standards nowadays.

The complexity of defining standard guidance

The complexity of defining guidance and blueprints for authentication is increasing year after year for various reasons:

- Increasing cloud adoption is leading big companies to take up a hybrid cloud model. The cloud is nothing more and nothing less than a data center, where the company can store cloud-native assets that need to co-exist with legacy applications. These cloud models are creating new authentication requirements for communication across data centers and cloud providers.

- The proliferation of APIs inside these big companies is creating new management needs and authentication requirements.

- The increase in software development speed, thanks to Agile practices and **Platform as a Service (PaaS)** cloud services, is creating more applications in less time, which is increasing the management footprint of a company much more quickly than before.

- The nature of cloud-native, serverless, and distributed applications requires authentication across different components. This is increasing the amount of management and governance required.

To summarize the preceding concepts, it is fair to say that in the IT world we left behind, there were fewer applications and APIs to manage, and they were developed slowly compared to today. This fact enables poor governance and poor control to be turned into technical debt in a very short timeframe, which in turn can get out of control quickly.

In the enterprise landscape of today, API development for heterogeneous needs proliferates at a scale that has never been reached in the past, and further attention is required to prevent too much complexity from arising within an organization due to multiple design choices. These choices in turn can include different authentication and authorization models.

Just to give an idea of the scale of the complexity we need to expect within a company, around 800 applications are developed and maintained on average at companies with more than 5,000 employees (each year, the number of applications developed is higher on average than the ones that are dismissed, and the trend is growing).

The vertical API approach

The code owned by the companies is usually developed by different teams. These teams can be either internal (employees of a company), external (contractors), or a combination of both. When is time to develop an API, the team assigned to doing so is commonly responsible, among the implementation itself, for the following aspects:

- Design decisions
- Security and authentication
- Documentation
- Change management
- Testing
- Monitoring
- Discoverability

All in all, we can state that different APIs are not just developed by different brains; they are also envisioned, implemented, and tested by different teams (we are going to refer to this process as a **vertical API approach**).

This kind of tight coupling between APIs and specific teams only works if the company needs to develop fewer APIs. Nowadays, organizations are facing disruption. The API landscape in a generic organization is clearly reaching a tipping point, and the vertical API approach described at the beginning of this section cannot be considered anymore for enterprises that need to scale. Let's see in the upcoming sections the implication of identity here and how existing standards play a crucial role in enabling scaling.

You can understand at this point of the book that a company with different teams to perform each API development task independently would lead to an anarchic model, where every API would be defined, tested, and documented differently. If we apply this to thousands of APIs, it is clear that the vertical API approach is going to lead to maintainability issues within the organization. At many companies we have worked with, the situation is already out of control.

What we have described is exactly what is happening in most organizations — a proliferation of APIs, without any guidance or blueprints defined, and a lot of technical debt to face in the upcoming year.

API landscape complexity

To fully understand the complexity of API proliferation and the related OAuth implications, let's start to enumerate what kind of API we can encounter today in an enterprise landscape.

The following table summarizes the most common use cases for APIs in an enterprise landscape:

API	Description	Example
Application frontend API	An HTTP endpoint that belongs to the application and is designed to be consumed by the application's user	**Single-Page Application (SPA)**
Application automation API	A publicly exposed HTTP endpoint that belongs to the application and is designed to be consumed by an automation service in a controlled way	Automatic processes need to query the application
Application backend API	An internally exposed HTTP endpoint that belongs to the application and is designed to be consumed by other applications' components	**Service Oriented Architecture (SOA)**, modular applications, microservice applications
Internal reusable API	An HTTP endpoint that does not belong to any specific application and provides a service that can be consumed	A company's CRM that needs to provide common information that can be consumed by different applications
Partner API	An HTTP endpoint that exposes internal services to external partners and companies	A Visa credit card company that exposes services to be consumed by partners to manage transactions

Table 6.1 – Types of API

The following diagram summarizes the types of API expressed in the table and will further outline the complexity that needs to be tackled:

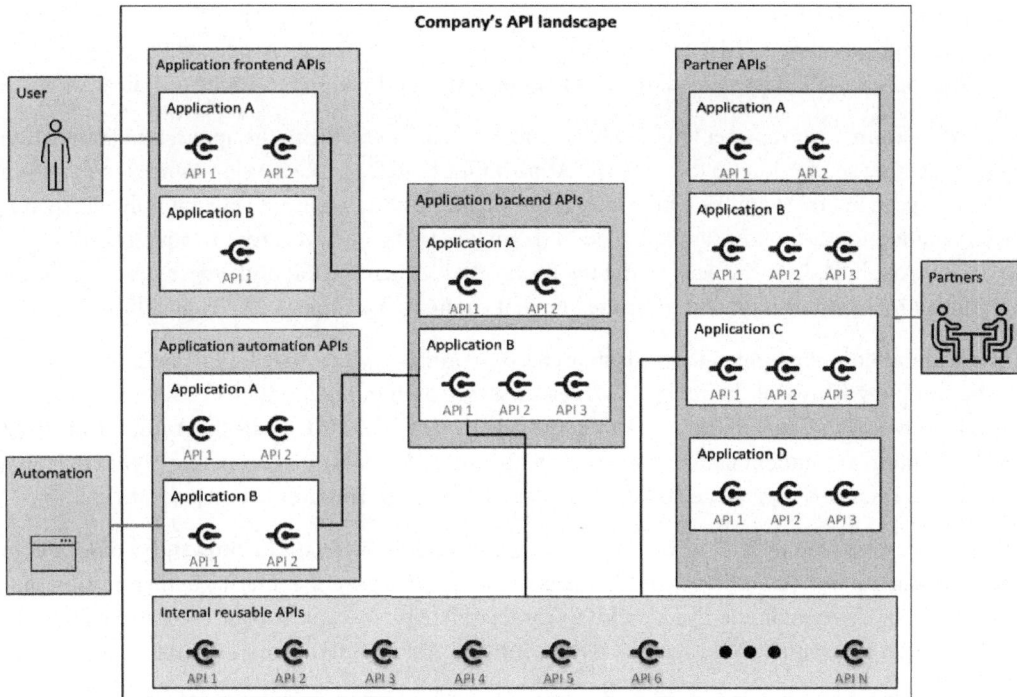

Figure 6.1 – A typical company's API landscape

As per *Table 6.1*, the diagram contains five boxes, one for each API type that we expect to find within an organization. The diagram has been extremely simplified for ease of readability, and it may not exactly reflect how all organizations work today. It is, though, reflective of our heterogenous experience from the retail, finance, public governance, and telecoms industries.

In the diagram, three external actors are represented — users, automation processes, and partners. The diagram represents a typical company's API landscape, which is the outer box with a white background. Within a company, different types of API are developed, as we mentioned in *Table 6.1*.

The three actors in the diagram (**User**, **Automation**, and **Partners**) interact with the related component (**Application frontend APIs**, **Application automation APIs**, and **Partner APIs**, respectively) that is supposed to publish assets to be served externally. The actors cannot interact with backend APIs or the internal reusable API layer, as they are not published and are only available for internal use. In the diagram, the lines represent the logical flow of communication that needs to be authenticated.

Before moving forward to explain the diagram in depth, it is important to note that the **Automation** actor and the **Partners** actor are usually represented by services and not humans. We mention this because it has authentication implications (systems cannot authenticate interactively among each other).

The **User** actor in the diagram, who ideally needs to interact with an API of a specific application (in the diagram, **Application A**, **API 1**), needs to perform interactive authentication. Interactive authentication with this application is represented by the **line that connects the user actor with Application A**.

The **Automation** actor represented in the diagram needs to interact with the application automation API of a specific application (in the diagram, **Application B**, **API 1**). The developers need to develop a service that can interact with the automation API and authenticate against it automatically in a server-to-server authentication flow (as explained in the previous chapters, this type of authentication can be done through the OAuth client credential flows). The authentication of the developer's service is not interactive, and it is represented by the line that connects **Automation** to **Application B**.

The **Partners** actor represented in the diagram needs to interact with a specific partner API published by the company. This will then trigger server-to-server authentication in a similar fashion to the **Automation** actor because it can use a different **Identity Provider** (**IdP**). Like the **Automation** actor, this is an automatic authentication flow that can be achieved in OAuth by using the client credential flow and, as such, it is represented by the line that connects **Automation** with **Application B**.

The diagram proposes internal server-to-server communication with **all the lines fully contained in the main central box** (**Company's API landscape**). This is because the internal authentication may differ from the external one, as different IdPs or even different protocols may be used. As an example, many internal communications systems rely on **mutual TLS** (**mTLS**) authentication rather than an OAuth flow (more details are provided in the *The service mesh and identity management* section).

It is important to note that the real world is usually more complex than *Figure 6.1*. As anticipated, multiple factors can complicate the design shown in the diagram even further.

The following is a list of complexities that are not captured in the diagram but that are common to find in enterprises. The following five items are exposed as points of reflection to help you envision the potential complexity of the diagram:

- The user actor can be internal to the company or external to the company. Accordingly, whether the user belongs to the organization or not, they can belong to a different IdP and, as such, the API authentication gets more complicated and an extra layer may be needed to hide this complexity. This degree of complexity and how to tackle it is better described in the *The multiple IdP dilemma* section of this chapter.

- The line that connects the **Application frontend APIs** box to the **Application backend APIs** box in the diagram represents server-to-server authentication (the API within the **Application frontend API** box needs to authenticate itself against the API in the **Application backend API** box). There may be use cases where the application backend API is designed to authenticate the user against the backend. Since the user cannot reach the backend directly, this is usually achieved by using a specific OAuth flow. This creates heterogeneous authentication flows in the backend, which goes beyond server-to-server authentication.

- We can also imagine that within the **Internal reusable API** box, the APIs are enabled to communicate with each other and can use a different authentication mechanism that is not represented in the diagram.

- Partner APIs may have their own backend layer, with another authentication round-trip, which is not part of the diagram.

- The automation frontend API may be consumed by an automatic service or by a human. The picture assumes that the API within the automation frontend API is consumed by an automatic service and not by a developer who interactively consumes the API. Both scenarios are valid; in our diagram anyway, the automatic service hits the authentication frontend API (with no human interaction involved). Moreover, it is important to note that the two assumptions (a developer or an automatic service) are not mutually exclusive. This means the diagram may have another box just for developers that will have access to extra features of the application through a dedicated portal. This isn't in the diagram.

An important factor to reflect on is that in the real world, the landscape proposed in *Figure 6.1* is the result of the development done by different teams at different points in time, across multiple business domains, developed across different platforms, and potentially with different technologies and methodologies.

Preventing the increase in complexity in API management is paramount to facilitating enterprise operations, keeping efficiency high, and reducing maintainability costs. By this point in this book, this concept must be clear.

What was just described has serious implications for authentication, and that's why it is important to define standards. Before doing that, let's analyze the public layer (by "public layer," we mean the layer on the diagram that has authentication from an external actor) in the next section.

The application frontend API flow

The application frontend API is the logical layer that hosts the APIs that are supposed to be consumed by the application's client. The flow is an extension of the single-page authentication pattern described in the previous chapter.

The following diagram outlines the subset of interactions reported in the previous diagram that involves this layer (the application frontend API).

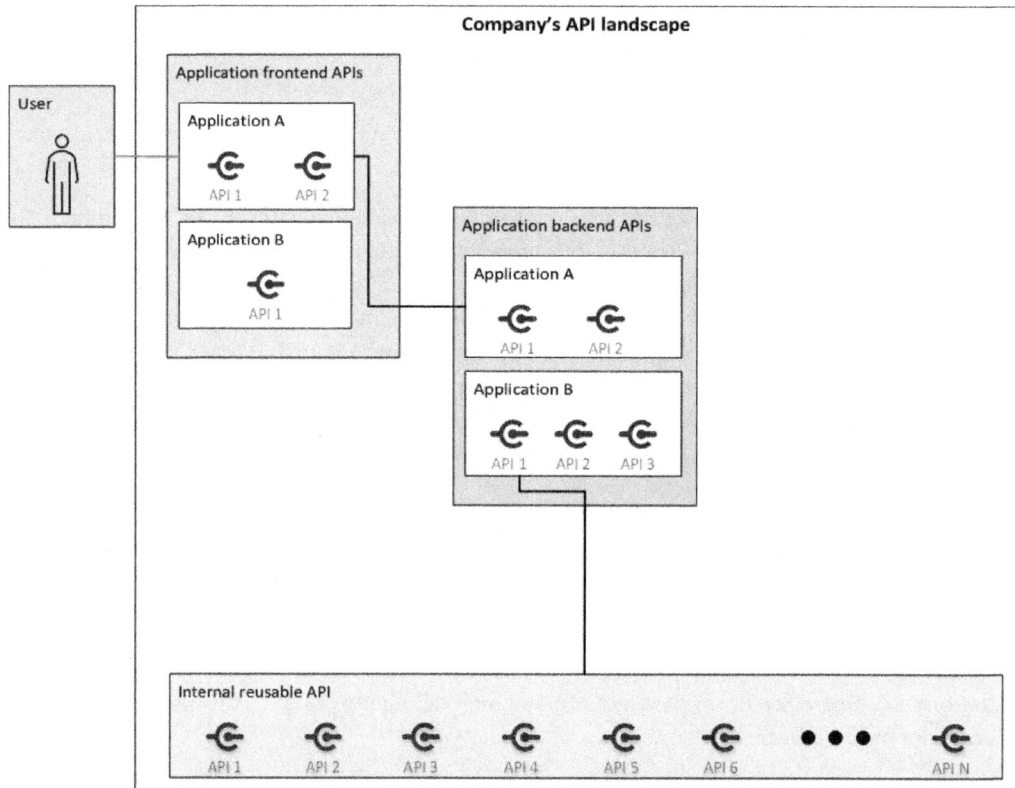

Figure 6.2 – Zooming in on the application frontend API

The frontend acts as a broker to send the request to a backend component synchronously or asynchronously, according to the application's design and the architectural pattern chosen.

The flow considered in such a diagram is composed of the following steps:

1. The user connects to the API, which we can assume is available on the internet. We can also assume that the user is using a SPA and the authentication flow represented by the line that connects the user to the application is the one discussed in *Chapter 5, Exploring Identity Patterns*, in the *Single-page authentication pattern* section.

2. The API within the application frontend API box authenticates the user, understands its intent according to the request made by the SPA, and sends the request to another API that is deployed in the application backend API. Unlike the previous step, the authentication flow between these two components is internal and not interactive (with interactive, we refer to human interaction), as it is a system-to-system flow. In a context such as this, if OAuth is adopted, the recommended flow to use is the client credential grant flow.

3. The application frontend API can take advantage of already developed logic by making a call to the internal reusable API layer. In the diagram, this flow starts from **Application B** only; taking advantage of the internal reusable API layer is an option for every application developed by the company regardless. This option has obviously been scoped out from the diagram, which is intended as a sample to outline a single round-trip. This is again a system-to-system authentication that, as outlined in the previous step can be achieved, in the case of OAuth, by adopting a client credential grant flow.

The flow described here is an example flow. We have worked with some customers that had the application frontend API connected directly to the internal reusable services for specific and exceptional requests that the API within the internal reusable services was able to serve without an intermediary. Although it is uncommon, in a portfolio of hundreds of applications, we are likely to find a use case like this, and this is another example of why it is important to define guidelines to have a uniform pattern across the company.

As a final note, it's important to understand that the application frontend API can sometimes be developed with more than one logical layer. Think, for example, of a multi-device application that can share the same API across mobiles, browsers, and potentially other devices. The response to be provided needs to be tuned according to the specific device. This logic is sometimes abstracted from the application by adding an extra layer (known as a **backend-for-frontend**) that is responsible for translating the responses according to the target device. In this kind of architecture design, the application frontend API should be divided into two: one layer to receive, resend, and translate the request, and another layer to perform the API logic and act as a broker to send the requests to the application backend API.

The application automation API

The application automation API is designed to enable the automatic service to retrieve information from applications. One example could be an insurance portal, where customers (users) subscribe to a specific insurance policy by using the insurance website, developed as a SPA, and following the flow described in the previous chapter. At the end of the day, an automatic process calls the application automation API to retrieve all the insurance contracts finalized during the day by the customers for forecasting or reporting purposes. This specific example is also applicable to the partner automation API, where a partner of the insurance company needs to use an API to perform backend activities, retrieve data, or update contract clauses.

From a technical perspective, the partner automation API and application automation API usually use the same authentication flow due to a matching requirement: an automated service needs to be authenticated. What could change in the partner automation API is that the partner may belong to a different organization and as such use a different IdP. This may have implications for application registration. More information about this scenario can be found in the *The multiple IDPs dilemma* section later in the current chapter. For the sake of technical understanding of the authentication flow, we are going to describe the application automation API layer, but the concept is also relevant to the flows in the partner automation layer.

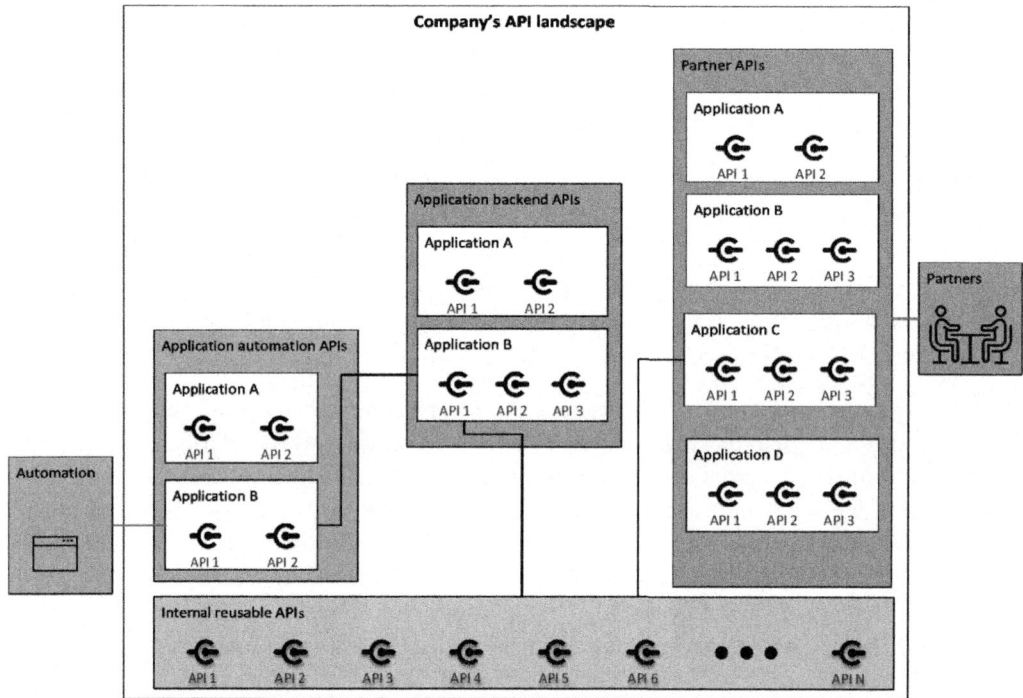

Figure 6.3 – Zooming in on the application automation APIs

In this flow, a service is authenticated in a non-interactive and unattended manner against the API. In OAuth, this is done by using the client credentials grant flow. Then, the server-side interactions (the lines fully included in the main box, **Company's API landscape**), follow the same patterns already described in the previous section, *The application frontend API flow*. Here, a backend service is going to be triggered, as evident from the **Application backend APIs** box, which, in turn, can take advantage of an internal API. If the OAuth protocol is used for internal authentication, as before, the recommended flow to adopt is the client credential grant flow because it is a system-to-system authentication pattern.

As explained, in the real world, there may be circumstances where multiple IdPs are involved, which, of course, has implications for the authentication flow. Let's look at this topic in more depth in the next section.

The multiple IdP dilemma

Having to deal with multiple IdPs is not as uncommon as one may think. Dealing with multiple IdPs can be the result of intended but also unintended design.

As mentioned previously in this chapter, the most notable side-effect of API proliferation is that different teams work in different ways, using different techniques and technologies, and sometimes this means using different IdPs. This is an example of unintended or unwanted IdPs, where a company needs to deal with multiple IdPs not because of a design choice but because of a lack of initial governance. There may be circumstances where multiple IdPs are the result of a design decision. It's important to understand that collaboration extends beyond the enterprise.

Multiple IdPs are usually involved when an application's scope spans multiple companies collaborating to achieve the application's business logic, which needs to harness features provided by external APIs or applications outside the perimeter of an organization. However, this is not the only use case where multiple IdPs are brought into the picture. As a matter of fact, it is common to encounter them within the same organization for reasons that are summarized as follows:

- Typically, different user categories are stored and maintained within dedicated IdPs. Common examples include the following types of users:

  - Employees

  - Partners

  - Customers

  Each of such categories may have a dedicated IdP to serve authentication to the users it stores.

Figure 6.4 – Example of user categories

- The same user category (for instance, employees) can have multiple IdPs serving authentication, with each IdP storing a separate overlapping (duplicated) set of users or identities. This usually happens in large organizations that, over the years, have developed and deployed several authentication systems without having a centralized governance strategy to wisely and uniquely manage a specific user category. The net result is that clusters of applications rely on a single IdP and **Single Sign-On (SSO)** is only provided to clusters that share the same IdP, making it difficult to enhance productivity in scenarios where a user has to access applications that trust different IdPs.

There is no magic wand or formula that can easily fix the issue of having multiple IdPs. The main problem with having multiple authentication systems is that they are not easy to maintain and most of the time, they must be kept in sync so that the latest information about a user is always up to date. This process usually identifies one of the available IdPs as the source of authority for a specific identity, and this is often the seed from which the requirement to consolidate all existing identities into a single, authoritative authentication provider within an organization grows.

When we talk about IdPs, we refer to authentication systems that implement modern authentication protocols such as OAuth 2.0, OIDC, SAML, and WS-Federation, but we need to keep in mind that other authentication systems leveraging legacy protocols may still exist within a big enterprise – so, how do we get rid of this complexity?

The most recent approach to the problem is identifying the IdPs and, in general, the authentication systems that should provide the source of the information concerning the different user categories that the organization manages. The first iteration of this analysis may identify authentication systems that serve specific user categories and authentication protocols. The second, and the most time-consuming, iteration involves assessing all existing company applications together with the different types of users accessing them. At the end of these iterations, we will have a comprehensive map of the existing applications, the types of users accessing them, and the IdPs that provide authentication to each application and user. With all this valuable information, we can start planning to consolidate the existing applications, users, and IdPs by using the following guidelines:

- **Identify the number of IdPs according to the different user categories**: At first, it could make sense to have an IdP dedicated to each user category that is relevant to the organization. Common user categories are employees, business partners, and customers. This means that we may end up with three IdPs, but this is just a rule of thumb that does not account for the different applications an organization has, which may decrease or increase the number of IdPs needed.

- **Consolidate IdPs according to common user categories accessing the same applications**: In an enterprise, it is very common that an application has been designed just for internal users (for example, a pay slip web portal). That's why it always makes sense to have an IdP that serves authentication to all the organization's employees. It is, on the other hand, less common for an organization to have applications that are only accessed by external collaborators (for example, a web portal where a business partner can retrieve important documents published by the organization). In these cases, the involvement of multiple IdPs (internal employees and partners) could be an option.

In the latter scenario, since the application must logically serve two types of users, we could take advantage of having a single IdP storing and serving both user categories so that the application is not overloaded with the burden of orchestrating the authentication between two or more IdPs. The choice to have both employees and external collaborators stored in a single IdP must be considered carefully because it may introduce the risk of inadvertently allowing external users to access internal applications. IdPs such as Azure Active Directory provide additional tools and features (such as **Conditional Access**) that assist an administrator in separating the duties each user has between the objects defined within the IdP (mainly the applications). The identities of an organization's customers are very often stored in a separate and dedicated IdP instead because of the different requirements of a customer's identity. Usually, it requires different privacy and security settings, access to applications an employee usually does not need to use, login with social IdPs (such as Facebook and LinkedIn), and so on.

- **Federate existing IdPs**: The main goal of reducing the number of IdPs is to reduce the management effort of having identities spread across multiple authentication systems. Applications benefit from this approach too; with a reduced number of IdPs, applications only need to federate with a single IdP, which will authenticate the users so that they can be authorized by the application to access all its functionalities. Even if the previous guidelines have already been implemented, there may still be applications that need to be accessed by users belonging to different IdPs. In this scenario, the application can provide the means to be federated with these IdPs but, in most cases, the best solution would be to give the illusion that there is only one IdP (this concept will be further expanded in the *Frontend authentication* section in *Chapter 9, Exploring Real-World Scenarios*) and hide the complexity of retrieving and validating user credentials to the application. This will push the IdP complexity out of the business logic and enhance the application's maintainability over time. This is possible thanks to the capabilities provided by the modern authentication protocol that we discussed in the previous chapters, such as the concept of delegating the authorization of the OAuth protocol.

An IdP can function both as an IdP and a service provider. This enables an IdP to be the service provider of another IdP.

How does this help when we have different users belonging to different IdPs? That's straightforward: the application will federate with just one IdP – let's name it IdP A (for example, the IdP containing customers' identities) – and IdP A, on the other hand, will federate with another IdP; let's name it IdP B (for example, the IdP containing the employees' identities). In this scenario, once an unauthenticated user lands on the application, it will redirect the user to IdP A, where the user will be asked to either authenticate using an identity stored in IdP A or to use the identity of the federated IdP B (some vendors, such as Ping Identity, refer to this as a federation hub):

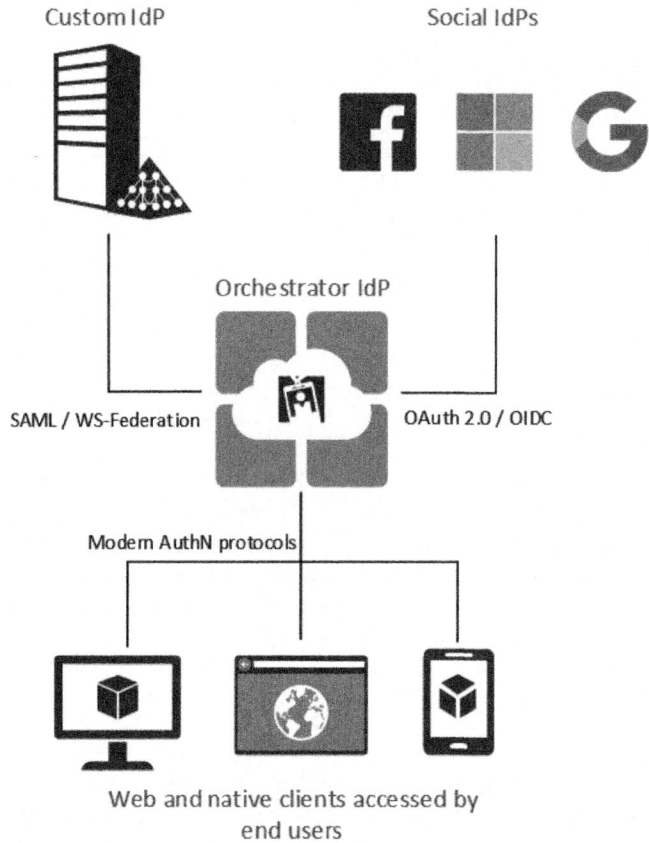

Figure 6.5 – Example of an IdP federating with multiple IdPs

We have talked about how to handle user credentials among different IdPs within the same organization, but what happens when different IdPs are managed by different companies?

When this kind of authentication involves user interaction, then a federation can be put in place so that the IdPs can trust each other and consequently allow the applications to accept credentials from users belonging to both companies.

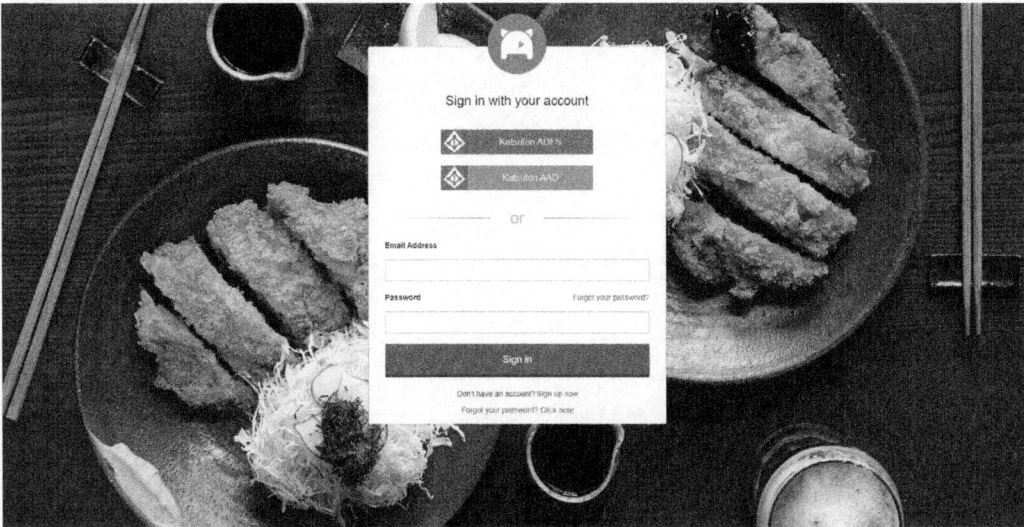

Figure 6.6 – Example of a login page of an IdP federated with other IdPs

When a user is not involved in the authentication process, then the answer becomes trickier — when does an application need to access an API that is registered in a different IdP? There is no straightforward answer. Either the application is also registered in the external IdP and starts using the credentials provided by the external administrator to retrieve an access token that the API trusts or a different type of authentication must be used. The most common alternative authentication method is using certificates in this case, typically mTLS, which is not covered by this book.

As discussed so far, having a way to design, develop, and maintain the services in a standardized fashion can help an organization reduce the overhead around the life cycle of a service or API. The next section will expand on this crucial topic.

Defining enterprise standards for identity

First and foremost, it is important to outline that defining standards or blueprints that are universally valid is not possible. This is because every company has different internal processes and different teams, and adopts different technologies. Most importantly, each company has a different business and, as such, they may have different priorities on how to manage internal APIs and services in general. Hence, this topic cannot be covered exhaustively with a single guideline. This section aims to expose the important principles and provide the items needed to define customized guidelines within a company to plan how to define services and APIs and, therefore, to dictate the authentication guidelines among these services.

The business impact of properly managing APIs and services depends on the strategy of the organization as well as the business context. Just to provide an example, there are companies that sell APIs to third-party developers as their main business. The standards to be defined in this context may be different from a company that mainly uses internal APIs in a service mesh for internal purposes to boost its internal business (there's more about the service mesh in the next section).

Developing an API, in a structured way, requires standardizing multiple decisions. There are many pillars that can be seen as a minimum set of decisions an enterprise architect needs to address at a company level.

The following table contains some of the important concepts that a company needs to be aware of when creating a new service or API:

Pillar to structure the company's APIs	Description
Discovery	As reported previously, regardless of its physical location, for an API to be adopted, it is important to keep an internal registry within the company that can help the developers to find an API they may need to reuse to facilitate their development. As we're going to see in upcoming chapters, certain technologies have this capability out of the box.
Monitoring	An API cannot be managed efficiently without live information that can report how it is being used and expose performance metrics. There are many tools that can help to define the monitoring pillar, and plenty of telemetry technology the API can take advantage of. As for the other pillars, it is extremely important to have a good level of consistency across the enterprise to simplify the maintenance and troubleshooting by the ops team, which should not switch from one tool to another according to the target API they need to monitor. It is important to understand that this pillar is usually connected with the development pillar because a technology choice can constrain what monitoring tools can be adopted.
Security	This is a hard topic to create a standard for. The reason is that each API can have different security requirements. For example, one API can expose sensitive internal information, while another API may be intended for public use to access information that isn't sensitive. The advice here is to create different security tiers to enable the architect that is planning the API to choose the proper security tier according to the API target usage and requirements.

Pillar to structure the company's APIs	Description
Authentication	This pillar needs to outline what an API consumer needs to do to authenticate against the API. The most important aspects this pillar needs to clarify are as follows: • It needs to report whether the authentication needs to be based on OAuth and whether application registration is required • It needs to report whether the authentication logic needs to be implemented within the business logic or offloaded to an external component, such as the API management layer of a service mesh Ideally, across the organization, it is recommended to adopt, if possible, a single IdP that needs to be defined by this pillar. This can help to simplify the processes and the overhead reported in the *The multiple IdP dilemma* section.
Deployment	This is usually connected to the DevOps practices adopted by the company, and it is recommended to be consistent with them. It is important that the whole deployment process is immutable and automatic to deploy and promote the API across different environments. If the API needs to be exposed externally, it is recommended the automation takes care of not only the deployment but also its exposure, and if OAuth is involved, the registration across the specific IdP.
Testing	This relates to what needs to be tested on an API and how it is supposed to be tested. Generally speaking, each API needs to be developed with unit testing. If the API is part of a microservices application or is in the general part of a serverless flow or an end-to-end flow, it is important to also define the integration tests needed to ensure it will work. Performance testing is an important aspect as well, and it is important to outline whether a distributed load test is needed and if so, what the benchmark is. Testing an API also has authentication implications because the test needs to mimic the caller and replicate the authentication flow of the caller, whether an OAuth client credential flow or a different protocol or flow.

Pillar to structure the company's APIs	Description
Development	The development pillar is maybe the widest one in terms of what decisions need to be made. It defines, for example, which frameworks and technologies the company intends to support. It is important to note that these choices may have specific implications relating to monitoring, security, and testing, as they can, in turn, be based on technologies (such as libraries and SDKs) that need to be compatible with this pillar.
	Another important factor to decide how to define this pillar is the development cost. There are specific technologies that are easy to adopt for API development; other technologies where, for example, it is hard to find skilled developers; and others that are widely used but may require further overhead in API development. All of these aspects need to be carefully considered.
	It is important to outline that an API can be written in any technology without impacting the consumer, who just needs to access the HTTP endpoint. From a maintenance perspective, a company cannot have all the APIs developed differently because it would create issues in the future to find proper staff for maintenance purposes.
Design	The external design (the interface) should be well-defined. This can define the degree of re-usability and enable the client to properly consume the API. As part of this pillar, the team needs to define what message patterns and protocols the API will adopt (such as REST or GraphQL).
Strategy	This is the tactical goal of the API, as in, what value the API will bring to the organization and how much of a strategic impact is measured. It is paramount to define its life cycle and to be able to evaluate in the long term when it is time for the API to be removed or redeveloped.
Documentation	The developer should be able to start using the API easily with specific guidelines. (For example, how to reach the API on the network. Is it on the internet or the intranet? Is it hosted on a cloud service and if so, does it require any further security enablement, such as firewall exceptions?)

Table 6.2 – Decision pillars

Describing the pillars of creating API guidelines within a company in detail is beyond the scope of this book. What is important is to understand the implications of authentication and, as stated, it is important to keep the number of IdPs adopted by the companies as low as possible and prevent teams from adopting IdPs that were not previously approved by the enterprise architect (or the team accountable for this approval). The proliferation of IdPs inside an organization is typical of many companies we have worked with, and it is usually the result of a lack of process and governance within the organization. Having multiple IdPs will lead to the consequences reported in the *The multiple IdP dilemma* section. If a single IdP is adopted, then authentication across services within a company becomes easy. As outlined, the typical design is to have one IdP to register the API/services and enable the OAuth client credential flow to happen in the following way:

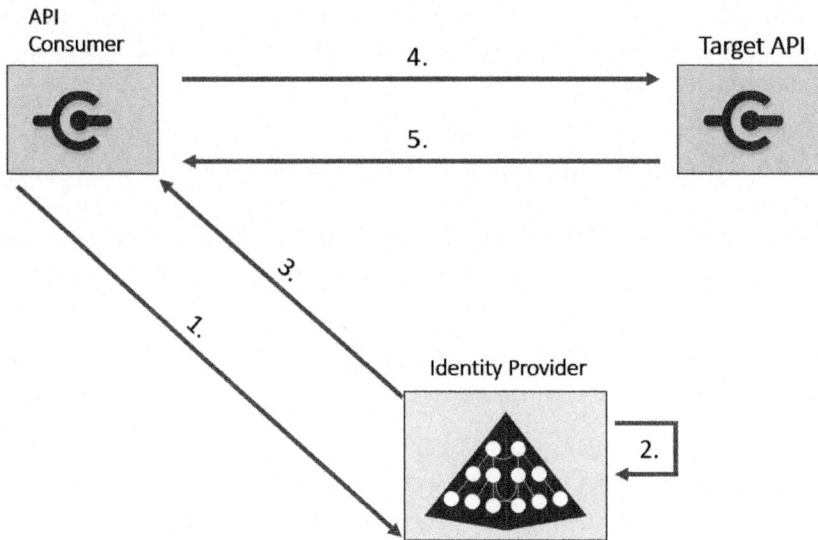

Figure 6.7 – API authentication with OAuth

For the sake of completeness, the following list will describe what happens in each iteration of the diagram:

1. Authenticate with the client ID and the client secret to the token's endpoint.
2. Validate the client ID and the client secret and forge the access token.
3. Deliver the access token.
4. Request data from the target API by adding the access token in the HTTP request (the bearer authorization header).
5. The target API provides a response to the caller.

It is implicit that it is mandatory to register the API consumer reported in *Figure 6.7* because the application needs to have its own client ID and client secret to be able to request the access token from the IdP. It is not mandatory to register the target API (unless the API needs, in turn, to call another API) because the token can be validated without needing to contact the IdP.

In the next section, we are going to see how current technologies can facilitate and, in some circumstances, even remove the overhead required to define service-to-service authentication and authorization practices across the organization.

The service mesh and identity management

It is important to note that *Figure 6.1* is the logical representation of how different types of APIs can be distributed within the organization for different purposes.

In the real world, the logical box represented in the diagram is usually distributed across different locations and data centers, and it is typically hosted on-premises or in the cloud, in a containerized platform, or more often a combination of all of them.

Nevertheless, what companies want to achieve is a simplified view that can hide complexity and enable the ops team of the company to manage the services easily, regardless of the physical distribution. We have recently encountered a trend of having the API deployed on the same hosting platform, which is typically a containerization platform (e.g Kubernetes). In the rest of the chapter, we are going to refer to a containerization platform as one cluster or a set of clusters that take advantage of the same technology stack (for example, *Kubernetes* or *Istio*).

Having a central view creates obvious benefits for management, as the ops team of a company can take advantage of a unified way to observe, manage, and deploy the APIs and services across the company.

Another important advantage is that, despite the fact that services can be distributed among multiple locations, this is transparent from the perspective of management and consumers (who consume the service or the API). Most of the complexity is hidden and handled by the containerization platform, which has the important duty of hiding low-level complexity and enabling the companies to focus on service deployment and management.

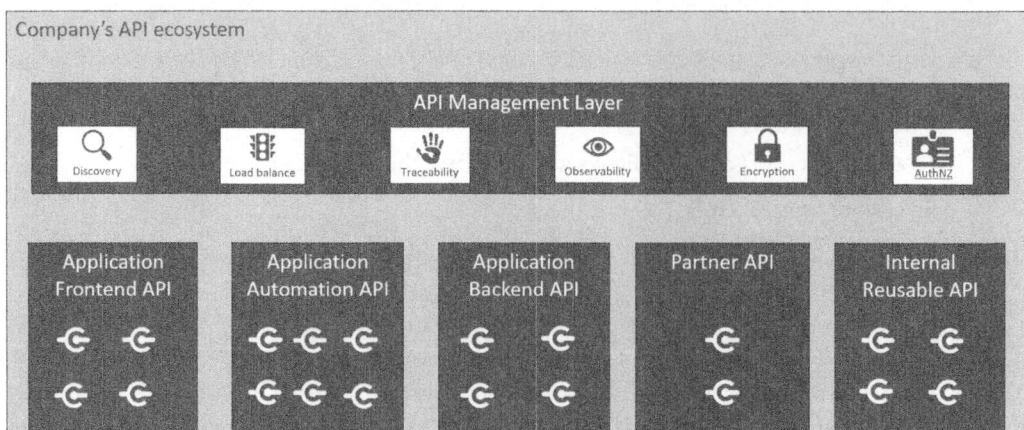

Figure 6.8 – Logical API grouping in a single-pane-of-glass fashion

As shown in the preceding diagram, all the APIs within the company can be reached through a single management layer. This management layer hides the network complexity of the API layers below. The layers below are typically hosted in a cluster on top of a software-defined network or, most typically, in multiple clusters. Using multiple clusters is usually done by adopting a combination of a physical network for cluster communication and a software-defined network to reach the internal services.

Technically speaking, it is important to outline that usually, containerization platforms such as Kubernetes, Mesos DC/OS, Docker Swarm, and Service Fabric do not have these capabilities out of the box. These capabilities are usually accomplished by including third-party products in the cluster, such as Istio, which is specifically designed to extend the capability of the Kubernetes containerization platform to include this management capability and, most importantly, enable multi-cluster management. From an infrastructural perspective, multi-cluster management is achieved by using techniques that are beyond the scope of this book, which is focused on authentication. If you are interested in going deeper into how to control multiple clusters, we recommend you learn about the sidecar pattern and understand how these kinds of patterns can be adopted to control the behavior of multiple distributed services (as tools such as Istio do).

The advantages of multi-cluster management do not stop with physical abstraction. If you think about it, you have a homogeneous way to expose, manage, and secure your company's assets.

Figure 6.8 groups APIs in a unique view; this grouping is done regardless of the physical locations of each API. The view provides an abstraction that can enable the management to see all the clusters as one and focus on the API/services only. This is the most important purpose of a service mesh.

In our experience, the service mesh concept is interpreted differently across enterprises. For certain companies, the service mesh must only contain the API consumable internally. Other companies use the same logic definition to also include publicly exposed applications; this is done by taking advantage of the management layer capabilities to secure the service mesh. On another occasion, we observed companies that adopted two different types of containerization platforms — one that was strictly a service mesh focused on hosting the internal API managed centrally, and another that had a containerization platform for hosting public applications that are not supposed to be consumed by other services internally. The latter approach creates two different levels of management, which, in turn, adds some management overhead. The additional management overhead is sometimes justified to enhance security: having a single way to administer and manage APIs can expose a very sensitive attack surface (the administrator can edit services regardless of cluster locations and privileges). On the other hand, abstracting the services into a single management layer has the advantage of enabling an API, service, or application hosted in one cluster to interact with a service hosted in a different cluster out of the box.

For the sake of completeness, since we already stated that *Figure 6.8* represents only a logical view of services that can be located in different places (and connected by a unified management layer), we are going to represent this concept in *Figure 6.9* in a mixed view that is composed of both logical aspects (the API management layer) and the physical view. This will highlight that services can be hosted in different clusters, which can, in turn, be located in different data centers, or on top of cloud providers such as Microsoft Azure or Amazon Web Services:

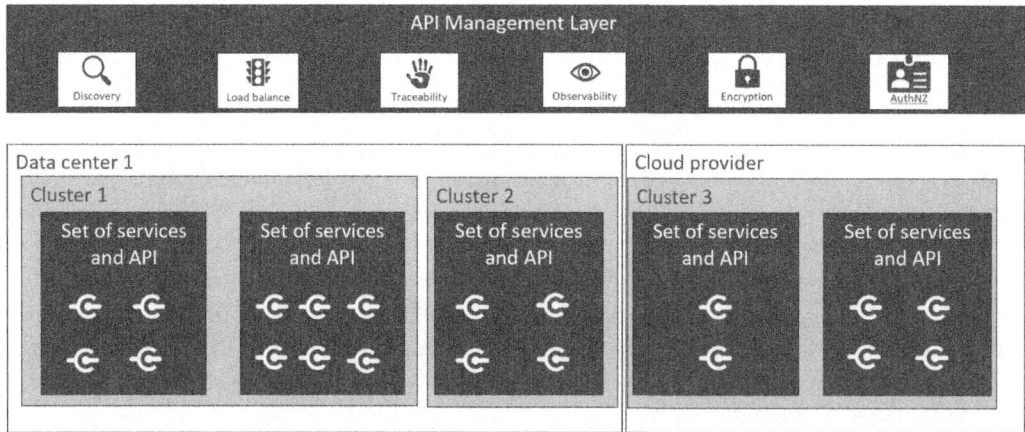

Figure 6.9 – Logical and physical view of a service mesh

Regardless of the service mesh definitions and configurations, it is important to review the management pillars offered by a service mesh. We are going to see that this adoption has implications for authentication and, often, adopting OAuth authentication for communication across services within a service mesh can be an unnecessary over-complication in this context. This concept will be better explained in the rest of the chapter.

The preceding diagram outlines the following pillars that represent the duties of the platform required to enable the management of the services in a unified view:

Pillar	Description
Discovery	The discovery or service discovery has duties similar to the ones of the **Domain Name Service (DNS)**. In other words, when a service or API needs to communicate with another service within the cluster, it needs to locate it. The orchestration platform provides the *discovery service* to enable each service to locate and reach the target API/service. This concept is even more important when there are multiple physical clusters in place. The goal of discovery is to abstract from the physical layer and let the API management layer route the traffic to the target service regardless of its physical location. In other words, the API management layer always knows how to route the traffic to reach a specific service in a specific cluster, and the service is located in the node of the cluster.

Pillar	Description
Load balance	It is important for a company, especially when the logical view represented in *Figure 6.8* is made up of multiple physical clusters, to control the traffic among the API by implementing rules and performing advanced operations, such as blue-green deployment.
Traceability	The ability to trace requests, store them, and reproduce them enables companies to have an important asset that they can reproduce easily with the goal, and analyzing it, to either improve the quality, spot bugs, or boost their troubleshooting capabilities.
Observability	Having real-time telemetry for each deployment is paramount to enable a company to scale and introduce more APIs without losing its effectiveness to troubleshoot. Generally speaking, services, nodes, and clusters need to be consistently monitored at any point in time to enable the API to grow and keep the management overhead small at the same time. Unlike traceability, usually, observability is intended to be a high-level view of the service that is above the network stack.
Encryption	The messages exchanged between the services within the containerization platform should be encrypted and decrypted in a way that should not impact the logic of the services or APIs. Offloading the encryption to the containerization platform is a great benefit.
AuthNZ	Authentication and authorization, the ability to enable one service to communicate with another, can be centrally managed by the containerization platform.

Table 6.3 – The service mesh pillars

Now that we have a clear understanding of the tendency of companies to keep increasing the number of APIs and services they have, it is time to focus on the authentication implications relating to the service mesh.

Authentication implications in a service mesh

Unlike the typical way of designing an OAuth flow, which needs to be designed according to the specific needs of the service or application, the service mesh has the advantage of having out-of-the-box capabilities to oversee authentication.

According to our experience, the *killer use case* to take advantage of the service mesh for authentication is **service-to-service** authentication, which, as outlined in the previous chapter, is typically achieved in OAuth by using the client credential flow. This is not how the service mesh typically handles authentication across services. If both services reside in the service mesh, authentication is usually performed by taking advantage of mTLS. The downside to using a certificate as a means to mutually authenticate services is the management of these certificates, which are supposed to expire eventually. A service mesh usually has the capability to automatically manage certificates, which eliminates the hassle of manually handling certificate renewal. This aspect enables a company to delegate the complexities of certificate management and mutual authentication to the service mesh product capabilities managed in a centralized manner.

Anyway, if the source API or service (the caller) that intends to consume the target API or service is hosted outside the service mesh, it may not be possible to completely delegate the authentication mechanism to the management layer of the service mesh. As such, we may lose the benefit of managing all the authentications homogeneously, and this is the reason why the trend right now is to host the APIs and services within the same service mesh.

Moreover, mTLS authentication, typically managed by the service mesh, is not always intended for interactive user authentication, which may need to take advantage of the OAuth flow reported in the previous part of the book. This often requires some ad hoc authentication. Authentication across components is a natural aspect of software design because each application, service, or API is designed for a different purpose, is supposed to be consumed by different stakeholders, and may need to be registered in an IdP.

For the *out-of-the-box service-to-service* communication provided by the service mesh, it is generally not necessary to register the service in an IdP. This is because the identity of the service is managed by the service mesh itself, and the service may not need to receive any OAuth-based authentication, as outlined in the following diagram, which is a sample taken from www.istio.io that describes how the Istio service mesh authenticates two services:

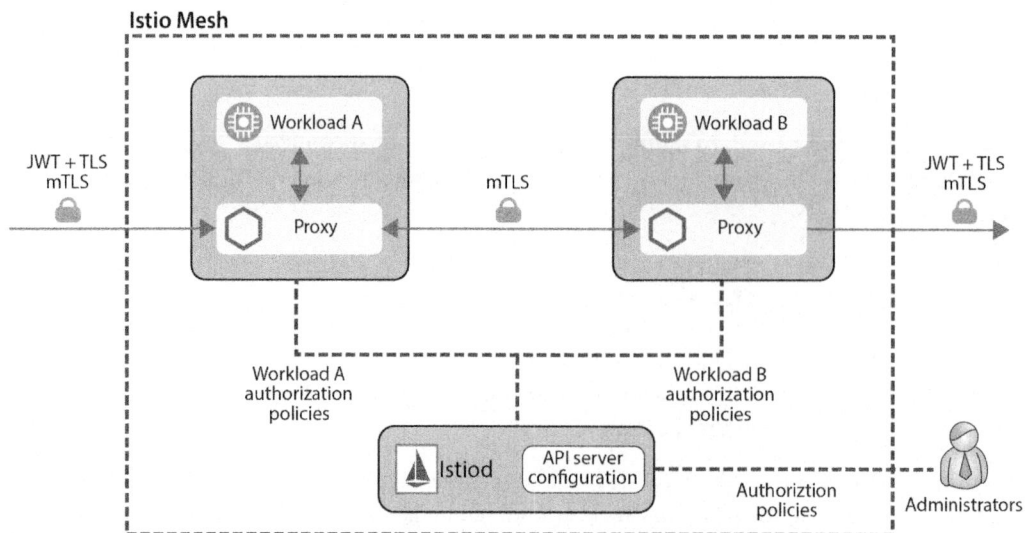

Figure 6.10 – Service-to-service authentication with Istio

In the preceding diagram, there are two services, **Workload A** and **Workload B**, which need to communicate with each other. It is not necessary to understand what the proxy is exactly; it is sufficient to see it as a component deployed by Istio in each service to control the services and implement the six pillars reported in *Table 6.3*. It is important to understand that in the diagram, the administrators (on the right side of the diagram) can centrally define authorization policies that will then be applied by Istio to authorize **Workload A** to communicate with **Workload B** and apply them without needing a dedicated IdP. The service mesh ideally takes care of all the related complexity.

We provided an example of Istio, as it is one of the most widely used service meshes across enterprises, but it is important to note that this is applicable, sometimes with subtle differences, to other technologies as well.

Now, we may wonder what happens if the service represented by **Workload A** in the figure is a web portal that users need to be authenticated against. In OAuth, this operation, as reported in the previous chapters, is usually achieved by using the auth code flow.

It is important to outline that the best implementation of a service mesh we were able to observe was focused on an internal service API. This means that in a service mesh, interactive authentication against a service may not even be needed. It is not uncommon to collapse multi-purpose APIs, applications, and services within the service mesh where interactive logon with OAuth is a relevant topic.

What the most widely used service mesh can do is validate the token before routing the request to the backend service or API within the service mesh. This means that if the client (for example, a browser) has the logic to authenticate the user against the IdP and gets the access token, then it is theoretically possible to enable the service mesh to validate the token and transparently route the request to the backend service without any authentication.

In many cases, this does not happen for the following reasons:

- From a security perspective, many companies do not want the access token to be released on the client side, and as such, it is not possible for the client to make requests with the access token against the API in the service mesh, which, in turn, cannot validate any tokens.

- From a portability perspective, if a client-facing application is developed by offloading the authentication or authorization logic to the service mesh, that application is not portable. This is because if the application is going to move to another containerization platform, a virtual machine, or a cloud PaaS service, it will lack the authentication and authorization logic that needs to be developed.

- The access token usually contains the claim audience, which reports the target service for which the token has been released; this would require some overhead to configure the service mesh to perform the checks.

- If the authentication and authorization logic is delegated to the service mesh, the target service would not be able to refresh the token.

These are some reasons why user authentication is usually still part of the application logic and is not delegated or offloaded to the service mesh. It should be clear that if a service within a service mesh needs to be part of the OAuth flow, it needs to obtain the user access token and it needs to be registered in an IdP. Regardless of where the user authentication is implemented, all the services/APIs must either have user authentication or server-to-server authentication implemented to prevent security issues. In other words, authentication needs to be implemented at every layer in any case.

As a final note in this section, it is important to outline that the service mesh is the hot topic of the moment. Features and functionality relating to this topic are evolving at a very fast pace. The service mesh is expected to gain some extra features and capabilities soon, and some of them may include evolution to facilitate user authentication.

Now that we have seen what the current trends are, in the final section, we are going to propose some practices to avoid pitfalls when it's time to define standards in your organization.

Common antipatterns

Think about an organization where the proliferation of APIs has created many different *islands* with different APIs made using different technologies and standards. It is very common to see different teams attempting to create standards that are not widely applicable.

A typical case we want to mention is something that happened to one of our customers. The infrastructure team had been empowered by the management to resolve the problem of API and application proliferation and to bring order to the APIs and the applications in the company's landscape. We are talking about a company that had more than 1,000 applications and APIs.

The infrastructure team defined a gateway to validate tokens and prevent any request from reaching the backend without the validation of a token, as follows:

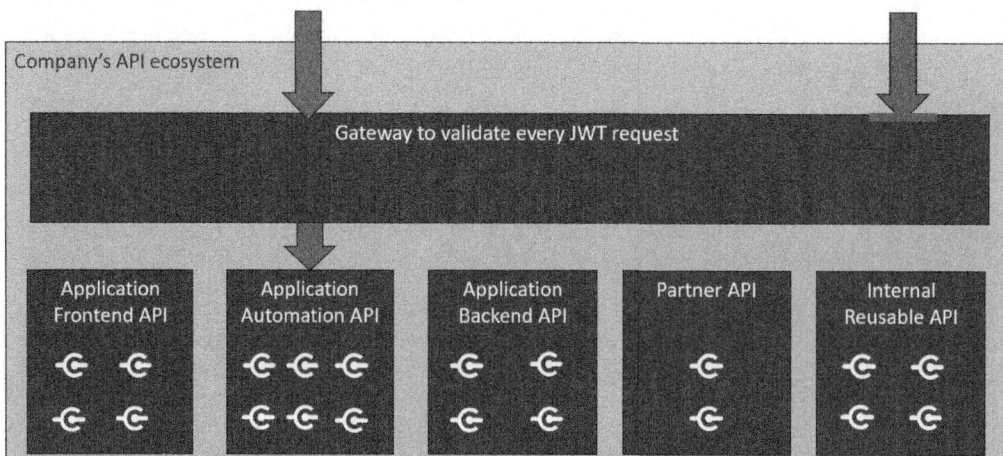

Figure 6.11 – Force check on every request

It is important to understand that this pattern has been applied to the entire application portfolio of the company in the development environment.

Despite the fact that, at first glance, it might look effective, it has created a lot of hassle and has never been promoted to the test or production environment.

The reason for this is that the problem has been trivialized too much by the infrastructure team. The application ecosystem of a company is extremely variable. Every application has different authentication requirements and a different OAuth flow. In general, it cannot be assumed all the clients are able to self-acquire an access token. This concept has implications for how the client is implemented, which protocol it is using, and if it's OAuth, which OAuth flow is adopted. As a matter of fact, many applications stopped working and this pattern has been abandoned.

This is the typical mistake of the *one-fits-all* assumption, which is wrong, especially in the context of authentication.

These bad practices also taught us a couple of important lessons:

- In a large organization, it is paramount to have cooperation between teams and not work in silos. It is very likely that an infrastructure team that's skilled in authentication may not be able to understand the complexity of the application's software design; likewise, the software team responsible for the application software design may not understand infrastructural concepts managed by the infrastructure team. Establishing cooperation and DevOps practices in a company is paramount for success.
- Creating an authentication design for APIs and services when teams have already released many applications without proper standardization creates challenges that are hard to tackle.

Summary

In this chapter, we had the opportunity to understand how the current trends map to the topic of authentication, when OAuth is required, and when tools can help to facilitate authentication without OAuth.

We started the chapter by outlining the API proliferation phenomenon and the related implications. We then showed you a diagram to outline how APIs are typically organized within a company and how they are classified, as well as the authentication requirements for each classification. We also reported the modern way to manage services and APIs with a service mesh and the related authentication implications.

This chapter also outlined bad practices, such as multiple IdPs, and provided an example of a real-world antipattern that we encountered during our work. In the next chapter, we're going to be a little more technical and focus on some of the most widely adopted cloud IdPs.

7

Identity Providers in the Real World

In the last chapter, we saw the most popular trends that describe the challenges that any enterprise architect should be aware of when designing an application nowadays.

This chapter will provide a list of the most prominent **Identity Providers** (**IDPs**) that are part of the modern identity landscape. We are going to briefly describe their capabilities in terms of use cases and the target audience they cover.

The objective of this chapter is not only to review the most prominent IDPs one by one but also to enable you to understand, appreciate, and evaluate technical and non-technical considerations when it is time to choose a provider.

We will cover the following topics in this chapter:

- The technical aspects
- The non-technical aspects
- Azure Active Directory (AAD)
- Azure Active Directory Domain Services (AD DS)
- Azure Active Directory B2C (AD B2C)
- Active Directory Federation Services (AD FS)
- Customer Identity from SAP Customer Data Cloud
- Okta (Auth0)

The technical aspects

There are many technical aspects in terms of the choice of which IDP to choose and it is not easy to scrutinize all of them.

We can definitely start with an initial distinction that connects the dots with the initial part of the book when we mentioned how the cloud era is affecting the identity landscape: one of the initial choices is whether to have a **hosted** IDP or a **cloud** IDP. By hosted IDP, we mean an IDP that needs to be installed and maintained by the enterprise on its server or in its data center. In this case, the enterprise is responsible from end to end and needs to have a dedicated team to take care of the entire stack. This is a legacy approach and companies tend to use SaaS IDPs in which the service doesn't need to be installed or updated, as it is part of the purchased service by the specific cloud provider. We're going to call these kinds of IDPs **cloud-based**, and there is a clear trend nowadays toward cloud-based IDPs.

Other important factors to consider are the following:

Decision factor	Description
Protocols	As mentioned multiple times in this book, each supported protocol enables a specific type of authentication workflow to be adopted by a specific company. This is usually one of the most important decision factors because protocols such as OIDC and OAuth 2.0 are a must. One caveat here is the way the OAuth specs are adopted and implemented by the IDP. This kind of evaluation may be pushed a level deeper to review not only the protocol implemented but also how close the IDP is to the RFC specs.
Federation	This is the ability of a specific IDP to be federated with another IDP using a protocol or out-of-the-box features such as the ability to invite external users from different IDPs as guests in the target IDP.
Multiple authentication factors	In the cloud era, with fewer network perimeters and more users, greater security depends on how authentication is protected. Having multiple factors of authentication is rapidly becoming a minimum requirement in many companies to enable users to be authenticated not only via a password but also via an SMS, a phone call, an email, certificates, authenticator applications, and other authentication systems.
Client-side libraries	When developers need to write an application that relies on a specific IDP for authentication, the support of the client-side libraries is an important factor. It's important to note here that many client-side libraries are protocol-based and not IDP-based. There are plenty of IDP-based client-side libraries that take advantage of specific features of IDPs. It's important that these libraries cover a wide range of coding languages.

Documentation	This is an important factor for all the technology choices, not just the IDP. Having good documentation means providing good support and references so that the developers can write code in a standard way and, most importantly, find answers to common problems. The documentation topic is not only for developers but, importantly, it also needs to be followed by the IDP administrator within the company to find answers and be supported in daily tasks (for example, guiding the registration of an application on an OAuth IDP).
Cost	Although it may not sound like a technical factor, the cost is still relevant because if the cost is low but the maintenance time required to support the IDP within the company is high, a low cost does not imply a better choice. The cost factor is usually a trade-off between the money requirement of the vendor and the overhead the company has to take into account to support the IDP operations.
Support	The availability of the IDP vendor to support the enterprise that chose to adopt a specific IDP is an important factor. This support is generally provided in various pricing tiers according to the SLA the enterprise requires.
Claims	The ability to affect claims before the token is forged by the IDP is typically an important technical aspect that needs to be considered. It is common for an enterprise to require a specific claim to be transformed or injected in order to be read by the final application, which needs to consume an access token or ID token.
API	APIs are usually required, especially by large enterprises, to automate different tasks (for example, application registration or renewing secrets). If APIs are not provided, the tasks need to be done manually, and this could be time-consuming, especially for big enterprises.
Customization	This feature is especially important for enterprises that want to adopt the IDP for their end customers. This functionality includes the ability to perform advanced actions, such as customizing the login screen for specific applications or creating and editing authentication workflows.
Hard limits	Each IDP has a limit in terms of how many users it can support or how many requests per second it can serve. This requires special attention from the enterprise architects, who need to be well aware of the requirements of the organization and the hard limits that can be tolerated for their application portfolio.

Auditing and reporting	Auditing and reporting is the ability to view reports of logins and logouts, enabling administrators to understand how many users access a specific application. One important example in this area is the ability to review suspicious activity: many IDPs raise an alert when, for example, a specific user logs in from the United States, and after a few minutes, the same user logs in from Europe in a timeframe not compatible with an actual relocation, which may indicate hacker activity.
Conditional access	Certain IDPs allow you to grant access to a specific resource not only based on the user identity but also based on what device the user is using, the region the user is connecting from, what their IP address is, or other custom criteria that can enhance the login security.
Provisioning	Users can be provisioned and de-provisioned in multiple ways. The bare minimum functionality is to have a portal that enables an administrator to provision new users. Then, there can be functionalities available via APIs or supported batch processes for onboarding or offboarding users from the IDP.
Self-service	This criterion encompasses all the actions that a user can do on their own without needing an administrator's help. Examples are self-service password resets (the user in this case is authorized by another factor), profile updates, or any self-management activities that can reduce the workload of the help desk.
Policies	An example of a policy could be a password policy such as configurable account expiration, the minimum number of characters, or the set of characters a password must contain. Policies are a broad concept and an IDP enables the administrator to establish advanced policies to manage it.
Extra features	This table thus far has covered the most typical technical factors of an IDP. Other features include temporary admin privileges, integrations, delegated administration, token signing, token encryption, and access restriction.

Table 7.1 – Technical decision factors

This list should not be considered exhaustive, but at the time of writing, it represents a good reference for the technical aspects an enterprise architect needs to be aware of when they need to choose the identity strategy of their company.

The focus of this chapter will be on IDPs that support modern authentication protocols (for example, SAML, WS-Federation, OIDC, and OAuth 2.0), and we will not cover all the technologies that implement legacy protocols (for example, Kerberos, LDAP, and NTLM), such as AD, based on Windows Server, or eDirectory.

Although many may think that having a standard protocol means that portability among solutions provided by different vendors is guaranteed, this is not always the case. It is actually pretty rare, so developers should know which features are portable and which are not.

Each technology has its own implementation details that make it slightly different from the implementation done by a different software vendor.

Sometimes, these differences do not cause any evident problems, and changing from one IDP to another is smooth and seamless. Other times, this can entirely break the authentication logic of an application in an unforeseeable way.

The most common nuances of protocol implementations within IDPs include custom query string parameters that are not defined in the specifications, custom token formats (JWT has nowadays become the de facto standard format for tokens, which, in the OAuth 2.0 specification, are just defined as opaque blobs that do not have any real meaning for the requesting client), the usage of the user endpoint in OIDC, and, in general, the decision to implement a particular protocol extension defined in separate specifications (for example, the RFC 8628 specification, where an additional OAuth 2.0 flow is defined – the device authorization grant flow).

Knowing the preceding criteria really helps an architect plan an application design because to avoid technological lock-in, they can discern the standard features a specific technology offers and decide whether they would like to create a fully standard application that only uses the capabilities defined in the authentication protocol specifications or not.

This decision is very important, especially when achieving application portability is one of the main goals of the application design.

That said, any of the IDPs we will present has pros and cons in terms of features and capabilities, which are usually not the key drivers for choosing one IDP over another. What happens is that, very often, a specific technology is chosen because of the existing technological footprint an organization already has so that they can harness the technical skills of their people.

This is true for every technology, although choosing a specific IDP has several implications that should be considered at the very beginning so that a comprehensive plan can be defined to overcome any limitations that the IDP might introduce.

Now that we have seen the technical aspects, before digging into the specific IDPs that we are going to cover in this chapter, we are going to discuss the non-technical aspects an architect should be aware of in the following sections.

The non-technical aspects

From an enterprise standpoint, choosing to adopt an IDP depends on many factors. Some of them are non-technical. As an example, regulatory compliance is usually a non-technical factor that can affect the choice of IDP.

An IDP's adherence to clear business standards, rules, or regulations is represented by its regulatory compliance. There are several reasons why these rules should be implemented. Existing business procedures should be improved, company resources should be secured, customer and employee privacy should be protected, and national and international legal obligations should be met. Customers are more likely to trust a product when it conforms to these laws. They can be sure that the product will perform as expected by the industry and won't cause them any unexpected trouble.

There are many rules and laws a specific enterprise wants to adhere to and they usually depend on the core business of the enterprise and its location.

One of the most important examples of regulatory compliance you may be familiar with is the **International Organization for Standardization (ISO)**. These certifications aim to establish the highest standards in quality management for proprietary, commercial, and industrial organizations. Another important example that is relevant to many enterprises is **System and Organization Controls (SOC)**. It revolves around protecting financial statements, improving operational efficiency, and maximizing compliance. A third example is the **Payment Card Industry Data Security Standard (PCI-DSS)**. The PCI-DSS usually applies to financial organizations.

If you want to learn more about standards and guidelines, a good source of information can be found in the **National Institute and Standards for technology (NIST)** documents: `https://pages. nist.gov/800-63-3/sp800-63b.html`.

The **General Data Protection Regulation (GDPR)** is another important regulation. It is pretty agnostic to the core business of an enterprise, as it needs to be followed by all European organizations and, therefore, all European enterprises. It was introduced by the European Union to protect the data and privacy of citizens residing in the European Union and the European Economic Area. The GDPR represents one of the most recent regulations, as it was introduced in 2016, and companies that don't follow it are subject to a fine of up to 20 million euros.

The reason why we wanted to bring these standards to your attention is that choosing a PaaS or SaaS that is managed by third-party companies or IDPs is usually a choice that does not focus only on technical factors. As an example, a SaaS IDP deployed in Europe could replicate sensitive data about its users in the United States for reliability purposes and may fail to comply with the GDPR. In this case, the technical capabilities of the IDP may not be relevant for an organization, even if they are technically better than the competition. This is because a SaaS that doesn't comply with the GDPR cannot be adopted by a European organization.

Then, there are the technical factors, and these are usually where an enterprise architect needs to step up and support its company for the best choice. There is not one single best choice; it depends on what scenario, level of service, protocols, and technical features a specific enterprise needs to support. During our experience, we have assisted customers who developed multi-factor authentication with custom code on top of the IDP. Recently, this scenario is becoming rare because many IDPs offer this feature out of the box, and a good enterprise architect prefers to focus development on what makes its business unique and differentiated rather than on capabilities than can be maintained by a third party.

When it is time to make a technology choice for an enterprise, business leaders use third-party organizations that offer an independent view of the market landscape and compare the products available on the market. Gartner is one such company, and in this chapter, we want to examine the **Gartner Magic Quadrant** for access management. It's important for you to note that the following diagram does not include all the available IDPs. This is because the inclusion criteria for the Gartner Magic Quadrant include many factors that not every IDP can offer, such as support for modern protocols such as OAuth 2.0, session management, profile management, delegated administration, and self-service capabilities:

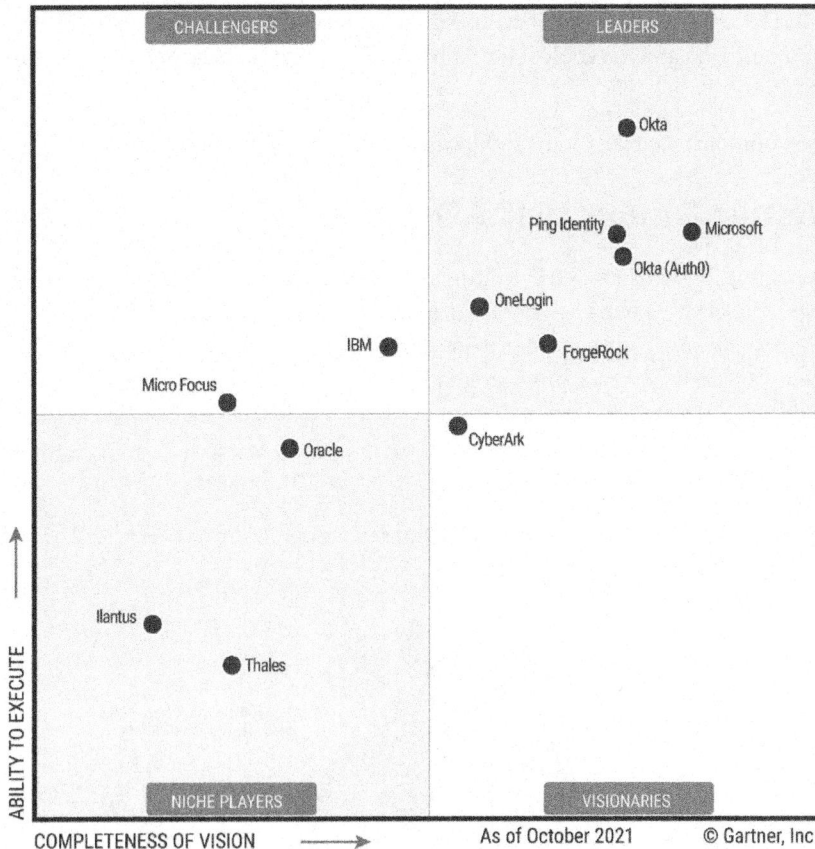

Figure 7.1 – The Gartner Magic Quadrant for access management

Describing Gartner's research on access management in depth is beyond the scope of this book, but it is important that you understand the methods and the technical and non-technical factors that can affect an enterprise's choice to embrace a specific technology and not another. The Magic Quadrant diagram is made up of four quadrants: *niche players*, *challengers*, *visionaries*, and *leaders*, according to Gartner. The further a technology is to the right side of the diagram, the more complete the vision of the vendor that provides the technology is. The closer to the top a vendor is in the diagram, the better a vendor can execute and apply its technology in the market.

Gartner's Magic Quadrant is just an example; there are many independent companies that support business leaders in making technology choices, such as Forrester or IDC.

Research by an independent company should be used just as support and cannot replace the judgment and the evaluation of an enterprise architect of a company. It is not rare to see companies that adopt vendors and technology that are in the *niche player* quadrant of a Gartner assessment. This is because being positioned in an unprestigious quadrant doesn't disqualify a vendor from consideration. Each technology has specifications, advantages, and disadvantages that may or may not fit the company's objectives and purposes and the choice should be 100% tailored to these objectives and the business of a specific enterprise.

Let's now start our journey through the modern landscape of some IDPs.

Azure Active Directory (AAD)

When you encounter Microsoft's AAD for the first time, the most common (and wrong) idea is to think of AAD as simply the cloud counterpart of AD DS. AAD and AD DS are two completely different technologies that can work together but provide different authentication services. AD DS is a service that comes with Windows Server; it provides an LDAP directory, Kerberos, and NTLM authentication (along with other enterprise features, such as group policy management). AAD, on the other hand, is a modern IDP that doesn't really know what those protocols are because it implements different ones, such as OAuth 2.0, SAML, WS-Federation, and OpenID Connect.

This means that AAD can be considered a hub centered within Microsoft's services, as shown in the following diagram:

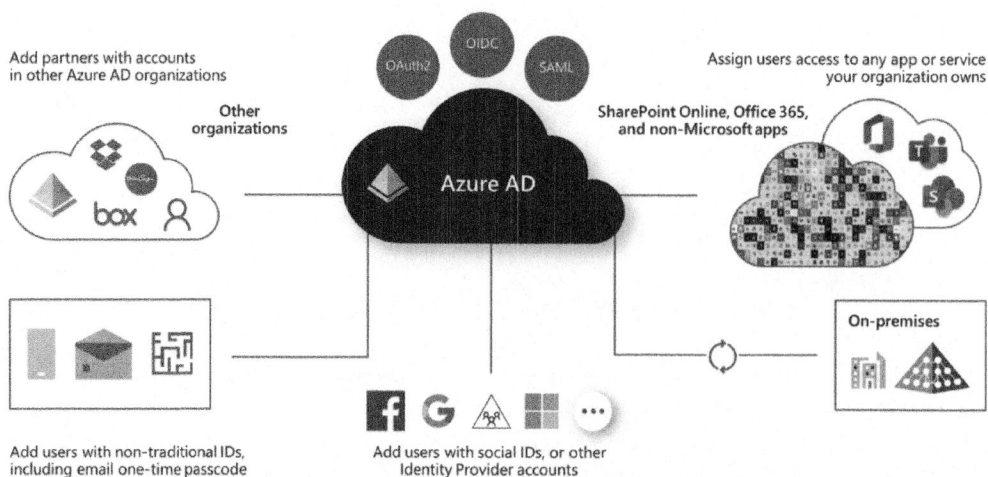

Figure 7.2 – AAD overview

Any AAD object can be accessed through a REST API called Microsoft Graph, which allows you to create, update, and delete users, groups, and any object type AAD manages.

AAD protects users from credential theft and privilege escalation by greatly increasing the security posture of the overall authentication footprint through several built-in features, including the following:

- **Conditional access**: Conditional access receives information from different signals during a user's authentication process to make and enforce decisions according to an organization's security policies. Signals include the user's location, the user's client operating system, the client applications used, and many other things.

- **Identity protection**: Thanks to the large number of signals Microsoft receives every day in its cloud systems, identity protection provides continuous protection against modern identity threats by constantly learning new attack patterns. Users and sign-in attempts are classified with a risk level (low, medium, and high) together with recommendations that suggest actions to mitigate the risks.

- **Identity governance**: Identity governance allows an organization to perform the following tasks:

  - Govern the identity life cycle

  - Govern the access life cycle

  - Secure privileged access for administration

  This is achieved using entitlement management and access reviews. Entitlement management allows us to create a pre-defined set of applications and permissions that a specific category of users typically needs. These users can then request these entitlements (or access packages) through a self-service portal. Access to access packages can be continuously monitored through access reviews, which are scheduled events that ask the owner of the applications included in an access package to validate or revoke the permissions that have been granted to the user.

- **Privileged Identity Management**: By implementing the principles of *least privilege* and *just-in-time administration*, Privileged Identity Management protects an organization against privilege escalation and lateral movement attacks by not assigning permanent administrative roles. Administrators can choose the role that is most appropriate to perform a specific task and set the amount of time they need to have this role. An administrative role request can also be controlled by an approval workflow where multiple people can decide whether the request is legitimate or not.

- **Managed identities**: A managed identity is an AAD-specific type of service credential that can be assigned to Azure (Microsoft's public cloud) services. The strength of this identity type is that the password is not visible to the users that would like to use it because it is automatically rotated by AAD without the user's intervention. This solution greatly reduces the attack surface because, for instance, a developer using this kind of identity does not have to write the password anywhere and instead, just uses the identity to access whatever resources they have been authorized to access.

It's worth mentioning that AAD and several other IDPs are gradually inserting the possibility to use other standard ways of authentication, such as OATH tokens (which must not be confused with OAuth 2.0!), compliant devices with FIDO2 technology, and passwordless authentication, which, as the name suggests, removes the password from the authentication process by replacing it with other authentication mechanisms, such as something a user has, a user is, or a user knows.

AAD provides integration with on-premises AD DS installations by allowing the synchronization of the users belonging to such installations with its own user repository. This greatly simplifies the migration of on-premises authentication systems and enables the concept of hybrid identity, as discussed in *Chapter 2, The Cloud Era and Identity*.

If AAD mainly serves the authentication of an organization's employees, on the other hand, it also enables **Business-to-Business (B2B)** collaboration and **Business-to-Consumer (B2C)** scenarios by allowing several types of external users to seamlessly access applications that are federated with AAD. A lot of enterprise applications already support AAD as an IDP, and they can be integrated directly through the AAD application gallery for user authentication and to enable user provisioning scenarios to and from the aforementioned applications. AAD implements the **System for Cross-domain Identity Management (SCIM)** protocol to offer a solution for users, groups, and roles provisioning HR systems and end user applications. All these capabilities fall under the umbrella of identity provisioning, another topic we discussed in *Chapter 2, The Cloud Era and Identity*:

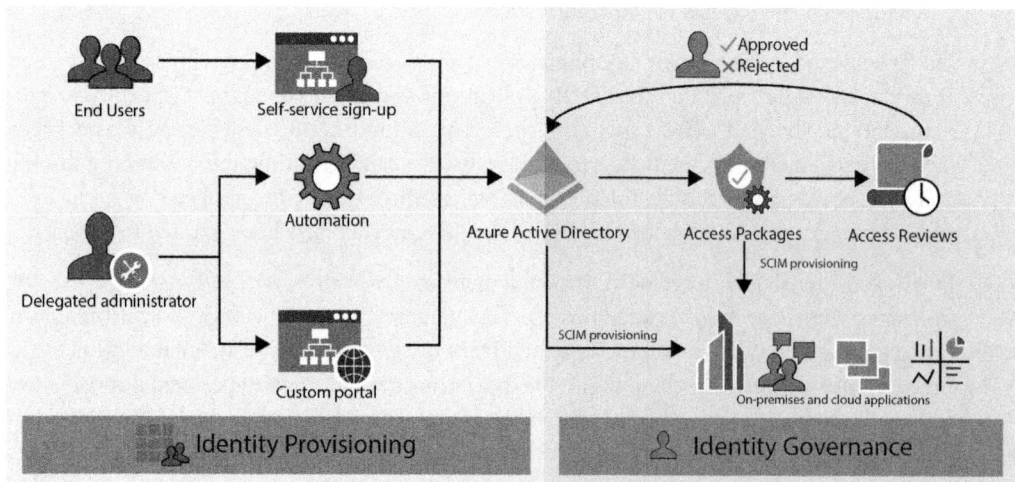

Figure 7.3 – Identity and access life cycle example

It is also important to mention that in order to use Microsoft applications such as Office 365 and Azure, having an AAD tenant is mandatory.

Azure Active Directory Domain Services (AD DS)

Even if AD DS is not an IDP that provides modern authentication capabilities, it is worth mentioning it because of its integration with AAD. AD DS is a *managed* service that relies on AAD identities to provide a managed AD DS installation (that is, managed Domain Controllers servers) in the cloud. It offers all the basic capabilities that AD DS offers by deploying a pair of Domain Controllers within a private network (an Azure Virtual Network) created through the Microsoft public cloud, Azure. As the non-managed counterpart service that can be deployed through Windows Server, AD DS provides Kerberos, LDAP, and NTLM authentication and simplifies all the *lift-and-shift* migration scenarios that involve tasks such as moving on-premises workloads (file servers) to Azure. AD DS does not provide the level of customization that a full installation of AD DS offers (the AD schema cannot be extended), but it has been designed for specific use cases that are typical of cloud migration initiatives where velocity and simplicity are key to success.

Azure Active Directory B2C (AD B2C)

AD B2C is a separate Microsoft offering that provides a dedicated AAD tenant with additional capabilities tailored to specific use cases that mainly involve interaction with the customers of an organization. In other words, AD B2C is a **Customer Identity and Access Management** (**CIAM**) solution that enables an enterprise to effectively engage with its customers.

In the following diagram, we can see how AD B2C integrates with a heterogeneous group of external systems and acts as an identity orchestrator that can hide the complexity of where those systems are, which language they support, and what type of users they manage:

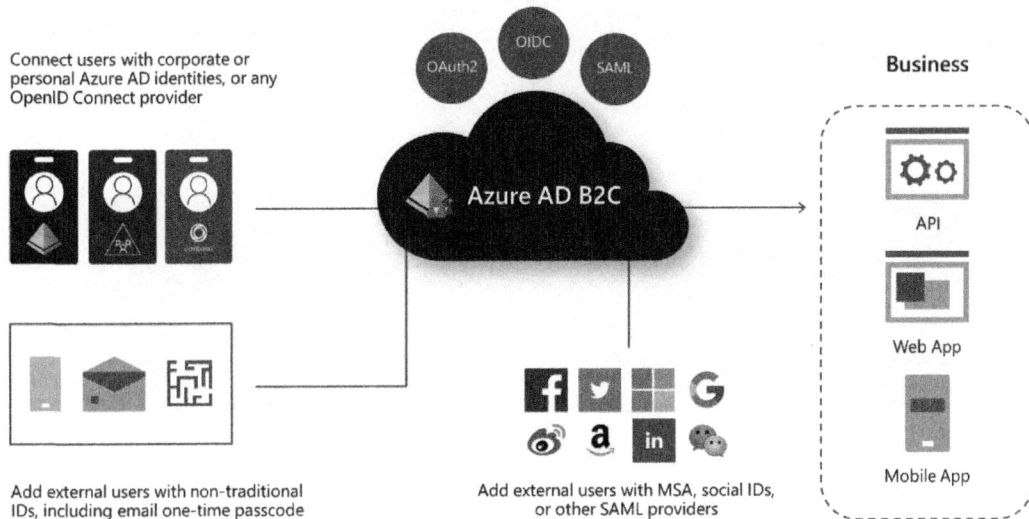

Figure 7.4 – AD B2C overview

AD B2C offers most of the core AAD features and adds the following capabilities on top of them:

- **User flows**: A fully guided experience that allows us to create different flavors of flows that guide the interaction of a user with the AD B2C tenant during scenarios such as sign-up, sign-in, profile edit, and password reset. User flows are entirely configurable with a UI but provide limited functionality when compared to custom policies that can be created through the **Identity Experience Framework (IEF)**.

- **IEF**: A highly customizable framework that can be used by means of a meta-language based on XML files to create custom policies.

  Custom policies are configuration files that specify how an AD B2C tenancy behaves. For the most frequent authentications, user flows are specified in the AD B2C portal; however, custom rules may be fully customized by an identity developer to handle a variety of duties. A custom policy orchestrates the interaction between entities in standard protocols, such as OpenID Connect, OAuth, and SAML. To expand the capabilities of these protocols, a custom policy can also interact with generic external systems that expose a REST API to exchange claims. The whole flow defined in a custom policy is dubbed the user journey and is made up of sequential steps. Each step receives some claims as input and generates some claims as output. Each step invokes an entity called a technical profile, which embeds the logic to interact with a specific standard protocol or external system.

  A custom policy is managed as one or more XML-formatted files. These XML files refer to each other hierarchically. Within the XML, there are elements that define the building blocks, the interaction with the user, other parties, and the business logic:

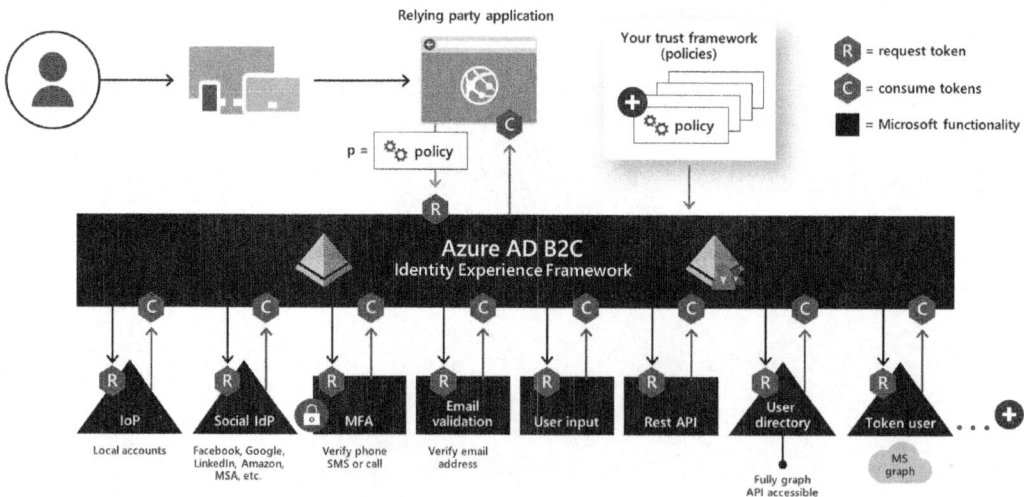

Figure 7.5 – AD B2C holistic overview

Compared to an AAD tenant, AD B2C is equipped with built-in tools that simplify the integration with external IDPs by the means of standard protocols. The list of these external IDPs is constantly changing. At the time of writing, it is possible to natively integrate with Apple, Amazon, Facebook, Twitter, Google, and LinkedIn, among other things. AD B2C can also integrate with generic IDPs that implement SAML, OAuth 2.0, and OpenID Connect from their end.

Getting familiar with the language and syntax of a custom policy and the IEF can be cumbersome and discouraging at the beginning, but in the end, mastering it will give you access to a comprehensive set of tools that can change the way a customer engages with all the services offered by an organization.

Active Directory Federation Services (AD FS)

Historically, AD FS has been Microsoft's solution to federated authentication. AD FS tightly integrates with AD DS by acting as a sort of protocol translator that allows federated applications to use modern protocols, while, under the hood, actually authenticating the users against AD Domain Controllers through Windows authentication (Kerberos or NTLM) without the application being aware of where the user's credentials are stored.

The infrastructure of AD FS is very simple and is made up of a pair of server roles: AD FS servers and AD FS proxy servers. The former are installed within a company's internal network and provide their functionality, including **single sign-on** (**SSO**), to users connecting from within the organization premises or connected through a **virtual private network** (**VPN**). The latter are typically installed in a **demilitarized zone** (**DMZ**) network, which is logically separated from the internal network and usually has stricter network rules because of its role as the entry point into the corporate network from the internet.

The following diagram represents a typical AD FS infrastructure architecture:

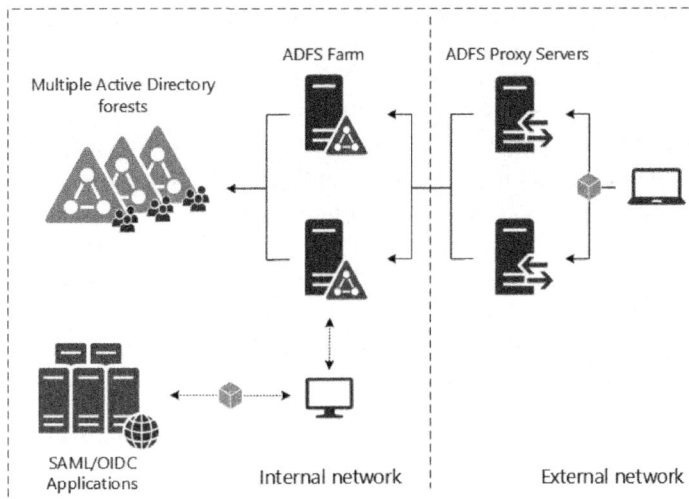

Figure 7.6 – ADFS architecture

ADFS comprises several features that allow you to customize a user's (and sometimes a device's or a service's) authentication experience:

- **External attribute stores**: Through a set of built-in connectors, AD FS can augment the claims issued in a token. These native connectors provide integration with LDAP and SQL Server external systems; however, it is also possible to develop a custom **Dynamic Link Library** (**DLL**) to integrate with potentially any type of external attribute store, such as a REST API.

- **Claim provider trusts**: A claim provider trust represents an external IDP to which AD FS can delegate the authentication. A claim provider trust can be an authentication system that "*speaks*" SAML, WS-Federation, or LDAP. AD FS receives the claims from the IDP and can either relay them to the application as they are or manipulate them according to the application's requirements.

- **Multi-factor authentication**: AD FS can integrate with external multi-factor authentication systems to strengthen the authentication process. AD FS natively allows you to configure **certificate-based authentication**: user credentials are validated by challenging the user's browser session with a request to provide a valid user certificate that was previously installed on the user's device by their organization. A user certificate installation is typically done by means of a Group Policy through AD (if it's a Windows device) or by web enrollment services that implement the **Simple Certificate Enrollment Protocol** (**SCEP**).

- **Custom claim rule language**: Thanks to a built-in claim rule language, AD FS can manipulate the information that needs to be sent to an application within the security token. Claims can be augmented, transformed, merged, deleted, or issued only if specific conditions are satisfied according to what the application needs.

- **Access policies**: AD FS is mainly used for user authentication, but it can also provide authorization according to specific conditions the user must meet. Access policies have been designed with this goal in mind and they can block or allow access to an application through controls over the user's location, group membership, and other criteria.

Along with the evolution of Microsoft's technologies, AAD is the service that gradually replaced all the AD FS features listed here, and there are still some gaps left to be filled. AAD provides a much more comprehensive set of security features that align with the zero-trust approach to identity protection (and security in general) and that are a good fit for the modern enterprise landscape.

Customer Identity from SAP Customer Data Cloud

Customer Identity is a CIAM solution from SAP Customer Data Cloud that enables organizations to engage with their customers and connect them with their web applications.

Customer Identity provides a comprehensive list of features that simplify the collection of user information and the overall management effort of maintaining an enterprise CIAM solution:

- **Registration and login options**: There is a large number of built-in registration and login options, which include social login (such as Facebook, Twitter, Google, LinkedIn, Amazon, and Microsoft) and federated login using the SAML or OpenID Connect protocols. It is also possible to configure passwordless phone and push authentication and, to increase the security posture, risk-based authentication.

- **Screen-Sets**: Screen-Sets are sets of screens that govern the user interaction with Customer Identity by defining a user-facing flow. Flows typically belong to the following types: login and registration, forgotten passwords, profile updates, re-authentication, lite registration, or account linking.

- **UI customization**: Customer Identity has several tools that come in handy when the UI has to be customized. The powerful UI Builder allows you to easily customize the UI of each screen defined in a Screen-Set, which, together with CSS and markup personalization, allows you to create conditional workflows and visualize each message in the user's preferred language.

- **Integration tools**: Through the IdentitySync **Extract, Transport, Load** (ETL) service, Customer Identity offers an API-based way to transfer data in bulk between platforms.

   Furthermore, Customer Identity provides pre-built integrations with many notable CMSs, CRMs, and other systems.

- **Admin tools**: Several out-of-the-box tools ease administrative tasks by providing reports, customer insights, and audit logs.

Customer Identity provides all the capabilities needed to build a strong trust-based relationship with an organization's customers.

Okta (Auth0)

Unlike Microsoft, Google, and Amazon, Okta is a company that we can call IAM-born. The core business of Okta is identity management; 100% of their business relates to identity management and, as a consequence, all the effort of the company is focused in this direction. In March 2021, Auth0 was acquired by Okta, another company that is focused on identity and the ecosystem around it.

Okta built its customer experience on top of the following pillars:

- **Directories**: The directory is the basic pillar of an enterprise that intends to adopt Okta. The directory is used to host resources, users, and groups. An Okta directory enables their customer to store an unlimited number of users, devices, and groups in a single and structured view. In the Okta language, a universal directory usually represents the main instance of the Okta IDP. Customers may use multiple directories if a company has multi-tenant ambitions.

- **Integrations**: This pillar encompasses the ability of the IDP for provisioning, de-provisioning, and federation with other IDPs. These integrations can represent the enablement of SSO capabilities thanks to protocols such as OIDC and SAML, or more advanced scenarios, such as automated user provisioning and integrations with Okta's API.

- **Insights**: This pillar is connected with the *Auditing and reporting* decision factor reported in *Table 7.1*. The insights pillar refers to the ability to gain insights from user activities, be alerted to suspicious logins, and analyze the user's behavior for business purposes (this capability can enable a business decision-maker to understand how many times a user logs in to a specific application and collect data that could be relevant for the business to understand where to focus the development investments).

- **Identity Engine**: Okta's Identity Engine is the pillar for creating tailored user journeys. With a context-driven user journey, enterprises can address a wide range of identity use cases with minimal custom code.

- **Workflows**: Similar to Identity Engine, this pillar is more focused on those who aren't developers to enable organizations to customize user journeys without writing a single line of custom code. The philosophy is "*Enable anyone to automate identity-based processes and drive innovative new user experiences with a low/no-code interface and extensible platform service*" (`https://www.okta.com/platform/workflows/`).

- **Devices**: Okta enables advanced features to enforce device security and enable a passwordless scenario whereby users can log in without entering their password by authenticating themselves via a device. Okta also provides multi-factor authentication capabilities with its own authenticator.

As highlighted in the Gartner Magic Quadrant diagram in *Figure 7.1*, Okta plays a crucial role in the identity market. It is considered a leader with a greater ability to execute its technology than anybody else. That's the reason why Okta must be seriously considered when it is time to choose the IDP to use in an enterprise. The recent acquisition of Auth0 outlines the healthy status of the company, and the future, at the time of writing, seems to be good and completely focused on identity, unlike many of its competitors.

This section just scratched the surface of Okta's features and capabilities. If you need to evaluate it as an IDP, we recommend going even deeper and directly browsing `okta.com`, which can provide up-to-date and more detailed information.

Summary

In this chapter, we reviewed the criteria for how a company should evaluate the IDP that they will choose. We discovered that there are not only technical factors at play in this choice but also regulation policies for specific businesses playing an important role. We reviewed all the technical aspects that should affect the choice of which IDP to use.

We also had the opportunity to describe, from a very high-level point of view, some of the IDPs that have a good standing on the market.

In the next chapter, we are going to move a step further and a level deeper: we are going to describe in detail how one of the most important IDPs works, look at its features, discuss the advantages and disadvantages of adopting it, and see the benefits an enterprise can obtain by leveraging features that are built on top of the OAuth protocol when choosing this IDP. We are going to have a closer look at AAD.

8

Real-World Identity Provider – A Zoom-In on Azure Active Directory

In previous chapters, we went through a theoretical overview of how modern authentication protocols work and how they can simplify the way that users interact with an application .We analyzed the pros and cons of each authentication flow that these protocols provide, how they fit into the modern application landscape from a technical perspective, and the main challenges that an enterprise faces every day in the real world.

Having shared a list of the most famous identity providers that can be found on the market today, we would like to take a deep dive into one of them: **Azure Active Directory** (**AAD**).

In this chapter, we will explain many of the features that AAD offers, starting with the features that relate to the implementation of the underlying authentication protocols that we now know and understand. Then, we will go ahead with a list of features that have been built on top of the basic identity provider capabilities that, nowadays, are implemented by any identity solution on the market. Finally, we will have a look at what the future of AAD might be and which identity trends Microsoft is investing in and implementing in its main identity platform.

We will cover the following main topics in this chapter:

- An overview of AAD
- AAD basics
- Supported authentication protocols
- Registering and configuring applications

An overview of AAD

AAD is a unique identity and access management service and unified control plane solution that provides authentication, authorization, and security capabilities to all of Microsoft's first-party cloud solutions, such as Azure, Microsoft 365, and Dynamics 365, and a plethora of third-party applications. Third-party developers can easily publish their applications into the **AAD Gallery** (and hundreds already have) to allow AAD administrators to seamlessly integrate applications into their enterprise and grant access to end users. If an application cannot be found in the gallery, the application can be manually added to an AAD tenant leveraging the underlying authentication protocols' implementation.

AAD users can use **single sign-on** (**SSO**) to access all AAD applications so that they are not forced to re-enter their credentials each time they access a new application: an administrator can configure which applications a user or a group of users needs to have access to (authorization).

On top of the aforementioned authentication and authorization capabilities, AAD implements a long list of security features that help strengthen the security posture of an enterprise and reduce the attack surface for a malicious user. Using **zero trust** as the guiding principle, AAD intensively leverages machine learning algorithms that analyze and study the behavior patterns of a user while they interact with the AAD platform so that it's easier to detect anomalous behaviors and identify and distinguish between legitimate and non-legitimate traffic (using **Identity Protection**) as early as possible. Administrators can also input their own security controls in order to prevent all the behaviors that the internal security teams usually prohibit (using **Conditional Access**), and they can also configure tailored administrative roles to be active only for a limited time (using **Privileged Identity Management**).

We know that collaboration with external companies is paramount to any enterprise – to this end, AAD provides the ability to trust identities coming from other AAD tenants and other external identity providers. Since, typically, a user in an AAD tenant is an employee that belongs to the company that owns the AAD tenant, external users belonging to external companies are usually contractors, suppliers, or simply business partners that need to access applications and services published by the enterprise they need to do business with.

With all the challenges that are involved when managing such a diverse set of users, it is fundamental to have full control over what these users can and can't do. Furthermore, user life cycles must be organized so that a user will only have access to a resource for the amount of time they need to perform a specific task; with the **Identity Governance** feature, AAD allows us to review and validate user access to AAD resources by unburdening IT administrators of this responsibility and effectively delegating it to the proper business decision makers.

Automation and the ability to programmatically access all AAD features are important, and AAD provides several tools to accomplish this. **AAD PowerShell** and the **AAD CLI** are command-line tools that allow us to interact with an AAD tenant programmatically, and they can be used together with the publicly available **Microsoft Graph** RESTful API through the many **software development kits** (**SDKs**) provided by different programming languages.

In the following sections, we will define the types of objects that can be created in AAD, their relationships, and the features that are built on top of them. This chapter does not aim to be a comprehensive and detailed description of all Azure features; we will mainly focus on all the authentication-related features, particularly how the concepts we've learned about throughout this book are the foundation of all modern identity providers. The goal is for you to recognize how these concepts underpin the implementation of a real-world identity provider, in order to become familiar with them and be able to recognize them regardless of the technology or the vendor providing the service. Cloud services such as AAD also change at a very fast pace, and therefore, some of the topics described in this chapter might change slightly in the future.

AAD basics

AAD is a globally distributed identity and access management service organized so that each customer that would like to start using it can create their own separate and isolated instance, which is also referred to as a **tenant**. Each AAD tenant has a unique GUID and a unique tenant name that is written in the following format: `tenantname.onmicrosoft.com`. The tenant name is also called the default domain of the tenant.

Before diving into the description of the AAD objects, it is worth refreshing the concept of a **security principal**. It's common to encounter the concept of security principals when talking about identity. In simple terms, a security principal can be defined as any entity that can be authenticated, that can be assigned permissions to do something, and that can be the target of a permission. Typical examples of security principals are users and groups.

AAD provides the ability to create and orchestrate the interactions of different types of objects. The list of objects includes the following:

- **Users**: A user represents (most of the time) the identity of an individual. A user contains a list of attributes used to store a user's information, such as first name, surname, office address, and email address, and attributes used for user authentication, such as user principal name, password, and **Multi-Factor Authentication** (**MFA**) phone number.

  A user always has at least the following attributes:

  - **User Principal Name (UPN)**: This is the attribute that contains the account name an individual uses to log on when prompted by the AAD login page. The UPN format is something like `username@domain.com` and is made up of two parts: the prefix (the part before @) and the suffix (the part after @), which must be either the default domain or a custom domain registered by an administrator.

  - **Password**: This is the attribute that contains a user's password; it is only mandatory for cloud users.

  - **Display name**: This is the attribute that contains the display name for a user. Most of the time, it is a combination of an individual's first name and last name.

There are several types of users in AAD that are typically used for different and distinct use cases:

- **Cloud user**: A user that is created directly in AAD is called a cloud user; each user is identified uniquely by a UPN. A cloud user's UPN and password are stored in AAD, and their life cycle is entirely managed within AAD (using **Create, Read, Update, and Delete (CRUD)** operations).

- **Hybrid user**: A hybrid user is a user that has been synchronized by an on-premises identity system, which, most of the time, is one or more Active Directory forests. The official tools that Microsoft provides to perform this synchronization are AAD Connect and AAD Connect Cloud Sync, which read the user's information from the on-premises Active Directory forests and write it to AAD (more details about this process will be explained shortly). A hybrid user cannot be modified directly in AAD (excluding some specific attributes); it can only be modified on the on-premises system first so that the updates are then synchronized to AAD. A hybrid user may leverage different authentication types depending on whether the on-premises password hashes are synchronized to AAD or not (more details can be found later in this chapter).

- **Guest user**: A guest user is a user that has been invited to the AAD tenant. This is part of the External Identities set of features that orchestrate the interaction between AAD and external identity systems. AAD allows us to invite users belonging to external identity systems such as external AAD tenants, Microsoft accounts, Google accounts, and WS-Federation or SAML identity providers where the invited user must accept an emailed invitation before gaining access to the application published by the inviting tenant. Once the invitation is redeemed and accepted, the external (guest) user can start to access applications federated by the inviting AAD tenant. The user's credentials will still be managed by the external identity provider and authentication will still happen there. What happens is that the inviting AAD tenant will trust the token issued by the external identity provider and it will issue a new token for the final application (just as standard federation works). A guest user can be seen in AAD as a placeholder (a reference) for the real user, who still lives in the external identity provider.

- **Groups**: Groups are containers of users or, more generally, containers of security principals, which can include application identities too (see the *Applications* bullet point later in this list). Membership within a group can either be static or dynamic. In the former, members are added manually; in the latter, members are added according to predefined rules that can be customized to, for instance, add all the users that have a specific value or a specific attribute (e.g., all the users in the marketing department). Groups are security principals too.

- **Devices**: A device, typically the client machine used by a user, can be represented in AAD. A device object is created in AAD when a client machine is either registered, AAD-joined, or hybrid AAD-joined. Having a device representation in AAD allows us to create security rules that can allow or block access to a particular AAD resource, such as an application, according to the status (information) of the device, which can be classified as compliant or non-compliant to the aforementioned security rules. It is not the purpose of this book to provide a thorough explanation of how device management works in AAD. For additional details, visit https://docs.microsoft.com/en-us/azure/active-directory/devices/overview.

- **Applications**: The representation of an application in AAD can be tricky to grasp at first sight, so bear with us and it will become clearer in the end. We know that, because of how the federated authentication protocols work, an identity provider must be aware of the applications that delegate authentication to it. The process of application configuration in AAD is called **application registration**. When a user registers an application in AAD, a couple of things occur: an application and a service principal (which is another type of security principal) are created in the tenant, which is also referred to as the **home tenant**.

  You can think of the application object as the blueprint for all the properties that the application must have: redirect URIs for the OAuth 2.0/OIDC protocols, client secrets, allowed permissions (scopes) to other applications, and so on. The service principal is an instance of the application object from which it inherits a set of static values; the service principal is the real object to which the permissions are assigned.

  It is also important to explain the concept of the home tenant: applications in AAD can either be single-tenant or multi-tenant. The meaning is straightforward: a single-tenant application can only grant access to users in the home tenant, while a multi-tenant application can grant access to users belonging to external AAD tenants too. In the case of a multi-tenant application, a service principal is created in the external AAD tenant too with the same logic as the service principal created in the home tenant; it inherits all the properties and permissions the application object has defined in the home tenant.

  But when is the service principal created in an external AAD tenant? This happens when an external user tries to access the application. According to the permissions that the application needs in the external AAD tenant, the user is first asked to insert their credentials and then prompted with a consent web page, where they need to agree to or disagree with the list of permissions required by the application (something similar happens with mobile applications installed on smartphones). Some permissions may require the user to be an administrator; in that case, the administrator must be involved in the consent process before the end users can successfully start utilizing the application.

This flow is described in the following diagram:

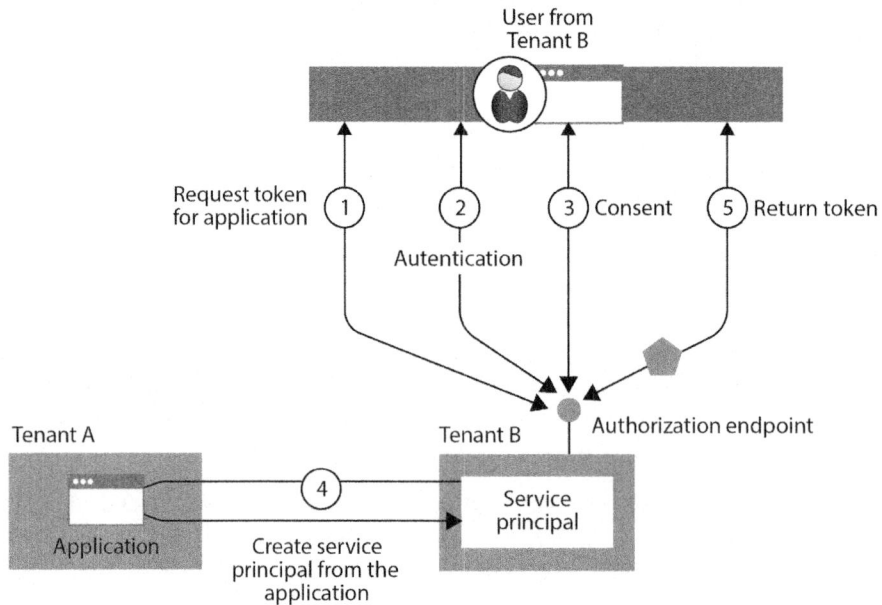

Figure 8.1 – Service principal creation flow in a multi-tenant AAD scenario

One particular type of service principal is the **managed identity**. A managed identity removes the need for developers to manage an application's or entity's credentials because the passwords (including their rotation) are completely managed by AAD. Managed identities are typically assigned to Azure resources so that they can, in this way, automatically request an OAuth 2.0 access token to use with other Azure resources, which must be registered in AAD as well. The only thing that is needed is for an administrator to create a managed identity and assign it to an Azure resource; from that moment, the developer using that resource can simply ask for an access token without specifying a client secret because AAD will verify whether the operation is allowed (authorization). **AD Domain Services** (**AD DS**) veterans will find the concept of managed identities very similar to **Managed Service Accounts** (**MSAs**).

- **Consent model**: When defining applications, it is possible to specify the permissions the application might need when interacting with another application. This is done by configuring scopes (merely strings) in the *server* application definition (operations that can be done within the application) and by authorizing a *client* application to request these scopes. When a client application requests permission to do an operation (scope) against a server application, the user is asked to grant their consent (i.e., authorize) for the client application to do what has been specified in the scope description. This happens after AAD has successfully authenticated the user, and consent can be granted by any user unless the scope has been explicitly configured to only accept consent granted by an administrator. In the latter case, an administrator can provide consent on behalf of the whole organization (the AAD tenant) so that no subsequent login attempts by any user will ask for consent anymore.

- **Administrative units**: Administrative units are logical containers that can only contain users, groups, and devices. They are not security principals, but they are used to organize and group the aforementioned AAD resources in order to delegate their management to specific people who do not need or do not want to be granted the full administration of all AAD objects indiscriminately. An example of administrative unit usage could be a business manager who has only been delegated the management of users, groups, and devices belonging to their team – so, for instance, they only need to be able to reset the passwords of the users they manage (those that belong to a specific administrative unit) instead of the passwords of all the users in the tenant.

Now that we know what the different types of objects in AAD are, let's discuss which authentication protocols AAD supports.

Supported authentication protocols

AAD supports several authentication methods. Here's the complete list at the time of writing:

- **Header-based authentication**: This authentication pattern, which involves forwarding HTTP headers from a client application to a destination web application, is supported only when using the AAD Application Proxy service. AAD Application Proxy is a service that comprises two distinct components, one of which runs in the cloud and one of which runs on-premises (through the means of a connector), that allows us to publish on-premises applications that still leverage legacy authentication protocols to the internet.

- **LDAP authentication**: Support for LDAP authentication is provided only through AD DS, which is a component, briefly described in the previous chapter, that must be deployed within an Azure Virtual Network and leverages identities that come from the synchronization of on-premises Active Directory forests. AD DS is useful in specific use cases, such as lift-and-shift migration scenarios, and for all those applications that still leverage the LDAP protocol and cannot easily be migrated to a modern authentication protocol.

- **OAuth 2.0 and OIDC authentication**: The OAuth 2.0 and OIDC protocols are fully supported in AAD. They can be used for application and user authentication/authorization, and they are tightly integrated with AAD security capabilities such as MFA and Conditional Access policies. We will go deeper into these two protocols and how they can be used later in this chapter.

- **RADIUS authentication**: AAD integrates with RADIUS authentication to add support for MFA to specific applications such as the following:

  - **Virtual Private Network (VPN)**

  - Wi-Fi access

  - Remote Desktop Gateway

- Virtual Desktop Infrastructure

- Any other service that depends on the RADIUS protocol to authenticate users

This means that AAD does not provide any endpoint that *speaks* the RADIUS protocol, but it simply provides the ability to integrate with an existing RADIUS server (specifically, a Windows Server installation with the Network Policy Service role) to add MFA controls during the normal authentication flow.

- **SAML authentication**: SAML is another protocol that is fully supported in AAD. Applications that still need to enable SSO through this protocol can easily integrate with AAD by sharing their federation metadata file or by simply exchanging all the information needed to create the federation (e.g., Entity IDs, Assertion Consumer Service URLs, and certificates).

- **Windows Authentication – Kerberos Constrained Delegation (KCD)**: Windows Authentication can only be used with AAD Application Proxy, which enables SSO to on-premises KCD applications that use **integrated Windows authentication (IWA)**.

With regards to the OAuth 2.0 and OIDC protocols, these are all the supported flows:

- Authorization code grant flows (with PKCE)

- Implicit grant flows

- On-behalf-of flows

- Client credentials flows

- Resource owner password credentials flows

- Device authorization grant flows

- Hybrid flows

All these flows have been discussed in *Chapter 4*, *Authentication Flows*, except for the device authorization grant flow, which is part of an extension of the OAuth 2.0 protocol defined in a separate RFC (RFC 8628), so let's briefly describe it.

The device authorization grant flow is typically used by a client application to obtain both an access token (or an ID token for OIDC) and a refresh token when it is not possible to input information coming from the user in the device where the client runs (e.g., an IoT device or smart TV). To complete the flow, the user must navigate to a web page on a different device and authenticate with their credentials after providing, as input, a code that identifies the authentication session created by the initial device. AAD uses a dedicated endpoint to support this flow: `https://login.microsoftonline.com/{tenant_name}/oauth2/v2.0/devicecode`.

The flow is described here:

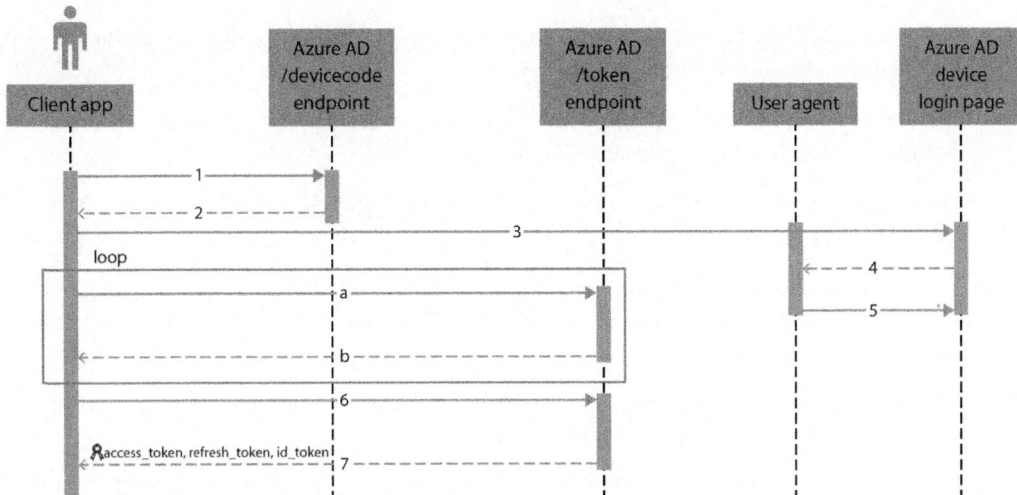

Figure 8.2 – Device authorization grant flow

Here are the steps that explain the flow in detail:

1. The client application sends a request to the AAD `/devicecode` endpoint in the background to initialize a new authentication session. This is what a request looks like:

```
POST https://login.microsoftonline.com/{tenant_name}/
oauth2/v2.0/devicecode
Content-Type: application/x-www-form-urlencoded
client_id=s6BhdRkqt3
&scope=openid%20resource_server_id
```

2. AAD responds with several parameters that are then used by the client application to continue the flow:

   - `device_code`: A string that is used by the client application and AAD to identify the current authentication session

   - `user_code`: The string code the user must input when prompted to authenticate against AAD to identify the authentication session initialized by the client application

   - `verification_uri`: The URL (`https://microsoft.com/devicelogin`) that the user must open in a browser window (in a device that is capable of using a browser) to insert `user_code` and authenticate against AAD

- `expires_in`: The expiration time (in seconds) before `device_code` and `user_code` expire

- `interval`: The number of seconds the client application should loop to wait for the user to successfully authenticate

- `message`: A human-readable message containing instructions for the user to successfully authenticate using the device authorization grant flow

The client application then starts a loop (steps *a* and *b*) where it constantly asks AAD for the outcome of the user's authentication.

3. The user opens the AAD device login page (received in the `verification_uri` parameter) in a browser (which, in this case, can be considered the user agent) where they insert `user_code` received by the client application.

4. After verifying `user_code` and consequently identifying the authentication session, AAD requires the user to authenticate with their credentials.

5. AAD validates the user's credentials and shows them a message containing the result of the authentication.

6. The client application sends another request containing `device_code` to AAD asking whether the user has been authenticated or not.

7. The client application receives confirmation from AAD that the user has been successfully authenticated and can end the authentication flow.

In the *Registering and configuring applications* section later in this chapter, we will describe the technical steps needed to configure each of these flows for an application registered in AAD.

User provisioning

In *Chapter 2, The Cloud Era and Identity*, we covered an overview of the different types of identities and described how those identities live in a cloud identity system. Let's now try to apply those concepts to AAD.

The complexity and the size of an enterprise company introduce challenges when it comes to using a cloud identity system such as AAD. Without getting into too much detail (more information on this topic can be found in *Chapter 2, The Cloud Era and Identity*), we should know that it is unlikely that there is a single identity system in the customer's premises, but a non-negligible number of different services likely provide authentication and authorization to the end users. Generally speaking, we can classify the user provisioning or synchronization process into four categories:

- Synchronization from on-premises to AAD

- Synchronization from a cloud HR system to AAD

- Synchronization from AAD to a cloud application

- Synchronization from AAD to an on-premises application/system

Let's describe them in greater detail.

Synchronization from on-premises to AAD

Luckily, most enterprises already have centralized on-premises identity solutions that are based either on AD DS or an LDAP directory. This common configuration has led the AAD engineering team to develop tools that facilitate the synchronization process of the users belonging to such systems to AAD:

- **AAD Connect Sync**

  AAD Connect Sync is the primary tool used to synchronize on-premises users stored in a single or multiple Active Directory forest environment. AAD Connect Sync is a standalone tool that needs to be installed on an on-premises Windows Server. As stated before, multiple Active Directory forests can be part of the identity source systems, each with a predefined set of synchronization rules that can be customized to filter out the users that are out of the scope of the synchronization (e.g., service accounts or built-in AD users). Users, groups, and devices are objects that AAD Connect Sync can synchronize to AAD. It's important to mention that one AAD Connect Sync installation can only synchronize those objects to a single AAD tenant, and an AAD tenant can only be associated with one AAD Connect Sync tool.

  Objects synchronized by AAD Connect Sync (flagged as *directory-synced*) cannot be modified directly in AAD (with the exception of a very limited set of attributes) and therefore any update must be made on Active Directory first, and you need to wait for AAD Connect Sync to propagate the update to AAD (by default, the synchronization interval is 30 minutes). AAD Connect also provides several other features that are sometimes mandatory to enable specific features in AAD (some of which will be discussed in the next paragraph), such as the following:

  - Device writeback

  - Directory extensions

  - Password hash sync

  - **Pass-through authentication (PTA)**

  - Group writeback

  - Password writeback

  It is possible to have multiple installations of the AAD Connect Sync tool in order to have a backup server in the unfortunate event that one server goes down and becomes unavailable, but only one AAD Connect Sync tool can be active at any one time. The active AAD Connect Sync tool is the only one performing the final step of the synchronization (i.e., the export of the users to AAD) while the secondary ones, configured in staging mode, will honor all the synchronization rules (they must be kept in sync with the primary one) without effectively exporting the users to AAD.

- **AAD Connect Cloud Sync**

    AAD Connect Cloud Sync is a lightweight version of the standard AAD Connect Sync tool based on the SCIM protocol. AAD Connect Cloud Sync currently does not support all the features that AAD Connect Sync does, but it does support all the scenarios that include disconnected on-premises Active Directory forests since multiple active installations are possible by means of a lightweight agent that can be deployed close to the resources that need to be synced. AAD Connect Cloud Sync can coexist with an existing AAD Connect Sync installation.

- **Microsoft Identity Manager**

    Microsoft Identity Manager (**MIM**) is an identity synchronization tool that provides a plethora of built-in connectors to provide all the capabilities needed to get different external identity systems in sync out of the box by defining which system takes precedence over conflicts and which identities must be merged, disconnected, or exported. In order to synchronize an LDAP directory to AAD, the only option is to use MIM and its built-in LDAP connector. This is an advanced configuration and requires a deep knowledge of the tool.

Synchronization from a cloud HR system to AAD

Cloud **Human Resources** (**HR**) systems are very common today, and the built-in synchronization engine available in AAD really helps to automate the user provisioning process. Examples of cloud HR systems are **Workday** and **SuccessFactors**.

The most common HR scenarios are as follows:

- The hiring of a new employee
- The termination of an employee
- The update of an employee's profile (attributes)
- The rehiring of an employee

The **AAD Provisioning Service** is a service that runs in the cloud and reacts whenever one of the preceding events is triggered by the cloud HR system. Depending on how the enterprise is organized in terms of on-premises identity systems, the AAD Provisioning Service can be configured to either synchronize the users directly to AAD (in a cloud-only scenario where no on-premises identity system is present or relevant) or synchronize the users to an on-premises Active Directory environment. In the latter case, users will, in turn, be synchronized through AAD Connect to AAD. The latter scenario is more common for an enterprise since it is rare to find a cloud-only environment when you are not in a newly established company that does not have to manage legacy identity systems that are rooted within the internal processes of an older company. The workflow described is shown in the following diagram:

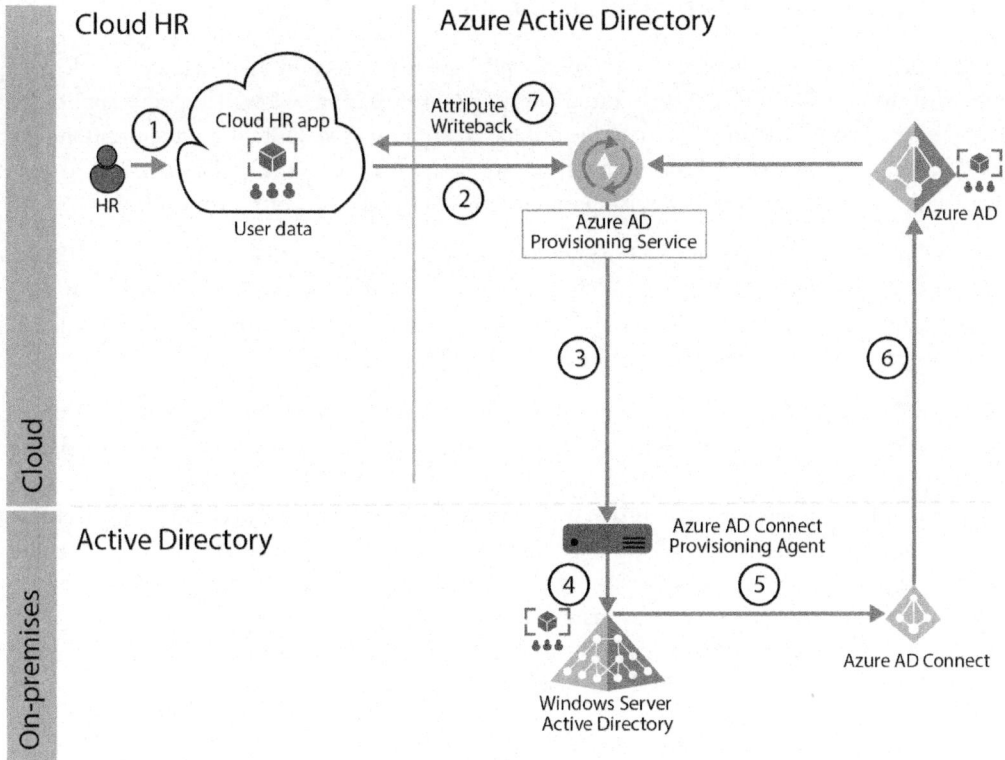

Figure 8.3 – Cloud HR app to on-premises synchronization flow

It is important when configuring the AAD Provisioning Service to plan its configuration based on the particular Active Directory topology and requirements a company might have. These are the things that must be planned or known upfront:

- Have a clear understanding of which attributes should be mapped from the cloud HR system to AAD or an on-premises Active Directory

- Understand the implications of the attribute writeback feature that enables the synchronization of a user's attributes from AAD to the cloud HR system

- Assess the on-premises Active Directory infrastructure in order to find the number of forests or domains and the presence of disconnected forests (forests that do not have direct network connectivity to other parts of the network)

Synchronization from AAD to a cloud application

Having a user in AAD is not sufficient to allow an application federated with AAD to undertake decisions about what the user can and can't do in the application (authorization). Nowadays, most applications have an internal data structure that maps the unique identifier received into the authentication token issued by AAD after a successful user authentication to a specific role in the application, which, on the other hand, enables the user to perform specific actions in the application's business logic.

Some applications available in the AAD gallery (the internal AAD store that provides out-of-the-box integration and configuration of applications published by third-party vendors) already support the automatic provisioning of users to AAD. Within their internal users' data structure, they implement an authorization model that is managed automatically by both the application and AAD.

This out-of-the-box synchronization is done through the SCIM protocol (already discussed in *Chapter 2, The Cloud Era and Identity*), which is preconfigured through a built-in connector with predefined attribute mapping rules when the application is integrated with AAD through the AAD gallery. This particular integration removes the burden of manual user provisioning into cloud applications and facilitates the AAD administrator job by automating the life cycle management process of the identities so that any update of the status of an existing user is synchronized into the application without any human intervention on either side. For instance, when a user is terminated, this mechanism allows us to disable the user's access to the external application by automatically informing the application that the user does not have the right to interact with the application.

Synchronization from AAD to an on-premises application or system

It's not uncommon that, once a user is created in AAD, it needs to be synchronized to an on-premises identity system or application. As a matter of fact, when it is not possible to consolidate all existing identity systems into one but, because of retro-compatibility with legacy applications, these systems must be kept alive, it is very common to have duplicated users. Duplicated users cause great administrative effort because they must be kept in sync and they need to be deleted, disabled, or modified on all identity systems to guarantee the consistency of the information across each application.

With this in mind, it's easy to understand why a tool that can keep all the users and identities aligned regardless of where they are stored is so important. AAD provides this capability using a couple of tools:

- **AAD Provisioning Agent**

  This agent can be installed on a Windows Server machine and must be registered to an AAD tenant. The agent supports the SCIM protocol and can be used to synchronize AAD users to an application or an identity system that supports the SCIM protocol and, therefore, provides a SCIM-compliant endpoint.

- **ECMA Connector Host**

  The ECMA Connector Host tool is used in conjunction with the AAD Provisioning Agent when the target application or identity system does not support the SCIM protocol. It translates the synchronization commands coming from the AAD Provisioning Agent into commands that are understood by the target application. ECMA Connector Host natively supports SQL-based applications and the LDAP protocol by providing two native connectors that can be configured to map users' attributes coming from the Provisioning Agent to the target user's attribute format. The following list of SQL-based applications is supported:

- Microsoft SQL Server and Azure SQL

- IBM DB2 10.x

- IBM DB2 9.x

- Oracle 10 and 11g

- Oracle 12c and 18c

- MySQL 5.x

The following LDAP directories are supported:

- OpenLDAP

- Microsoft Active Directory Lightweight Directory Services

- 389 Directory Server

- Apache Directory Server

- IBM Tivoli DS

- Isode Directory

- NetIQ eDirectory

- Novell eDirectory

- Open DJ

- Open DS

- Oracle (previously Sun ONE) Directory Server Enterprise Edition

- RadiantOne Virtual Directory Server (VDS)

At the time of writing, the ECMA Connector Host is still in **Public Preview**.

It's worth mentioning that it is also possible to develop a custom application that exposes a SCIM endpoint and implements the logic to synchronize the users to a remote application in the background by translating the SCIM calls it receives to synchronization operations in the remote application. This way, it is possible to use just the AAD Provisioning Agent and avoid using the ECMA Connector Host tool.

It's common for an organization to need to store specific information related to a user that requires the creation of a new user attribute. This often happens when all the existing attributes are already in use or there is no suitable attribute that can store that piece of information.

AAD allows us to extend the default set of attributes with **custom attributes** defined by an administrator. The operation can be delegated to the AAD Connect Sync tool, which will create an attribute with the name the administrator chooses. This is a convenient way of storing additional information related to an organization's identity that is needed by an application to implement its business logic (e.g., only show specific parts of the application to users that have a particular value within an extension attribute). These extension attributes are usually passed to the application as claims within a security token.

One thing that is worth mentioning is the fact that the use of extension attributes should not be abused because application-specific information about the user should, in general, be stored within the application itself (such as in an internal database) and not within the identity provider. An identity provider should only store information that is not specific to a single application but that can be utilized among different applications; that, ideally, is related to the identity of a user (e.g., a user's role); and that does not contain too much specific information for an application (e.g., the list of paid services a user has subscribed to).

Now that we understand how users are provisioned in AAD, we can discuss the different authentication types that are available and how to decide which one to use in different scenarios.

Authentication types

We now should know what the different user types are in AAD. Different authentication types can be used with specific user types according to the following table:

	MFA	Federated	Pass Through	Seamless SSO	Password Hash Sync	Passwordless	TAP
Cloud user	Yes	N/A	N/A	N/A	N/A	Yes	Yes
Hybrid user	Yes	Yes	Yes	Yes	Yes	Yes	Yes

Table 8.1 – AAD users' authentication types

Guest users do not feature in the table because they (and their credentials) do not live in the inviting AAD tenant and, therefore, their authentication type depends on how authentication has been configured in the external identity system (which could be another AAD tenant). The only authentication an administrator in the inviting tenant can configure is either to enforce MFA for a guest user or trust a guest user's MFA that has been done in the home tenant.

We will now describe each authentication method in the table.

MFA

First of all, let's start by saying that MFA is not a primary authentication method, but it is always used in conjunction with another authentication type that is used as the primary method.

When using MFA, the second factor of authentication is added to the primary one. To successfully implement an MFA authentication configuration, the two factors of authentication (the primary and the secondary) usually belong to two out of the three different types of credentials a user can use: something a user knows (typically a password, a PIN, or a code), something a user is (a biometric factor such as a fingerprint or the user's face), and something a user has or owns (such as a smartcard or an OATH token).

The user is challenged with the request to use the second authentication factor after they successfully authenticate in AAD through one of the authentication types listed in the preceding table. This allows an administrator to independently configure each of the authentication factors.

In AAD, given that the primary authentication is the user's password, the MFA's second factor of authentication can be one of the following:

- **Microsoft Authenticator app**

  The Microsoft Authenticator app as a second factor enables the use of push notifications to the user's smartphone. The user can either accept or deny access through the app if they think that the authentication attempt is fraudulent. The app also allows us to generate OATH verification codes (such as **time-based one-time passwords (TOTPs)**).

- **OATH software and hardware tokens**

  OATH (not OAuth!) is an open standard that specifies how TOTP codes should be generated. The codes can be generated either in software (such as the Microsoft Authenticator app) or directly into specialized hardware provided by a third-party vendor.

- **Phone verification**

  Phone verification can be done either with text message verification, where an SMS with a code is sent to the user's phone number (registered when an administrator has enabled MFA for the user), or with a phone call to the same phone number where the user has to press # on the keypad to accept the second-factor request. Phone verification is the least secure second-factor authentication method, and therefore, it is not recommended to use it unless it's the only option available.

MFA in AAD can be configured either per user or through a Conditional Access policy. In this case, the usage of Conditional Access policy is the recommended method.

Passwordless authentication is a particular type of MFA where neither of the two factors of authentication includes the user's password. We will describe it in one of the next subsections.

Federated authentication

Federated authentication can be used with hybrid identities that have been synchronized to AAD through the AAD Connect (Cloud) Sync tool. Companies that have already invested in on-premises identity provider solutions such as **Active Directory Federation Services (AD FS)**, **NetIQ Access Manager (NAM)**, or PingFederate (to name a few) can create a federation between AAD and the on-premises identity provider to delegate hybrid user authentication to the on-premises system. The federation is done through the SAML or the WS-Federation protocol and can be configured for each AAD-registered domain individually (federated authentication is not a tenant-wide configuration). With this setup, AAD acts as a relying party (in some flows online, you can find the relying party represented as the service provider). In a federated authentication scenario, the flow is as follows:

1. An AAD federated application redirects the user to the AAD authentication page.

2. The user inserts their `userprincipalname`, and AAD, according to the specific UPN suffix, decides whether the user must be redirected to the federated identity provider or can be authenticated locally.

3. The user is redirected to the federated identity provider login page where they enter their credentials.

4. Upon successful validation of the user's credentials, the third-party identity provider redirects the user to AAD with the authentication protocol-specific security token it issued.

5. AAD reads and validates the issued token, and then it generates and issues a new token enriched with the information needed by the application that initiated the authentication flow.

6. The user is finally redirected to the application, which, based on the information in the token, will authorize or deny access to the application.

The use of federated authentication is not the recommended way of authenticating hybrid identities since it adds complexity and increases the management overhead because of the presence of multiple on-premises servers that need to be maintained. Only organizations that have already invested in an on-premises identity provider should use this solution. Others should go with PTA or **password hash synchronization (PHS)** and Seamless SSO instead, which reduces complexity and increases security (as explained in the next subsections).

PTA

PTA is a lightweight solution for hybrid identity authentication that involves the installation of agents (three is the minimum recommended number) onto on-premises Windows Server machines. Hybrid users must have been synchronized by an on-premises Active Directory forest since PTA only supports validating a user's credentials against a Domain Controller. PTA can be configured through the AAD Connect Sync tool, which installs the very first PTA agent on the AAD Connect Sync tool machine. PTA agent-based installation is more secure than federated authentication because it does not introduce any inbound endpoints, but all the communication from the agents to AAD and vice versa happens within an outbound connection. The authentication flow is as follows:

1. An AAD federated application redirects the user to the AAD authentication page.

2. The user inserts their credentials (UPN and password) into the AAD authentication page. AAD pushes the credentials into a queue (based on a technology similar to Azure Service Bus).

3. One of the on-premises PTA agents reads the credentials from the queue (each of the on-premises PTA agents has the same likelihood of reading the credentials first – therefore, there is no guarantee that one PTA agent is picked over another).

4. Once the credentials are read, the PTA agent tries to validate them against an on-premises Active Directory Domain Controller.

5. Upon successful validation of a user's credentials, the PTA agent reports the outcome of the authentication to AAD, which, in turn, replies to the application with either a security token or an error message.

PTA authentication is triggered for users that do not have direct visibility from their machine to an Active Directory Domain Controller. This usually happens when the user is not connected to the corporate network and tries to access an application from the internet. When the user is connected to the corporate network, Seamless SSO authentication, if configured, is triggered instead.

PHS

As an alternative solution to authenticate on-premises Active Directory users (synchronized again by the AAD Connect tool), it is possible to use PHS. AAD Connect Sync can optionally synchronize Active Directory password hashes to AAD to allow a user's authentication to happen locally in AAD without installing any additional components (no agents and no federation servers). PHS can be used in combination with Seamless SSO and can also be configured as a backup authentication solution in all situations where the primary authentication method is not available (either the PTA agents are not responding, or the federations servers are not available). The synchronization of the password hashes is a secure process that the AAD Connect Sync tool implements by encrypting the hashes multiple times before they are synchronized to AAD.

Seamless SSO and Primary Refresh Token (PRT)

Users connected to their corporate network are used to not inserting their credentials when accessing applications that are federated with a third-party identity provider using a modern authentication protocol. This is because when the users are stored in Active Directory, the identity provider leverages IWA – and because the user is already authenticated on their corporate domain-joined machines to provide SSO (through the Kerberos protocol).

When using PTA or PHS authentication in AAD, there is no intermediate identity provider that can provide SSO to the end users. That's when the Seamless SSO feature becomes important. Seamless SSO allows users who have direct visibility of a Domain Controller (connected to their corporate network) to SSO into applications federated with AAD.

This is made possible because when configuring Seamless SSO (again, by means of the AAD Connect Sync tool), AAD challenges the user accessing the application in the corporate network to provide a Kerberos ticket through a 401 Unauthorized response. The user's domain-joined machine does the rest in the background by exchanging the Kerberos tickets it has already acquired during the user's login for a Kerberos ticket that can be used with AAD (during Seamless SSO setup, the AAD Connect Sync tool creates a computer account, AZUREADSSOACC, which represents the AAD tenant where the users have been synchronized. This account's service principal name is used to generate the Kerberos ticket).

Enabling Seamless SSO is only recommended when there are still legacy operating systems in an enterprise network such as Windows 7 and 8 devices. For Windows 10 and 11, SSO is guaranteed by the means of the PRT, which is a token retrieved by a Windows 10/11 device from AAD during a user's initial logon and is regularly renewed in the background without prompting any input from the user. The PRT is a **JSON Web Token (JWT)** that is issued to a device that is either AAD-joined, hybrid AAD-joined, or AAD-registered. It is out of the scope of this book to describe these different device states, but, for the sake of comprehension, you could imagine those different states as three different ways of registering a device identity in AAD. An enterprise, as a matter of fact, can independently choose which registration method best fits each of its devices according to the following (simplified) flowchart:

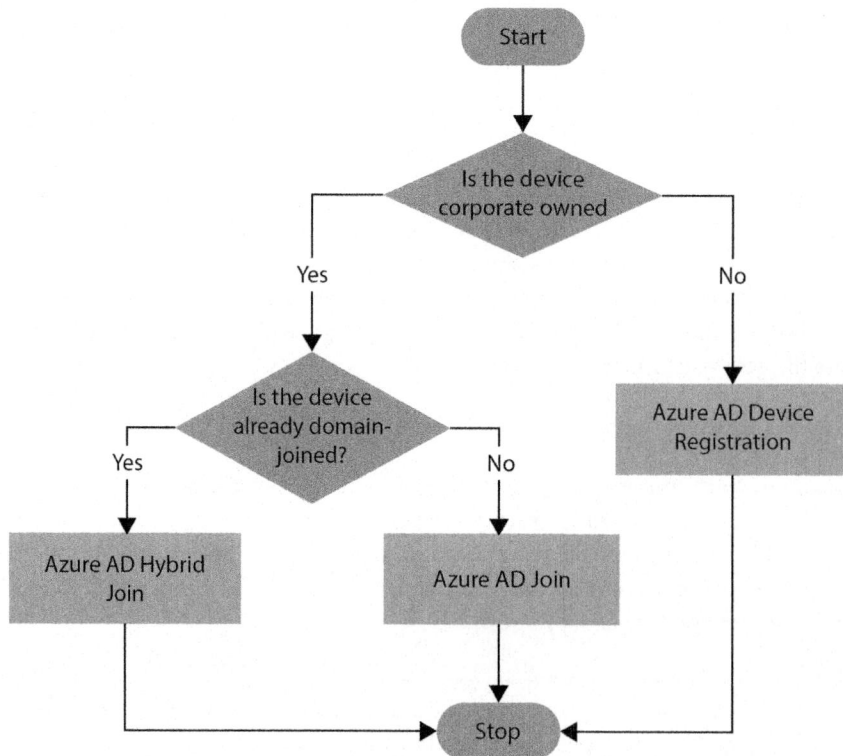

Figure 8.4 – AAD device onboarding decision flowchart

Passwordless authentication

Passwordless authentication is a form of MFA that can be configured in AAD to discourage and ideally remove the usage of passwords. Passwordless authentication can leverage the following technologies:

- Windows Hello for Business
- Microsoft Authenticator app
- FIDO2 security keys

Each of these technologies embeds two authentication factors to effectively implement MFA. Windows Hello for Business is a Windows technology that stores security encryption keys within a domain-joined device **Trusted Platform Module (TPM)** – something the user owns – which can either be unlocked using a biometric factor (something the user is) or using a PIN (something the user knows). The Microsoft Authenticator app is installed on a smartphone the user owns, which can be unlocked using a biometric factor (something the user is) or a PIN (something the user knows). The app uses number matching (a technique used to mitigate MFA fatigue attacks by making users more aware of their MFA prompts), which basically shows a number that must be inserted into the AAD login page when the user is prompted. FIDO2 security keys are pieces of hardware that store secure cryptographic keys (something the user owns) that are unlocked either through a biometric factor (something the user is) or a PIN (something the user knows). FIDO2 security keys must be registered upfront by the end user.

Passwordless authentication replaces password-based authentication types (PTA, federated, and PHS) by implementing a solution that is both secure and convenient.

As already explained in the *AAD basics* section, the AAD username is stored in the `userprincipalname` attribute. There may be scenarios where the user needs to authenticate with a username that is different from the synchronized `userprincipalname`, on-premises with the AAD Connect (Cloud) Sync tool. The on-premises Active Directory attribute that is mapped to the AAD UPN might not be a suitable attribute for all the on-premises Active Directory forests, especially in merger or acquisition scenarios where two or more companies probably have a completely different setup in their on-premises identity systems.

In these scenarios, one or more domains are likely registered in AAD and used both as UPN suffixes and mailbox domains. In the latter scenario, AAD provides the capability to use the `ProxyAddresses` attribute, an attribute containing all the user's email addresses, as the source of user's UPNs so that they can leverage any of their email addresses to log in to an application federated with AAD. This feature, named alternate login ID, is still in Public Preview (at the time of writing) and it has some limitations that do not make it suitable for every scenario, but it's a very convenient way to enable user authentication with an attribute, the email address, that almost every user already knows.

Before diving into the next section, here are some tips that might help you decide which is the best authentication type to choose for an organization:

- Use passwordless authentication whenever possible. It's the most secure and convenient authentication type that AAD provides.

- When passwordless authentication is not an option, avoid using password-based sign-in only and integrate an MFA solution to strengthen the authentication process instead.

- Use PTA whenever possible. It's a simple and lightweight solution that does not need the installation of any additional servers since the agents can be installed on existing servers.

- Use PHS as a backup authentication method or as the primary method when PTA cannot be used (for example, a disconnected forests scenario).

- Integrate PTA or PHS with Seamless SSO to create a smooth user experience.

- Use federated authentication only when your organization has already spent money on an existing identity provider solution.

We now understand the different authentication types that AAD provides to users. Let's see how AAD allows us to manage and configure applications in the next section.

Registering and configuring applications

In the *AAD basics* section, we analyzed the twofold nature of an application in AAD. We know that an application has a definition that lives in the home tenant (the tenant where it has been effectively created) and a service principal, which is an instance of an application definition that can live both in the home tenant and within an external AAD tenant, where it will be created as a dedicated new instance. The service principal inherits the application definition permissions and applies them to the resources that live in the same tenant where it has been instantiated.

AAD provides several ways to manage its services:

- AAD admin center (`https://aad.portal.azure.com`)

- Microsoft Entra admin center (`https://entra.microsoft.com`)

- AAD PowerShell

- The Azure CLI

- Microsoft Graph API

The examples that will be described in this paragraph use the Microsoft Entra admin center, which has been released recently and still has the same look and feel as the AAD admin center. This means that any example that you see here can be easily mapped between the portals.

To manage this twofold nature of an application, the AAD portal provides two different sections:

- **App registrations**: Lists the definitions of applications
- **Enterprise applications**: Lists the application instances

You can see in the following screenshot how **App registrations** and **Enterprise applications** are part of two different sections in the **Microsoft Entra admin center** portal:

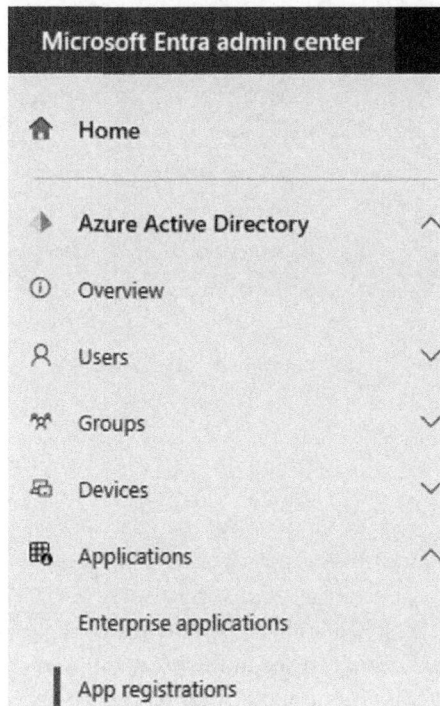

Figure 8.5 – Entra admin center

Let's now delve into the details of these two types of applications in the following subsections.

App registrations

When registering a new application in AAD through the **App registrations** menu, the only mandatory pieces of information are a display name for the application and the type of the application: single-tenant or multi-tenant. A multi-tenant application can grant access to users belonging to external AAD tenants, while a single-tenant application can grant only access to users belonging to the home tenant.

Once registered, this is what my single-tenant ClientApp01 looks like in the portal:

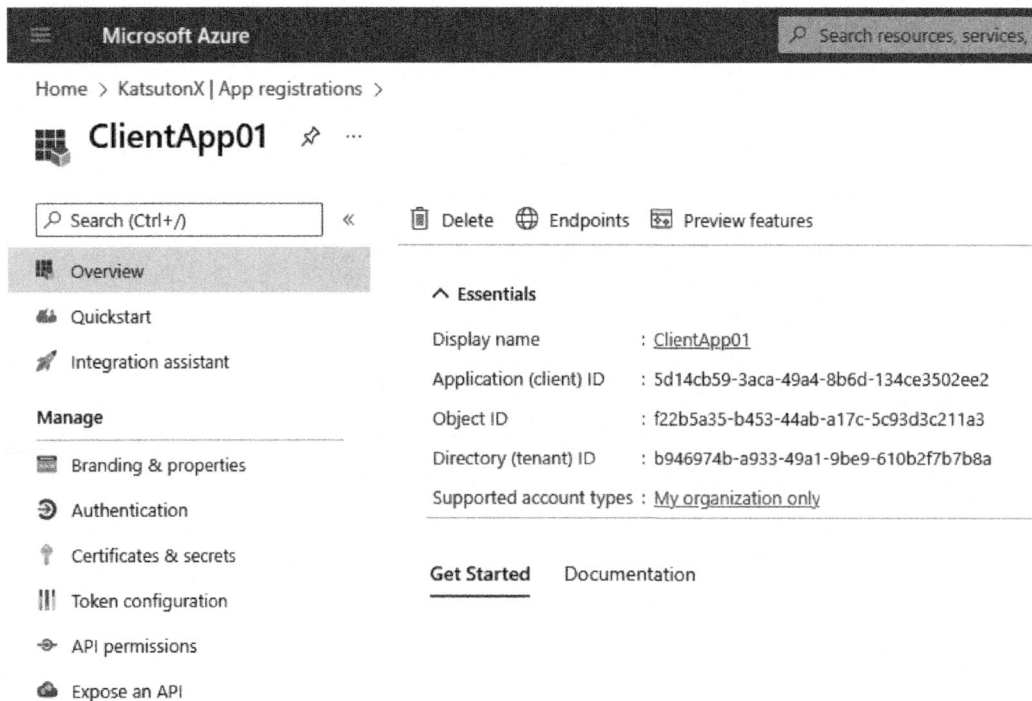

Figure 8.6 – An application definition overview

Within an application definition, it is possible to specify the configuration of the OAuth 2.0/OIDC protocols for the application. As you can see in the preceding screenshot, once an application is registered, AAD auto-generates a unique application ID (which also represents the client_id information used in OAuth 2.0/OIDC). We are not going to detail all the capabilities that the **App registrations** menu provides for an application; we will just focus on the parts related to the two authentication protocols to see how the concepts we've learned about throughout the book have been implemented in a commercial identity provider.

Authentication

In the **Authentication** menu, the following can be defined:

- **Redirect URIs**: This is the list of the redirect URIs that are used by the authorization code grant flow, the implicit grant flow, and hybrid flows. They are the application URIs to which AAD should send the JWT once it has been issued. For simplicity, they can be organized per platform (web, single-page application, iOS or macOS, Android, and Windows).

- **Front-channel logout URL:** This is the URL that AAD uses to trigger a logout inside the application when the logout request has been initiated by another application defined in AAD (also known as a single logout flow).

- **Implicit grant and hybrid flows:** By default, the implicit grant flow and the hybrid flow are disabled because they are deemed insecure. Some applications cannot use other flows, though, and AAD provides the capability to enable them and decide which types of tokens these flows can issue (access tokens and/or ID tokens).

- **Supported account types:** This setting defines which account types can log on to the application (either a single-tenant or multi-tenant application).

- **Allow public client flows:** This is another important setting that is disabled by default. When enabled, it allows us to use the resource owner password credential flow and the device code flow.

This is a screenshot of the **Authentication** menu taken for the `ClientApp01` definition:

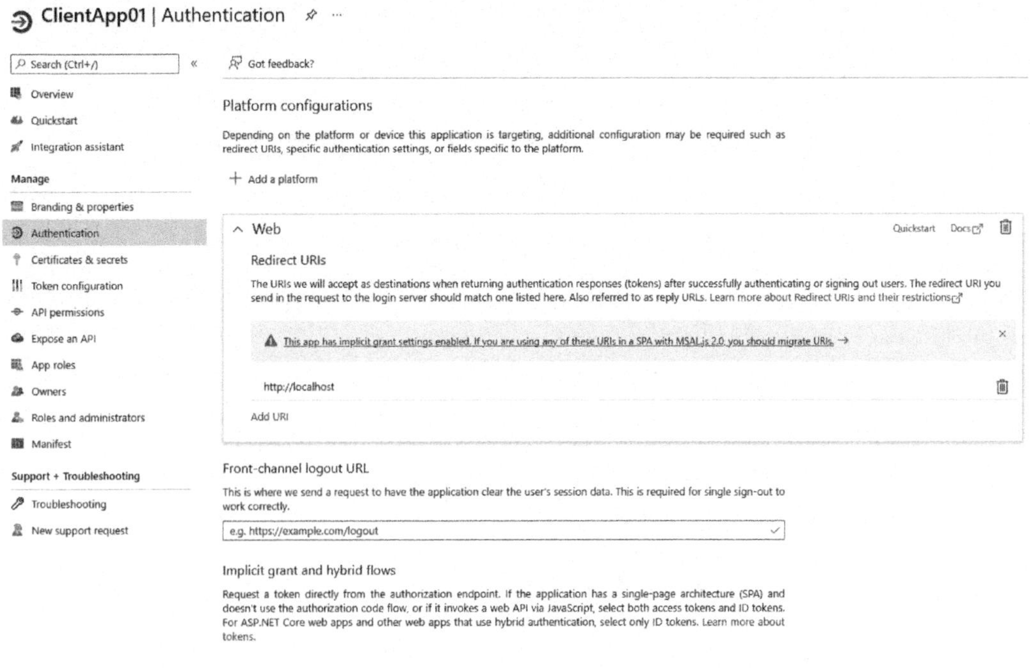

Figure 8.7 – Authentication menu for the ClientApp01 definition

Certificates and secrets

In this section, we will explain how it is possible to generate secrets (shared secure strings), upload certificates, and use federated credentials.

Secrets and certificates can be used in the `client_secret` parameter used in the authorization code grant flow and the client credentials flow, whereas federated credentials are built-in AAD features that allow us to trust tokens issued and signed by an external OIDC identity provider.

Here's a screenshot of the menu taken for the `ClientApp01` application definition where a secret has been generated:

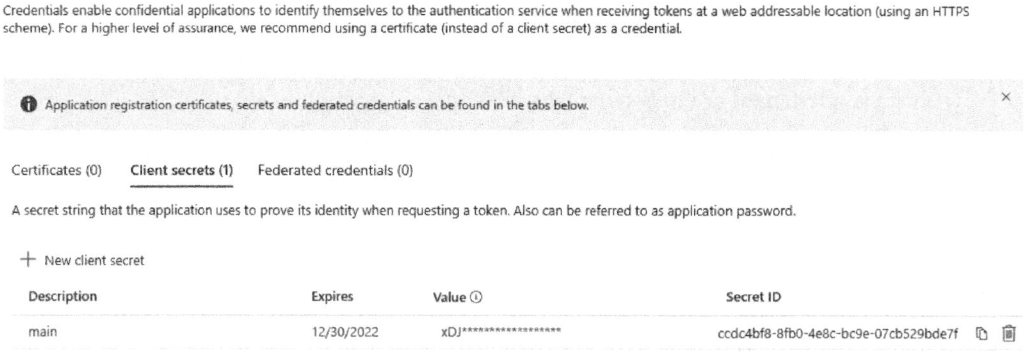

Credentials enable confidential applications to identify themselves to the authentication service when receiving tokens at a web addressable location (using an HTTPS scheme). For a higher level of assurance, we recommend using a certificate (instead of a client secret) as a credential.

ⓘ Application registration certificates, secrets and federated credentials can be found in the tabs below.   ✕

Certificates (0)   **Client secrets (1)**   Federated credentials (0)

A secret string that the application uses to prove its identity when requesting a token. Also can be referred to as application password.

╋ New client secret

Description	Expires	Value ⓘ	Secret ID		
main	12/30/2022	xDJ*****************	ccdc4bf8-8fb0-4e8c-bc9e-07cb529bde7f	🗋	🗑

Figure 8.8 – Certificates and secrets menu for the ClientApp01 application

Token configuration

In the **Token configuration** menu, it is possible to define additional claims to be returned within the access tokens and ID tokens issued by AAD upon a user's successful authentication. Here's a screenshot for the `ClientApp01` application:

Optional claims

Optional claims are used to configure additional information which is returned in one or more tokens. Learn more ⧉

╋ Add optional claim   ╋ Add groups claim

Claim ↑↓	Description	Token type ↑↓
email	The addressable email for this user, if the user has one	ID
email	The addressable email for this user, if the user has one	Access
family_name	Provides the last name, surname, or family name of the user as defined in the user object	ID
given_name	Provides the first or "given" name of the user, as set on the user object	ID

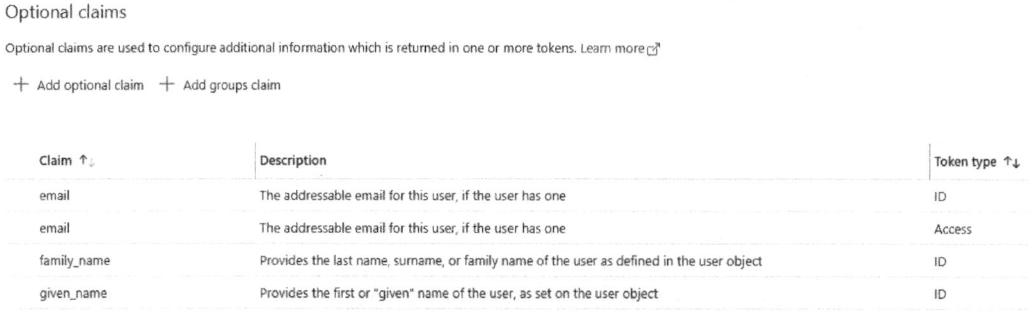

Figure 8.9 – Token configuration for the ClientApp01 application

API permissions

In the **API permissions** menu, it is possible to authorize the application to ask for specific scopes during an authentication request. The values defined here can be used as strings within the scope parameter used in all the OAuth 2.0/OIDC flows. To allow an application to request a scope, the scope must be defined within the application definition of the other application that accepts them. In the following example, there is a list of scopes that `ClientApp01` can request for two distinct applications: one set of scopes that can be requested to perform specific actions against the built-in Microsoft Graph API and another set of scopes for the custom `ServerApp01` application. The definition of the scopes in the `ServerApp01` application is done within the **Expose an API** menu (see the next section).

Keep in mind that the business logic that implements the authorization controls and the semantics behind each scope must be done within the application logic. AAD (and the OAuth 2.0/OIDC protocols) only defines an authorization model that describes the relationships between applications, enforcing which scopes can be requested by an application and adding them to the issued token to delegate their effective implementation to the application receiving them.

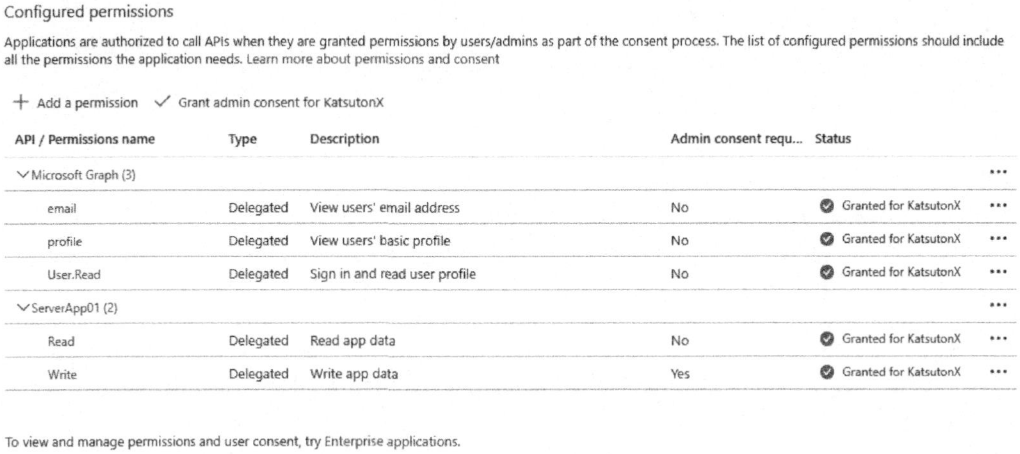

Configured permissions

Applications are authorized to call APIs when they are granted permissions by users/admins as part of the consent process. The list of configured permissions should include all the permissions the application needs. Learn more about permissions and consent

$+$ Add a permission $\checkmark$ Grant admin consent for KatsutonX

API / Permissions name	Type	Description	Admin consent requ...	Status	
$\vee$ Microsoft Graph (3)					•••
email	Delegated	View users' email address	No	✓ Granted for KatsutonX	•••
profile	Delegated	View users' basic profile	No	✓ Granted for KatsutonX	•••
User.Read	Delegated	Sign in and read user profile	No	✓ Granted for KatsutonX	•••
$\vee$ ServerApp01 (2)					•••
Read	Delegated	Read app data	No	✓ Granted for KatsutonX	•••
Write	Delegated	Write app data	Yes	✓ Granted for KatsutonX	•••

To view and manage permissions and user consent, try Enterprise applications.

Figure 8.10 – API permissions menu for the ClientApp01 definition

Exposing an API

Within the **Expose an API** permissions, it is possible to define a list of scopes that can be requested for an application. The implementation of the authorization controls behind the scope definitions in AAD (which are just strings) must be done within the application logic upon receiving the scopes as claims within the AAD-issued JWT. When a client application asks for a scope, the authenticating user must consent and allow the application to do what's explained in the scope description. Some scopes (application permissions) can be consented to by any user, while others require an administrator to intervene and consent for the user or the entire organization (all the users in the AAD tenant) to prevent AAD from asking for consent from the end users when they try to log in to the application.

Here's a screenshot for the `ServerApp01` application:

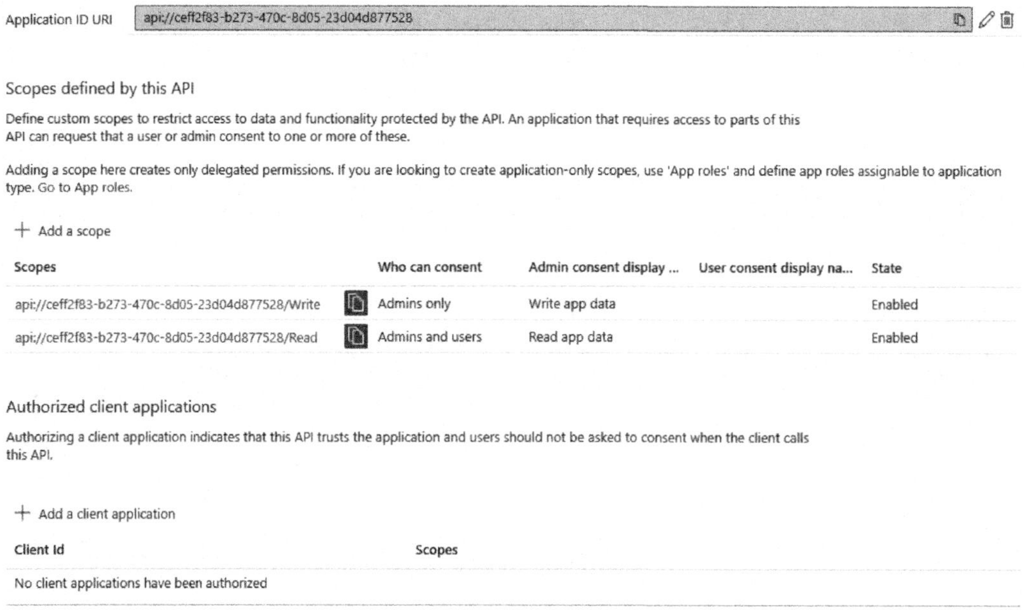

Application ID URI	api://ceff2f83-b273-470c-8d05-23d04d877528

Scopes defined by this API

Define custom scopes to restrict access to data and functionality protected by the API. An application that requires access to parts of this API can request that a user or admin consent to one or more of these.

Adding a scope here creates only delegated permissions. If you are looking to create application-only scopes, use 'App roles' and define app roles assignable to application type. Go to App roles.

+ Add a scope

Scopes		Who can consent	Admin consent display ...	User consent display na...	State
api://ceff2f83-b273-470c-8d05-23d04d877528/Write		Admins only	Write app data		Enabled
api://ceff2f83-b273-470c-8d05-23d04d877528/Read		Admins and users	Read app data		Enabled

Authorized client applications

Authorizing a client application indicates that this API trusts the application and users should not be asked to consent when the client calls this API.

+ Add a client application

Client Id	Scopes
No client applications have been authorized	

Figure 8.11 – The Expose an API menu for the ServerApp01 definition

AAD provides a set of endpoints that can be used to interact with it by means of one of the AAD-supported authentication protocols. Not surprisingly, the endpoints include the pointers to the federation metadata files that are used to establish the federation between AAD and an application and all the familiar endpoints defined by the OAuth 2.0/OIDC protocols specifications that we have analyzed throughout this book. As an example, here's the list of endpoints for the KatsutonX AAD tenant:

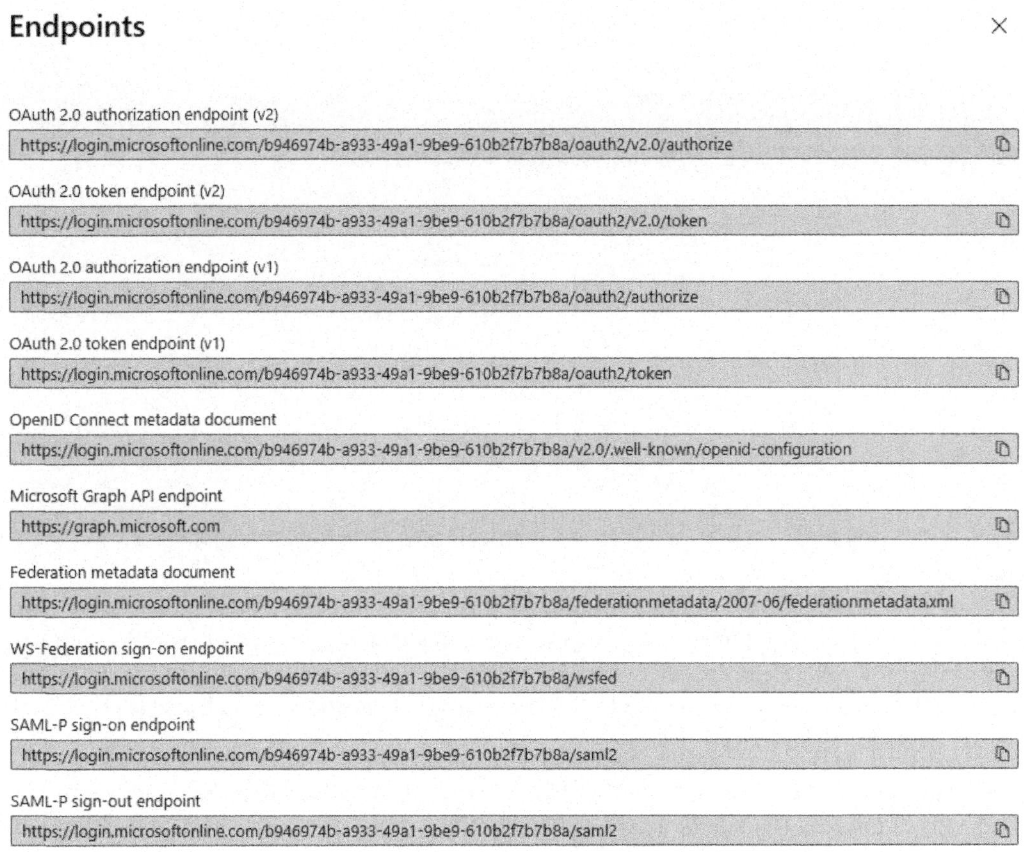

Endpoints   ✕

OAuth 2.0 authorization endpoint (v2)

https://login.microsoftonline.com/b946974b-a933-49a1-9be9-610b2f7b7b8a/oauth2/v2.0/authorize

OAuth 2.0 token endpoint (v2)

https://login.microsoftonline.com/b946974b-a933-49a1-9be9-610b2f7b7b8a/oauth2/v2.0/token

OAuth 2.0 authorization endpoint (v1)

https://login.microsoftonline.com/b946974b-a933-49a1-9be9-610b2f7b7b8a/oauth2/authorize

OAuth 2.0 token endpoint (v1)

https://login.microsoftonline.com/b946974b-a933-49a1-9be9-610b2f7b7b8a/oauth2/token

OpenID Connect metadata document

https://login.microsoftonline.com/b946974b-a933-49a1-9be9-610b2f7b7b8a/v2.0/.well-known/openid-configuration

Microsoft Graph API endpoint

https://graph.microsoft.com

Federation metadata document

https://login.microsoftonline.com/b946974b-a933-49a1-9be9-610b2f7b7b8a/federationmetadata/2007-06/federationmetadata.xml

WS-Federation sign-on endpoint

https://login.microsoftonline.com/b946974b-a933-49a1-9be9-610b2f7b7b8a/wsfed

SAML-P sign-on endpoint

https://login.microsoftonline.com/b946974b-a933-49a1-9be9-610b2f7b7b8a/saml2

SAML-P sign-out endpoint

https://login.microsoftonline.com/b946974b-a933-49a1-9be9-610b2f7b7b8a/saml2

Figure 8.12 – AAD protocol endpoints

Enterprise applications

When an application is registered (defined) in the **App registrations** menu, a service principal is created in the home AAD tenant and it will become visible in the **Enterprise applications** menu. Remember that a service principal is an instance of the application definition, which inherits the permissions that are defined in the application definition. As you can see in the following screenshot, the ClientApp01 service principal has been granted the permissions (scopes) that have been defined and consented for the application by a user or an administrator:

Permissions

Applications can be granted permissions to your organization and its data by three methods: an admin consents to the application for all users, a user grants consent to the application, or an admin integrating an to the application. Learn more.

To request additional permissions for this application, use the application registration.

As an administrator you can grant consent on behalf of all users in this tenant, ensuring that end users will not be required to consent when using the application. Click the button below to grant admin consent.

Grant admin consent for KatsutonX

Admin consent   User consent

🔍 Search permissions

API Name	↑↓	Claim value	↑↓	Permission	↑↓	Type
Microsoft Graph						
Microsoft Graph		email		View users' email address		Delegated
Microsoft Graph		profile		View users' basic profile		Delegated
Microsoft Graph		User.Read		Sign in and read user profile		Delegated
ServerApp01						
ServerApp01		Write		Write app data		Delegated
ServerApp01		Read		Read app data		Delegated

Figure 8.13 – ClientApp01 service principal's granted permissions (scopes)

If the application definition related to a service principal provides a SCIM endpoint for user synchronization, then it is possible to configure an automatic user provisioning workflow (entirely managed by the AAD Provisioning Service) through the **Provisioning** menu. This will basically create, update, and delete users within the SCIM-enabled application and delegate user life cycle management entirely to AAD.

In the **Single sign-on** menu, on the other hand, it is possible to configure the SAML protocol configuration if the application does not support the OAuth 2.0/OIDC protocols. This option is only available if the service principal is created first, directly in the **Enterprise applications** menu (this is a little bit counterintuitive, but it's how AAD works).

Example of an AAD-issued token

By taking as a reference the OAuth 2.0 configuration of the `ClientApp01` and `ServerApp01` applications described in the previous paragraph when discussing what a registered application was, here is an example of an AAD-issued access token obtained through the client credentials flow:

- **Request**:

```
GET https://login.microsoftonline.com/b946974b-a933-49a1-
9be9-610b2f7b7b8a/oauth2/v2.0/token HTTP/1.1
Host: login.microsoftonline.com
Content-Type: application/x-www-form-urlencoded
```

```
grant_type=client_credentials&client_id=5d14cb59-3aca-49a4-
8b6d-134ce3502ee2&client_secret=xDJ8Q~6QrdkVphZjTWkb9krIp5
eQXGh8qEO8rdyg&scope=api%3A%2F%2Fceff2f83-b273-470c-8d05-
23d04d877528%2F.default
```

- **Response body**:

```
{"token_type":"Bearer","expires_in":3599,"ext_expires_in":
3599,"access_token":"eyJ0eXAiOiJKV1QiLCJhbGciOiJSUzI1Ni
IsIng1dCI6IjJaUXBKM1VwYmpBWVhZR2FYRUpsOGxWMFRPSSIsImtpZCI6
IjJaUXBKM1VwYmpBWVhZR2FYRUpsOGxWMFRPSSJ9.eyJhdWQiOiJhcGk6Ly
9jZWZmMmY4My1iMjczLTQ3MGMtOGQwNS0yM2QwNGQ4Nzc1MjgiLCJpc3Mi
OiJodHRwczovL3N0cy53aW5kb3dzLm5ldC9iOTQ2Otc0Yi1hOTMzLTQ5YT
EtOWJlOS02MTBiMmY3YjdiOGEvIiwiaWF0IjoxNjU2NjA1NjUwLCJuYmYi
OjE2NTY2MDU2NTAsImV4cCI6MTY1NjYwOTU1MCwiYWlvIjoiRTJaZ1EQT1
JbnJqQnU4RUR3c1ZuLzhHNXJNTUFBPT0iLCJhcHBpZCI6IjVkMTRjYjU5L
TNhY2EtNDlhNC04YjZkLTEzNGNlMzUwMmVlMiIsImFwcGlkYWNyIjoiMSIs
ImlkcCI6Imh0dHBzOi8vc3RzLndpbmRvd3MubmV0L2I5NDY5NzRiLWE5MzM
tNDlhMS05YmU5LTYxMGIyZjdiN2I4YS8iLCJvaWQiOiI2NzI2M2NjYi1hOT
A5LTRkNWMtYjM2MC05ZmMyY2JkOGMzZTEiLCJyaCI6IjAuQVRzQVM1Zed1V
E9wb1VtYjZXRUxMM3Q3aW9Ndl84NXpzZ3hIalFVajBFMkhkU2c3QUFBLiIs
InN1YiI6IjY3MjYzY2NiLWE5MDktNGQ1Yy1iMzYwLTlmYzJjYmQ4YzNlMSI
sInRpZCI6ImI5NDY5NzRiLWE5MzMtNDlhMS05YmU5LTYxMGIyZjdiN2I4YS
IsInV0aSI6Ik5yTy16RHY4Q1Vxd1pRMVBMbEstQUEiLCJ2ZXIiOiIxLjAif
Q.Uv4SvZUSZye7LZvn93LrGtKVw3j-8TAZcVQgmlnX5_WWPx6LRPBrqh8sl
CC5y4hvHy1MV6rKbpepLSSo62U1-Ox6YxLyL_rxd3963Ue8P7voXAcvzQIt
veuPUDNe0Qhn7XPNuBvNIf-WiaSE-qSJE4n817qJ8cKXLNwNp-LqXCc38S9
NS6W0yRAE1qK5ZXOWgJbkBp0K5Td1NHA6hfBkaM7soDmvMuaADbGHRkGXxS
0QnxcLGaS-7s8VQjN82uG-XlnPEz6jMvvbLaomk1slCawYbTMqUgQqbB6mY
SEEhMVLZQ89hHbL3XpcDeFWgs45hBg6brlAIOzwV1JnPAaKRg"}
```

- **Decoded access token:**

```
{ "typ": "JWT", "alg": "RS256", "x5t":
"2ZQpJ3UpbjAYXYGaXEJ18lV0TOI", "kid":
"2ZQpJ3UpbjAYXYGaXEJ18lV0TOI" }.{ "aud": "api://ceff2f83-
b273-470c-8d05-23d04d877528", "iss": "https://sts.
windows.net/b946974b-a933-49a1-9be9-610b2f7b7b8a/",
"iat": 1656605526, "nbf": 1656605526, "exp":
1656609426, "aio": "E2ZgYDizmjtQvMnv0HdZwXUfBOYeAQA=",
"appid": "5d14cb59-3aca-49a4-8b6d-134ce3502ee2",
"appidacr": "1", "idp": "https://sts.windows.net/
b946974b-a933-49a1-9be9-610b2f7b7b8a/", "oid":
"67263ccb-a909-4d5c-b360-9fc2cbd8c3e1", "rh":
"0.AtsAS5dGuTOpoUmb6WELL3t7ioMv_85zsgxHjQUj0E2HdSg7AAA.",
"sub": "67263ccb-a909-4d5c-b360-9fc2cbd8c3e1", "tid":
"b946974b-a933-49a1-9be9-610b2f7b7b8a", "uti":
"0Y6Fozzet0aCs4veEArDAA", "ver": "1.0" }.[Signature]
```

In the *Registering and configuring applications* section, we explained the application management model that is implemented in AAD and its close relationship with the OAuth, OIDC, and SAML protocols. In the next section, we will go through a set of additional AAD features that integrate with its authentication capabilities through more enterprise-oriented features that enable collaboration scenarios with external organizations and increase the overall security posture of the organization.

Additional features

On top of all the authentication capabilities that AAD provides as an implementation of the OAuth 2.0/OIDC specifications, AAD has built a set of management and security features that ease the tasks of both governing identities and their life cycles and securing access to the assets protected by AAD, such as applications and the data behind them. In this section, we will give you an overview of these features. Some of them require additional licensing (AAD Premium 1 and 2) in order to be used.

Conditional Access

Conditional Access is a security feature that can decide to grant or block a user from accessing AAD-federated applications according to specific conditions that are evaluated during a user's authentication attempt.

The Conditional Access feature consists of creating policies where an administrator can define the conditions that trigger the policy and the actions that AAD must perform when those conditions are satisfied.

A Conditional Access policy comprises the following:

- A list of assignments that define the scope of the policy, which include the following:

  - The user or workload identities that the policy should be applied to

  - The cloud apps or actions the user is accessing or doing (registering security information, such as a telephone number for MFA)

  - The conditions a user should satisfy

- Access controls that specify whether the user is granted or blocked access and how the user session is treated (either a persistent browser session or the user has to authenticate after a specified amount of time)

A condition is also called a signal, and it can include the following:

- User risk level (part of the Identity Protection feature)
- Sign-in risk level (part of the Identity Protection feature)
- Device platforms (which operating system the user is using)
- Locations (which locations the user is trying to authenticate from)
- Client applications (which client applications, such as a browser or a native app, the user is connecting from)
- Filter for devices (additional filters to include or exclude devices by creating attribute filters)

So, basically, the logic is as follows: when a user authenticates against AAD because they would like to access an AAD-protected resource (such as a federated application), AAD evaluates all the active Conditional Access policies by looking at the defined assignments to understand whether that particular authentication session is within the scope of a policy. If all the assignments are satisfied (e.g., the user is a member of a specific group, accessing a specific application, and satisfying specific conditions defined in the policy's assignments), then the access control is triggered (the user is either granted or denied access) and eventually enforced if the policy is not set to **Report-only** mode (which only audits the effects of the policy without enforcing the access controls).

Here is a screenshot, taken from the Entra portal, of the Conditional Access policy creation wizard:

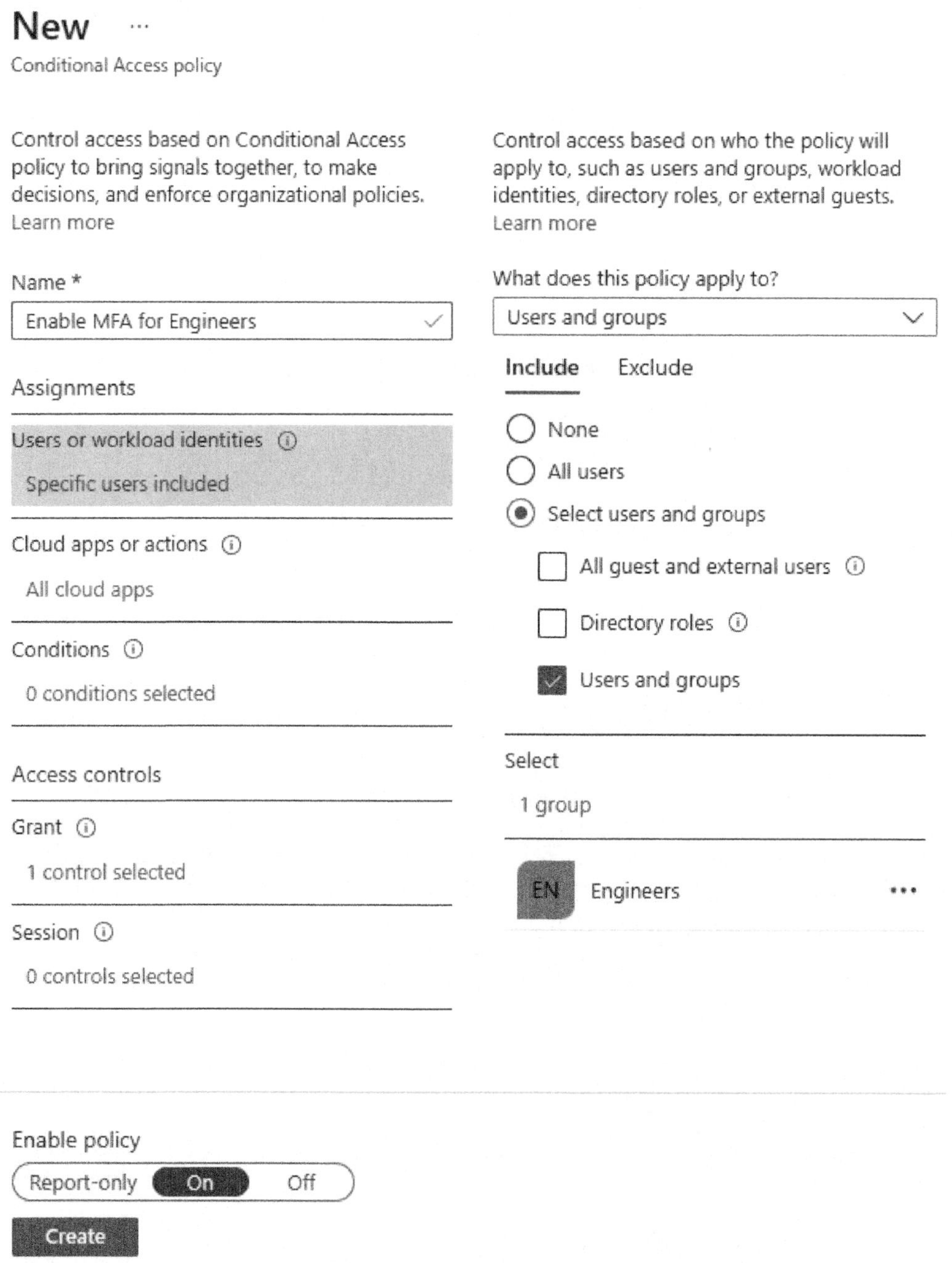

New   ⋯
Conditional Access policy

Control access based on Conditional Access policy to bring signals together, to make decisions, and enforce organizational policies. Learn more

Control access based on who the policy will apply to, such as users and groups, workload identities, directory roles, or external guests. Learn more

Name *

| Enable MFA for Engineers   ✓ |

What does this policy apply to?

| Users and groups   ⌄ |

Assignments

Users or workload identities ⓘ
  Specific users included

Cloud apps or actions ⓘ
  All cloud apps

Conditions ⓘ
  0 conditions selected

Include   Exclude

◯ None
◯ All users
◉ Select users and groups

  ☐ All guest and external users ⓘ

  ☐ Directory roles ⓘ

  ☑ Users and groups

Access controls

Grant ⓘ
  1 control selected

Session ⓘ
  0 controls selected

Select

1 group

| EN | Engineers | ⋯ |

Enable policy

(Report-only **On** Off)

Create

Figure 8.14 – Conditional Access policy creation

Identity Protection

Identity Protection harnesses the huge amount of underlying signals that AAD captures every day when users authenticate and use the platform. Once those signals are acquired, AAD applies complex **artificial intelligence** (**AI**) algorithms to extract relevant insights and build patterns that define a user's behavior when interacting with AAD and the connected services.

These patterns and behaviors are then used to find exceptions (outliers) that allow AAD to make decisions and flag a particular user or sign-in attempt that deviates from their standard pattern. As an example, it would be impossible for a real user to perform an authentication attempt from Rome followed by an authentication attempt from New York after only 5 minutes – in cases like this, AAD will highlight this log-in attempt as a security risk. Identity Protection uses three risk levels to label a user or a sign-in attempt as risky: low, medium, and high.

Specific actions can be associated with each of the preceding risk levels, such as blocking the account, forcing the user to change their password, or forcing the second factor of authentication. Identity Protection provides reports containing the decisions that have been made regarding a specific risk level, and it can also be integrated into a Conditional Access policy assignment.

Privileged Identity Management

Privileged Identity Management (**PIM**) embeds two common security principles that are considered best practices when it comes to assigning and defining permissions for a user:

- **Just Enough Administration (least privilege)**: A user should have the minimum set of permissions needed to perform a task
- **Just-in-Time Administration**: A user should have permission to perform a task only for the amount of time that is strictly needed to do it

AAD provides a set of built-in administrative roles that restrict administrative permissions to specific tasks, such as managing users (User Administrator role) or managing applications only (Application Administrator). AAD also provides very generic roles that can do a lot of things to different entities that are part of AAD. The most common example is the Global Administrator role, which has permission to do everything on a particular AAD tenant.

The temptation to grant the Global Administrator role to an administrator is high because it prevents any potential headaches related to the authorization errors that arise when a user tries to legitimately do something that their current assigned role does not allow. However, as per the principles stated previously, this approach is utterly wrong: the headache of tomorrow will be much worse if someone steals the credentials of a privileged user with the power to do everything on an AAD tenant.

PIM tries to help security administrators by providing built-in capabilities that allow role assignments to not be permanent but eligible: a user does not have an administrative role assigned to them but, with PIM, they can request a specific role that another administrator must already have configured for them so that they are allowed to request it for a predefined timeslot. A request for a non-permanent role assignment can also be subject to the approval of another administrator, and each request is audited to provide information about which user was assigned which role at which specific point in time.

External identities

Managing external identities (or guest accounts) can become tricky when the number of external users rises. Guest users are users that come from outside an organization's boundaries; as such, their life cycle is managed by an external identity provider. That's why AAD provides some built-in capabilities to manage those users.

The External Identities capabilities mainly fall into the following features:

- **External collaboration settings**

    With this feature, it is possible to specify basic authorization controls for guest users and who in the tenant can invite them (by default, every user in an AAD tenant can invite guests). It is also possible to allow invitations only to specific domains (companies) to prevent inviting all kinds of users into a tenant that might also belong to companies that shouldn't have visibility of your organization's data.

    Self-service sign-up is also possible. A user flow can be created to guide an external user to sign up and become part of your tenant if, for instance, your company has a web portal that is free for everyone to access and, therefore, you want people to be able to create an account without an administrator's intervention. Basically, in the **External collaboration settings** section in the Azure portal (see the following screenshot), define the constraints involved in the onboarding process of an external (guest) user:

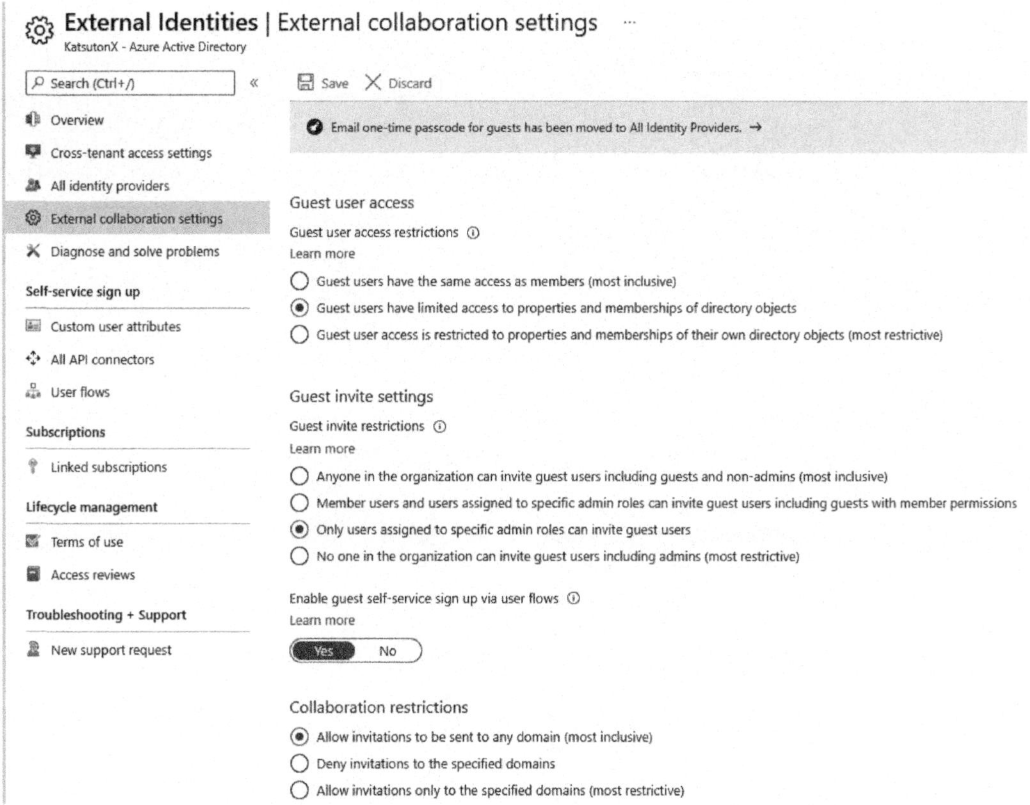

Figure 8.15 – AAD external collaboration settings

- **Cross-tenant access settings**

    Once a guest user is onboarded and is visible to the inviting AAD tenant, it makes sense to define common authorization controls for them. This is done by the cross-tenant access settings, which allow you to define which applications, by default, external users are granted or denied access to. It is possible to have both a default configuration that applies to all guest users and specific configurations that apply to specific external AAD tenants (defined by their registered domains).

    Cross-tenant access settings are a very convenient way to manage authorizing external users because they allow you to create a permission baseline that applies to all guest users without having to granularly specify explicit permissions for each guest user that has been invited to an AAD tenant. The following screenshot is of the **Cross-tenant access settings** section in the Azure portal:

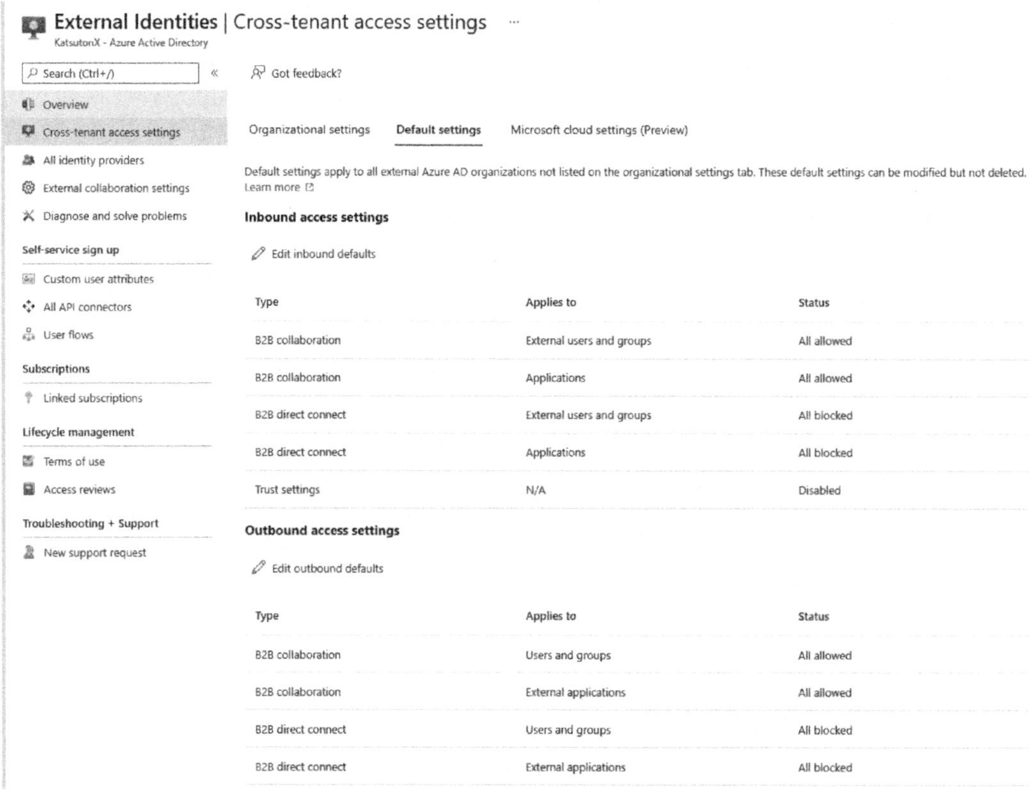

Figure 8.16 – AAD cross-tenant access settings

Identity Governance

The AAD Identity Governance umbrella comprises a framework for managing the life cycle of a user's authorizations regardless of the type of user (whether it is a guest or a member):

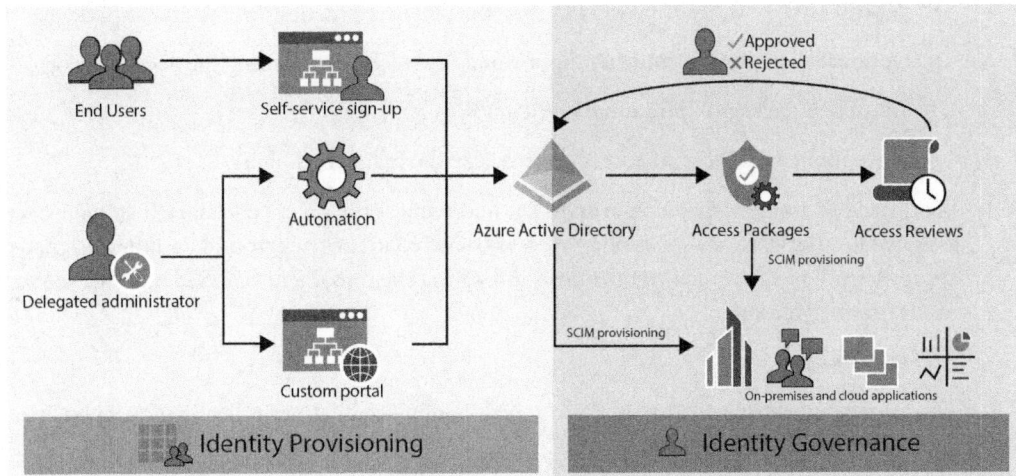

Figure 8.17 – An AAD user's life cycle

This is done using the following features:

- **Entitlement management**

  AAD's entitlement management is a workflow-based solution that enables a built-in identity governance process to manage internal and external users' life cycles. Permissions and access requests are defined in an entity called an **access package**, which is contained in a logical container named a **catalog**. A catalog can contain multiple access packages, and it defines a role-based access control model that allows you to delegate the administration of the catalog or the contained access packages to specific people in a company.

  This comes in handy when it is necessary to delegate the management of the permissions of a particular business unit to its business owner. The administrator generally doesn't know whether a user really needs access to a particular application; the business owner usually does. This model benefits both the administrators, because they are relieved of the burden of a dull task, and the business owners, who can improve their agility when managing their resources.

  An access package contains the following:

  - A list of resources and assigned roles that define what permissions a user will get for a specific resource when requesting the access package

  - A list of policies, each defining the following:

    - The users who can ask for the access package

- Whether one or more approvers must approve a user's request for the access package

- Optionally, questions requiring input from a user when requesting the access package

- The access package expiration date (if any)

- The optionally associated access reviews (see the following bullet)

Users need to access a specific portal to see and request the access packages they have been assigned to; afterward, an approval process is triggered in the background and the designated approvers will receive email notifications informing them that a new access package request needs their attention.

- **Access reviews**

    Access reviews, simply put, are built-in scheduled objects that periodically request business approvers to review the following:

    - A user's access to one or more applications

    - A user's membership in one or more groups

    - The validity of the permissions assigned to a user through an access package

    It often happens, as a matter of fact, that permissions remain assigned to individuals that have left the company, changed their role, or simply do not need access to some resources anymore. That's where access reviews help.

Verifiable credentials

Throughout the book, we have always referred to the federated authentication model, which involves different identity providers holding user credentials, and a trust model, which describes the interaction between applications and identity providers.

The verifiable credentials feature in AAD implements a new authentication model, the same one we briefly described in *Chapter 2, The Cloud Era and Identity*, which comprises the concepts of both **verifiable credentials** and **decentralized identities** (**DIDs**).

This new model tries to resemble the interactions that we commonly have in our real lives by digitalizing the concepts of issuer, holder, verifier, and wallet. Let's try to use these terms in a real-world example: when you are stopped by a police officer, among other things, you usually show them your driving license, the police officer verifies it, and then they usually let you go. In this scenario, you are the holder of your driving license (your credentials), which is stored in your wallet, and the police officer is the verifier of your credentials, which are issued by the government, the issuer.

This real-world authentication model, called the **presentation model**, can be translated into the digital world by representing each concept described here as different pieces of software. Let's see how AAD implements it. At the time of writing, the service is still in preview and it is named Verified IDs, part of the Microsoft Entra family. These are the components involved:

- **AAD tenant**

  AAD is the issuer of a verified ID that contains a user's credentials (cryptographic keys) and signed claims about the user. The Microsoft solution for verifiable credentials implements the **World Wide Web Consortium** (**W3C**) Verifiable Credentials Data Model 1.0 and DIDs V1.0. Part of an AAD tenant is the AAD verifiable credentials service, which enables you to issue and revoke verifiable credentials by provisioning and writing DIDs on the **Identity Overlay Network** (**ION**).

- **ION**

  ION is a public, permissionless Layer 2 DID network that runs on top of the Bitcoin blockchain.

- **Microsoft Authenticator application**

  The Microsoft Authenticator application acts as a digital wallet where the AAD-issued verifiable credentials are stored. It orchestrates the interaction between the user, the issuer, and the verifier. The application can only present to a verifier the portion of a verifiable credential that the user has consented to.

The presentation model is not likely to replace the existing federation model, which had and still has great success within small and large companies that have adopted it, but it's more likely that the two models will coexist for many years.

Microsoft Graph

Microsoft Graph is a gateway that allows programmatic interaction with every entity that belongs to a first-party Microsoft cloud service (i.e., AAD, Azure, Microsoft 365, and Dynamics 365).

Microsoft Graph exposes RESTful APIs that model the different objects that are used within the aforementioned cloud services. For AAD, the relevant objects are users, groups, and devices. Each entity is made up of a list of properties and methods that can be used to query the graph to retrieve information about a specific object.

The endpoint Microsoft Graph answers to is `https://graph.microsoft.com/`, and to use it, you have to obtain an access token from AAD by leveraging one of the supported OAuth 2.0 flows. Two types of permissions are available for an application to be granted the authorization to query Microsoft Graph, delegated and application permissions:

- **Delegated permissions**

These permissions involve the interaction of a user with the identity provider during the acquisition of the access token. Basically, the application that is assigned delegated permission to Microsoft Graph needs to be authorized by a user to perform the action granted by that permission. For instance, if an application registered in AAD is assigned the `User.Read.All` delegated permission, then only an OAuth 2.0 flow that involves a user authentication (e.g., the authorization code grant flow) can be used to obtain an access token. The user must also have the same permission that the application is asking for in order for the delegation to be successful. In other words, if I assign the `User.Read.All` delegated permission to an application, *then* also, the user *must* be assigned the very same permission to the Microsoft Graph (which is done by assigning a specific AAD role to the user) in order for the delegation to succeed.

- **Application permissions**

  This is a type of permission that is assigned directly to an AAD-registered application that does not need any user interaction to be honored. The access token can be obtained by an OAuth 2.0 flow that does not involve a user's authentication, such as the client credentials flow.

As an example, let's see how a user entity is modeled within Microsoft Graph and how it is possible to interact with it. User properties include the following:

- `accountEnabled`
- `assignedLicenses`
- `businessPhones`
- `city`
- `companyName`
- `country`
- `createdDateTime`
- `department`
- `displayName`
- `givenName`
- `identities`
- `mail`
- `mobilePhone`
- `onPremisesDistinguishedName`
- `onPremisesSameAccountName`
- `onPremisesUserPrincipalName`

- passwordPolicies

- preferredLanguage

- proxyAddresses

- state

- surname

- usageLocation

- userPrincipalName

- userType

Methods, which allow you to interact with a user's object, include the following ones (each method is associated with a specific HTTP verb):

Method	Description	HTTP verb
List users	Get a list of user objects	GET
Create user	Create a new user object	POST
Get user	Read the properties and relationships of the user object	GET
Update user	Update the user object	PATCH
Delete user	Delete the user object	DELETE

Table 8.2 – Microsoft Graph user object methods

Here's an example of how it is possible to retrieve the list of properties associated with a user by leveraging the get user method, assuming that the access token, which must be sent in the authorization HTTP header, has already been obtained through an OAuth 2.0 flow according to the permissions model explained previously:

- **Request**:

```
GET https://graph.microsoft.com/v1.0/users/me
```

- **Response**:

```
{
    "@odata.context": "https://graph.microsoft.com/
v1.0/$metadata#users/$entity",
    "businessPhones": [
```

```
        "4250000000"
    ],
    "displayName": "Fabrizio Barcaroli",
    "givenName": "Fabrizio",
    "jobTitle": null,
    "mail": "kadmin@katsutonx.onmicrosoft.com",
    "mobilePhone": null,
    "officeLocation": null,
    "preferredLanguage": null,
    "surname": "Barcaroli",
    "userPrincipalName": "kadmin@katsutonx.onmicrosoft.
com",
    "id": "57f25ecb-d0ff-4707-8211-b1ab756696c0"
}
```

Each method, when invoked, can be enriched with additional parameters to filter the result only by the information that is needed. For instance, it is possible to restrict the number of attributes that are returned when querying Microsoft Graph for a user object.

Microsoft also provides several SDKs in different programming languages that ease the task of interacting with Microsoft Graph:

- C#
- PowerShell
- TypeScript/JavaScript
- Java
- Go
- PHP
- Python

When interacting with AAD, it is inevitable to meet Microsoft Graph at some point on the journey. The good news is that whatever your technical background, Microsoft Graph will simplify the management of all AAD-related resources thanks to its standard and scalable architecture.

Summary

In this chapter, we've seen how OAuth 2.0/OIDC concepts are implemented in a real identity provider, AAD. We've seen how all the different parts of the protocols can be configured in AAD, including redirect URIs, secrets, flows, and tokens. The purpose of this chapter was to give an overview of how a commercial identity provider, at the end of the day, effectively implements a standard authentication protocol so that you can easily navigate the same concepts in other identity providers too.

In the next chapter, we are going to focus on real-world scenarios, starting with a holistic view of the identity challenges a company needs to deal with, going through the many implications the identity strategy has within a company, and going in depth to see the anatomy of a cloud-born application.

Exploring Real-World Scenarios

To better be able to focus on what real-world scenarios involve, first, it is important to holistically see the concept of identity within an enterprise.

To provide a broader view, first, this chapter will introduce all the features that a modern enterprise needs to consider regarding identity. This will help you to understand the implications and complexities to be expected in the real world.

The rest of the chapter will then present scenarios we come across in an enterprise when developing solutions, with a particular focus on modern applications. The examples that will be shown will demonstrate microservices applications designed with **domain-driven design** (**DDD**) principles in mind.

Most of the assets in a modern enterprise should be authenticated and authorized. The following are some use cases that are purposely very different from each other:

- Employees who need to access their mailbox

- Applications that need to query a database

- The mobile phone of an employee that needs to be registered to enable them to access sensitive information

- An enterprise application that an internal employee is required to access (e.g., an HR application)

- An enterprise application that customers are required to access to consume a service

- An unattended job or process that requires access to sensitive information

- An employee from an external company who needs to access resources within our company

- A customer from an external company who needs to access the API exposed by our company

Such a differing and complex landscape presents multiple scenarios that a typical medium-large company has to handle. It is quite normal for identity management to be inefficient due to the number of heterogeneous situations to handle. Moreover, digital transformation is evolving exponentially; large companies are known for their slowness and most of them cannot keep pace.

As an enterprise architect, it is important to distinguish between these two different levels of complexity: one where we have all the requirements a company needs to guarantee and secure the authentication and authorization of miscellaneous assets within the enterprise, and another where we have what has been the main focus of the book – the ability to guarantee a scalable and easy identity pattern when we, as architects, design an application.

We will cover the following main topics in this chapter:

- The identity features within an enterprise in the real world
- The implications of the company's structure
- Frontend authentication challenges in the real world
- Backend authentication challenges in the real world
- Authentication challenges for microservices integration

The following section will present an exhaustive view of the identity-based features that a modern organization needs to care about. Going in-depth on each of the bullet points presented in the next section is out of the scope of this book; what is important to understand is how complex the company identity landscape is in the real world.

The identity features within an enterprise in the real world

For the sake of understanding all the complexities related to real-world scenarios and to better capture what a holistic view of identity in a big enterprise may look like, we are going to enumerate all the topics related to identity that a modern enterprise needs to consider:

- **Privileged access management** (**PAM**): PAM consists of identity strategies and technologies to manage the full life cycle of elevated (privileged) users who have access to highly confidential corporate or government information and can become targets for cybercriminals.

- **Endpoint security**: Endpoint security solutions protect user devices that can compromise corporate network security via the valuable identity data stored in them.

- **Identity governance and administration** (**IGA**): IGA systems merge identity administration (which addresses account and credentials administration, provisioning, and entitlement management) with identity governance (which addresses the segregation of duties, role management, analytics, and reporting).

- **E-signatures and certifications**: E-signatures are the digital equivalent of hand signatures and are a legally binding demonstration of consent. Digital certificates are electronic documents that validate claims made by an entity about identity.

- **Network and infrastructure security**: Network security solutions enable intelligent traffic filtering, performance monitoring, and threat detection to safeguard all the data traversing the network and respond to unauthorized network intrusions.

- **Master data management (MDM)**: MDM helps companies maintain a single source of truth for digital assets, such as customer data. It ensures the accuracy, accessibility, and accountability of shared data across an enterprise.

- **Workforce IAM**: Workforce identity solutions provide full life cycle management and administration for an organization's employees, partners, and contractors. Solutions include user registration, authentication, **single sign-on** (**SSO**), and access controls.

- **Identity of Things**: Identity of Things solutions focus on managing device identity credentials, permissions management, endpoint security, and data protection for billions of internet-connected devices.

- **Consent management platform (CMP)**: CMPs obtain and manage proof of consent to collect, share, or sell personal data; they help companies comply with data privacy and protection regulations, such as GDPR and CCPA.

- **Behavioral biometrics**: Behavioral biometrics is a class of authentication solutions that use dynamic identifiers based on human behavioral patterns. Distinct from *traditional* biometrics, which uses absolute identifiers such as fingerprints and facial features, behavioral biometrics can be kinesthetic or device-based.

- **Identity graphing and resolution**: ID graphs map deterministic and probabilistic datasets to correlate online and offline identifiers with consumer identities. Identity resolution matches disparate records and data attributes to create a single, 360-degree customer view.

- **Customer IAM (CIAM)**: CIAM solutions focus on identity management for end users and provide a centralized and managed view of each customer across registration, authentication, authorization, federation, and data capture.

- **Biometrics**: Biometrics measure a human's physical characteristics to verify and authenticate an identity. Biometrics encompasses several physiological modalities, including fingerprints, faces, irises, palm veins, and voice.

- **User-generated content (UGC) moderation**: UGC moderation is how platforms protect their audiences from illegal and inappropriate content. UGC moderation can identify whether an account is human or non-human, providing the ability to remove bad actors before they have a chance to be disruptive.

- **User and entity behavior analytics (UEBA)**: UEBA expands upon traditional cybersecurity tools, looks at the behavioral patterns of humans and machines (e.g., routers, servers, and endpoints), and applies algorithms to detect anomalies and potential threats.

- **Mobile identity device intelligence**: Mobile identity includes user data (e.g., biometrics and account information) and mobile device data (e.g., location data and device number). Together, solution providers can determine risk signals, prevent fraud, and improve customer experiences.

- **Identity theft protection**: Consumer identity theft protection solutions monitor personal data for anomalies (e.g., social security numbers and credit card accounts) and provide paths for identity restoration in the event of theft.

- **Alternative credit and financial identity**: Traditional credit scoring processes exclude millions of potential borrowers who don't have a sufficient credit history to be scored. Alternative credit promotes financial inclusion by using a more comprehensive range of data attributes to determine a person's creditworthiness.

- **Fraud prevention and risk management (FPRM)**: FPRM solutions use risk-based approaches to analyze transaction history and network-related activity in order to identify potentially fraudulent or risky behavior patterns.

- **Identity wallets**: Identity wallets are smartphone-enabled applications that allow individuals to manage their digital identity credentials and data. Digital identity wallets offer control over what information is shared, when, and with whom, facilitating privacy, security, and consent management.

- **Identity proofing**: Identity proofing is a step up from identity verification and document authentication. It confirms that a user's identity is associated with a real person and answers the question, "*Are you really who you say you are?*"

- **Regulatory compliance transaction monitoring**: **Anti-money laundering** (**AML**) transaction monitoring helps financial institutions and money service businesses monitor customer activity and information, such as transfers, deposits, and withdrawals, to prevent financial crime.

- **Identity verification (IDV) and document verification**: IDV is the process of confirming that a user's identity is associated with a real person. IDV includes document authentication, which establishes an individual is who they say they are through a government-issued identity document.

- **Self-sovereign identity (SSI)**: SSI promotes the usage of **decentralized identifiers** (**DIDs**) that are decoupled from federated solutions, centralized registries, and **identity providers** (**IdPs**). With SSI, individuals can maintain ownership of their own portable, interoperable, and consented digital identity attributes.

- **Background screening**: Background screening is the process of looking up and compiling the employment, criminal, commercial, and financial records of an individual or an organization.

- **Enterprise master patient index (EMPI)**: EMPI solutions assist healthcare enterprises with managing patients' holistic healthcare records, which may be housed across disparate databases, systems, or entities.

For the purpose of this book, it is not mandatory to understand each of the bullets proposed in the preceding list in depth, although it's important to keep in mind the whole ecosystem of operations and processes beyond application authentication. In the upcoming section, we are going to review the implication of the company's structure in terms of software design and choice of IdP.

The implications of the company's structure

In *Chapter 6, Trends in API Authentication*, we have already seen the drawbacks for an organization to have, maintain, design, and pay for multiple IdPs to serve the multiple application architectures in its portfolio.

The purpose of this section is to understand the common reasons why this phenomenon occurs.

This aspect is usually connected to the structure of an organization. Mature companies already embrace DevOps, which is the practice of breaking down silos within an organization to ease collaboration and boost productivity. Companies that still work on silos with a lack of DevOps practices applied are more likely to suffer the IdP proliferation problem explained in *Chapter 6, Trends in API Authentication*, in the *The multiple IdP dilemma* section.

The reasons are straightforward: lack of communication and cooperation cannot produce a common strategy for a company, and this can result in different views on different areas that span design patterns, cloud providers, technology stacks, and, of course, identity strategies.

Such concepts are perfectly captured by Conway's law:

> *Any organization that designs a system (defined broadly) will produce a design whose structure is a copy of the organization's communication structure.*

Therefore, the very first step to moving toward a defined identity strategy in the application's design is to focus on how the organization works.

This is where DevOps practices come into the picture; they can be leveraged to support an organization to be more efficient in the long term if properly applied. They can also be leveraged to break down silos, define common strategies, and, in general, enable a company to produce more homogeneous deliverables with shared principles, especially in terms of security and identity – typically across the whole application portfolio.

When it comes to speaking about DevOps, we find commonly agreed principles but we cannot find any "magic receipt" or "golden bullet" that explains in detail what steps a company needs to apply in order to boost their productivity with these theoretical principles.

The DevOps model an enterprise needs to adopt varies from company to company; if we want to summarize the DevOps principles, we can definitely find cooperation and collaboration as a common denominator within every successful DevOps model. Place collaboration at the center of the enterprise strategy, as it's a concept that cannot be bypassed to successfully call an organization a DevOps organization.

If you want to explore effective delivery models for your own organization further, it is recommended to read the article at `https://web.devopstopologies.com/`. This article outlines the advantages and drawbacks of the most typical DevOps patterns and can be an important source of ideas to be refined further and applied to a company.

It is not uncommon in our job to meet customers with different approaches to DevOps and Agile practices.

Agile is a methodology to manage projects in a lean and faster fashion. Agile methodologies (Kanban and Scrum) distinguish themselves from legacy methodologies (Waterfall) with short iterative cycles that can tune the outcome of Agile projects in a few weeks, unlike a legacy methodology, in which tuning the outcome could mean re-evaluating the initial requirements of the project.

The typical scenario we find is where Agile project management concepts are forced within individual teams but every team is a silo by itself. Applying Agile concepts within a team is necessary but not sufficient to have well-defined company strategies and success in the long term. It is underestimated how important it is to have principles, guidelines, and blueprints shared across teams that need to cooperate well on high-level decisions.

Some may complain that Agile project management practices require the team to be self-sufficient, and the preceding statement (regarding cross-team cooperation) can limit the productivity of single teams and can be seen as an Agile anti-pattern. This is not true and it is a matter of trade-offs; dependencies between teams should be limited but not completely removed. This concept is paramount because a wide organization with hundreds of teams, different and potentially contradicting choices, and divergent architectural styles would lead an organization to the following potential drawbacks, among others:

- **Economics**: Paying multiple licenses for different products to serve the same purpose due to different choices or team philosophies.

- **Heterogeneous skill sets**: Different choices can lead to divergent types of tech adoption, which would, in turn, imply divergent skill sets across teams. This can limit the ability of a company to swap resources across teams according to market demand (as an example, one team could use Okta as an IdP, with the frontend coded using Angular technology and the backend in Node.js; another team could use Azure B2C as an IdP, with the frontend in Svelte technology and the backend in Java).

- **Solutions maintainability**: Adoption of different technology will force the production environment to deal with divergent problems of different natures at different points in time. This can span from a punctual technology bug that needs to be fixed to technology updates. The latter would occur at a different point in time according to the technology adopted and its life cycle. This has an impact on multiple areas – not just on identity or security but also on monitoring. For example, a company would have different ways to observe and monitor the solutions in production. All of these can lead to unsustainable maintenance for large firms.

In some circumstances, we noticed that a company still falls under a silo model (multiple teams and divergent strategies) due to a misinterpretation of the Agile principles that suggest a team be able to work independently. It is indeed important to understand that these principles don't imply the teams don't work together. It is important to design strategic decisions in a centralized way. If a strategic decision is made within a single team, the company may benefit in the short term but as said, there is definitely a high price to pay in the medium-long term due to the potential gaps between teams or silos, different decisions, different technologies to maintain, and, potentially, **different IdPs** being chosen. This simple concept may not be straightforward to every firm due to the interpretation (or misinterpretation) of Agile best practices.

If every single team works on its own strategy part independently, then they will likely produce different ways to approach topics such as security, identity, and the technology stack and reference architectures to follow. When this happens, we have a model similar to the one represented in the following figure:

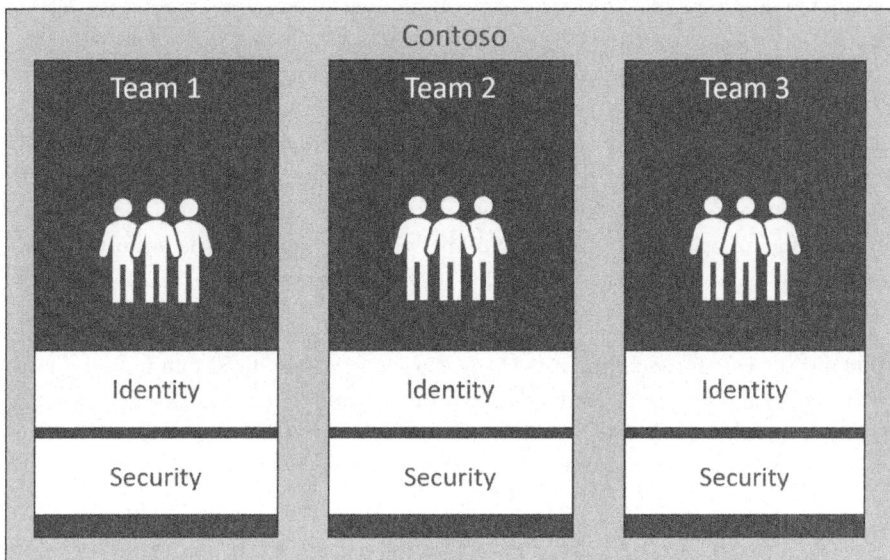

Figure 9.1 – Real-world example of independent teams, independent strategy

The preceding diagram provides an example to represent an organization with efficient teams with their own security standards, IdPs, and, potentially, identity protocols chosen.

The following diagram is an example of individual teams that share common strategies for high-level topics. Despite this slightly limiting the freedom an individual team can have, the end result of adopting this kind of model is an easier enterprise to maintain and there is a reduced cost to maintain the solution in the long term. The price to pay is that teams are not fully independent. As an example, they are not going to have the freedom to choose a specific IdP, to put in place different security practices, or even to choose the technology they wish; these high-level topics need to be mutually agreed upon:

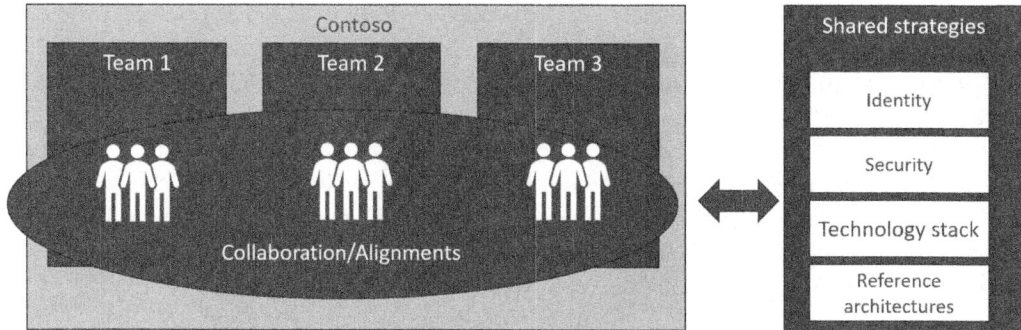

Figure 9.2 – Real-world example of independent teams, shared strategy

It is important to understand that any shared strategy reduces the freedom the Agile team is supposed to have and as such, it is recommended to force a shared strategy only on three or four pillars important for specific companies, such as the ones proposed in the preceding figure, and leave everything else up to individual teams. An extreme efficiency model (teams being 100% self-sufficient) leads to a proliferation of technology that, in the long term, requires more money and overhead to maintain. An extreme consistency-based model (teams follow shared strategies for all the choices) introduces processes and governance that lead to a static organization and remove most of the benefits of Agile project and product management. The trade-off between these extremes is important, and in any case, processes and governance practices need to be almost transparent for the model not to be an Agile anti-pattern.

This section didn't cover any technical aspects, just aspects that are important to keep in mind that involve IdP choices and that can be extended to other common areas such as security. With these preconditions in mind, we can now return to the technical part and review frontend and backend authentication in the following sections.

Frontend authentication challenges in the real world

As outlined in *Chapter 6*, *Trends in API Authentication*, multiple IdPs for the same purpose within the same organization will lead to several side effects. When we refer to *IdPs for the same purpose*, we mean an IdP applied to common audiences or channels, such as consumer authentication, employee authentication, or app authentication, each of which represents a different purpose. The IdP for consumer authentication may be different from the one used for employee authentication; indeed, it would be inefficient to have multiple IdPs for employee authentication.

Mixing IDPs for the same purpose is hardly ever done on purpose. Most of the time, this anti-pattern occurs as a result of poor strategy in an organization and decisions siloed by team, as described in the previous section.

Just to give an example, let's try to imagine an organization with multiple IdPs authenticating customers to their end services; it would create hassle and overhead for the company to manage, and moreover, it requires workarounds to mitigate **user experience (UX)** impact.

As an example, a customer or consumer who wants to access a service provided by a bank (e.g., the website of a bank) may use an IdP optimized to host consumer identities chosen by the architect who designed the bank's platform. In a context such as this, customers may and should use an IdP for their customer identity. The same enterprise architect may have chosen a different IdP for the internal employees, which, in turn, may be different from the IdP chosen to host internal web applications that need to authenticate between each other (server-to-server authentication). This scenario is not optimal (we don't have a unique IdP across the organization) but is acceptable and sometimes advisable for security purposes (we have different IdPs for different purposes, which, in turn, provides some security boundaries around different kinds of identity: customers, employee, and web app).

What would generate overhead is to have different IdPs for the same purpose. As an example, imagine a scenario where different internal applications need to authenticate with other internal applications that are hosted on another IdP. Another example that generates overhead is when the same customer needs to access a different service from the same company and its identity is hosted on a different IdP, which requires the customer to be hosted twice, having two different identities, and likely, two different passwords.

To understand the concept better, we're going to have a look at a concrete example with a graphical diagram. Let's imagine a company that provides both banking and insurance services to customers and, as such, has two web applications.

If customer-facing applications of this kind are developed by two different teams that implement two different IdPs, the high-level architecture would look like the example represented in the following figure:

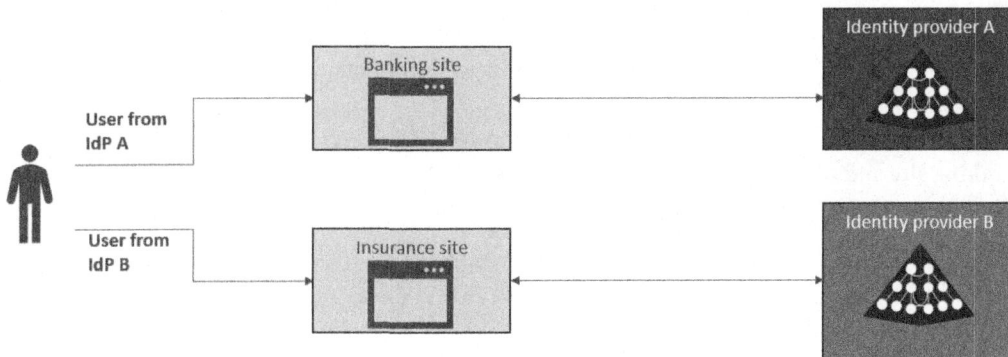

Figure 9.3 – Multiple customer-facing IdPs

This kind of scenario (as represented in the preceding figure) has the following two major drawbacks:

- **Company overhead**: Different IdPs to manage, different secrets, application registration, access token format, and any drift that two different IdPs may have

- **UX**: A user needs to use one identity for website A and another identity for website B, which leads to a more complicated experience and can impact the business due to fewer interactions with the customer

This scenario is not uncommon for many companies. Often, minor adjustments to the preceding architecture are performed to resolve any issues that might otherwise affect the UX and perception of the company's brand. As a matter of fact, the preceding diagram requires the user, a customer of the bank, to have two different identities and to remember two different usernames and passwords, and likely two multi-factor authentications. When a situation such as that occurs, companies tend to mitigate the issue by adding an extra layer to the architecture, taking advantage of SSO techniques to enable the user to use just one identity for access, as represented in the following figure:

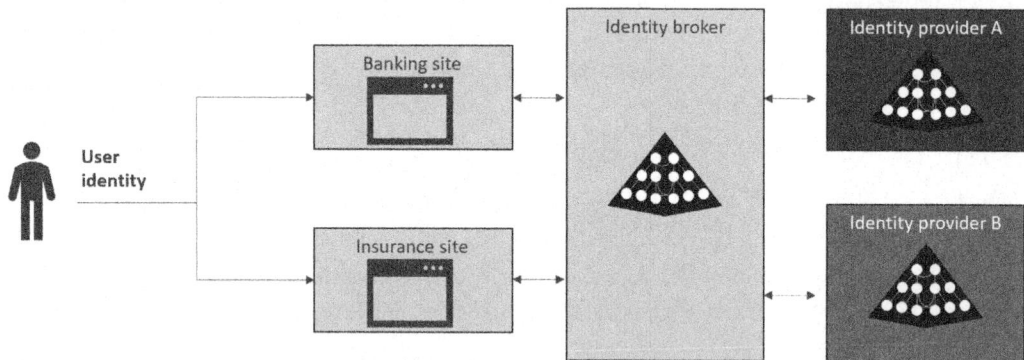

Figure 9.4 – Enhancing the UX with an identity broker

In the preceding figure, the **identity broker** is seen from both the applications (in this example, the **banking site** and the **insurance site**) as the reference IdP to be used to authenticate users to both platforms, even if, under the hood, the users belong to any two different IdPs.

From a high-level point of view, the workaround represented in the preceding figure is commonly implemented with any of the following two techniques that we have come across in our experience:

- **Synchronization**: With the synchronization option, the identity broker is a full IdP and the identities that belong to both IdP A and IdP B are copied into the identity broker. This is usually achieved with a third-party system that is designed to sync identities. This makes the identity broker completely self-sufficient to release tokens toward the applications in real time without referring to the source IdP that actually hosts the identities. This approach has sync overhead and requires always keeping the sync between the IdPs up to date.

- **Token delegation**: In the token delegation option, both applications still trust the identity broker as the IdP. Like the synchronization workaround, with token delegation, the complexity of having multiple IdPs is transparent from the application's and the developer's point of view. This time, the identity broker needs to check the user identities against the target IdP in real time, which, in the example in *Figure 9.4*, can be either IdP A or IdP B. It is important to note that in this kind of scenario, the identity broker completely relies on the other IdPs and is not able to release any token if these IdPs are not reachable for any reason. This has an impact on the **service-level agreement** (**SLA**) of the solution, which is directly proportional to the number of layers that belong to the solution.

In both cases, the access token released to the application (or to the user, according to the chosen protocol and flow) is forged and signed by the identity broker itself.

This is just an example of what companies tend to do to mitigate the proliferation of unwanted IdPs within their application portfolio. This workaround simplifies the application development, as well as the UX, more importantly, which, in turn, affects customers' perception of the company.

From an enterprise architect standpoint, it is important to understand that the aforementioned scenario intrinsically generates overhead within the enterprise, which needs to cover multiple assets (IdPs) to serve the same purpose twice.

In fact, in this kind of scenario, the users of the companies are likely to be present on both IdP A and IdP B. It should be obvious that this pattern should be avoided, as long as there are no important security restrictions that recommend IdP segregation, which justifies the overhead addition.

The drawbacks to having multiple IdPs to host the customers of a company are, among others, as follows:

- Duplicates the effort to implement, monitor, and maintain multiple IdPs
- Decreases customer satisfaction and perception with the double IdP and the need to add an extra layer as a workaround (SSO, as shown in the example of the preceding figure)
- More complex architectures, which may include an identity broker or, in any case, an additional layer to implement, monitor, and maintain
- An impact on the SLA of the solution due to the extra layer(s) required

Let's come back to the example of the two applications – the banking site and the insurance site – within the same company and see how the architecture would look with a unified IdP:

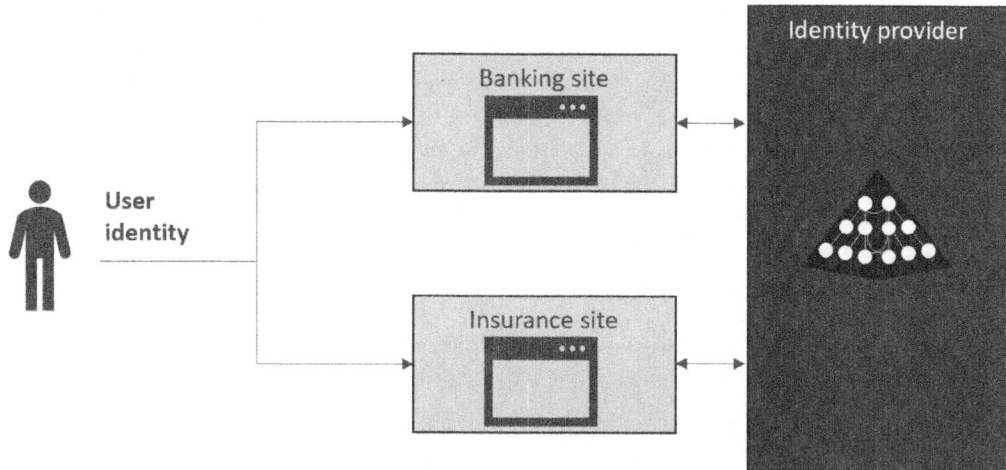

Figure 9.5 – A common IdP for consumers

As you can see, this proposed diagram contains fewer elements to produce a cleaner and more efficient architecture that is more reliable in the long term. This diagram, moreover, will likely have a better SLA due to fewer layers involved.

Before finishing this section, we want to outline once again an important aspect that we have covered: even by implementing the workaround of the identity broker and the addition of the extra layer, we are only going to be able to improve customer perception. Under the hood, the company still needs to deal with multiple identities and IdPs. This will result in a less reliable architecture. It is important to outline that although it may seem counterintuitive to a junior architect, adding layers to applications usually does not improve the reliability of the application; indeed, the overall reliability is generally reduced. This is because the more layers an application has, the more items are required to work (and need to be maintained) to enable the application to serve the requests, a scenario that a good enterprise architect wants to avoid.

In the next section, we are going to make similar considerations, but this time, for backend authentication instead. Backend authentication is a wider topic to analyze compared to the frontend due to the multiple ways an application can be designed. Because of its complexity, we have sliced the section into subsections, where each subsection is a different pattern, which will help you to appreciate the pros and cons of each of them.

Backend authentication challenges in the real world

In the previous section, we focused on how the number of IdPs used to authenticate the customer of a company can affect the design.

In this section, we are going to be focused on server-to-server authentication, a topic that is becoming even more important with cloud-born applications.

In the consumer example proposed in the previous section, having multiple IdPs for backend authentication (or server-to-server authentication) within an organization can lead to an even worse scenario than the one analyzed in the previous section.

Let's forget user, consumer, or customer authentication for a minute; in other words, let's forget the interactive authentication made by a human that was covered in the previous section, and let's go deeper into analyzing backend authentication.

As covered in *Chapter 1, Walkthrough of Digital Identity in the Enterprise*, digital transformation and the cloud are impacting the way we design applications. Nowadays, new applications tend to be more distributed and, as such, composed of different slices, services, and layers. This means that we now have new challenges that weren't relevant a few years ago.

To understand the argument better, let's take an example of a monolith from the legacy era; in this case, the business logic sat on top of the same process that was supposed to serve views to the end user, as well as data classes. As a matter of fact, the most used pattern for legacy applications was based on **Model-View-Controller** (**MVC**). MVC is an architectural pattern implemented by different frameworks and technologies.

This kind of architectural pattern aims to distribute code components between three layers:

- **Model**: Code that is usually responsible (depending on the technology and framework chosen) for dealing with the database and materializing data into a concrete class usable inside the code.

- **View**: Code that is responsible for returning the view to the client.

- **Controller**: A component that is responsible for most of the business logic; it usually interacts with the view and the model.

With this common framework implementation, the pattern segregated the code. In the early 2000s, we assisted in the proliferation of MVC frameworks to support many different backend technologies: Java Spring, Ruby on Rails, ASP.NET, and CakePHP, just to mention a few of the most famous technologies. Anyway, the three layers (Model, View, and Controller) need to strictly interact with each other to enable the full logic of the application to work, and there is usually a strong dependency between code. This meant the MVC framework segregated the code, but not the hosting platform. This framework helped developers have clean and well-organized code, but it didn't help from a hosting point of view, as this kind of code was usually compiled together and run on a single hosting platform. As a consequence, many developments on top of this kind of framework produced artifacts to run on top of a single application server known as a **monolith**.

In other words, a web application used to belong to the same compute process within the same application server. This means that no authentication was usually required between application components (e.g., the model didn't need to authenticate against the controller, as it ran in the same process).

You may understand at this point that adopting an MVC framework led to code that was well-organized but wasn't scalable, distributed, or able to scale independently. In the legacy world, authentication was still a hot topic, especially for integration (where an application needed to call an external API from the application itself) or in **Service Oriented Architecture (SOA)**, but it is far from the requirements we have today in a world where most new applications are distributed by design.

In this new generation of cloud-born applications, we are dealing with applications that are distributed by design across different hosts, containers, and, generally, different processes; serverless applications are an extreme example of this. This means that, potentially, every time we have a portion of an application that needs to speak with another portion, authentication needs to occur.

To understand this concept better, let's see an easy example aided by a diagram. We are going to consider a banking company that exposes a banking portal to its customers; we refer to the example proposed in the previous section again but elaborated further with a focus on backend authentication. This time, we are also going to represent greater complexity on the backend logic– we are going to split the backend into portions to simulate an extremely simplified distributed architecture:

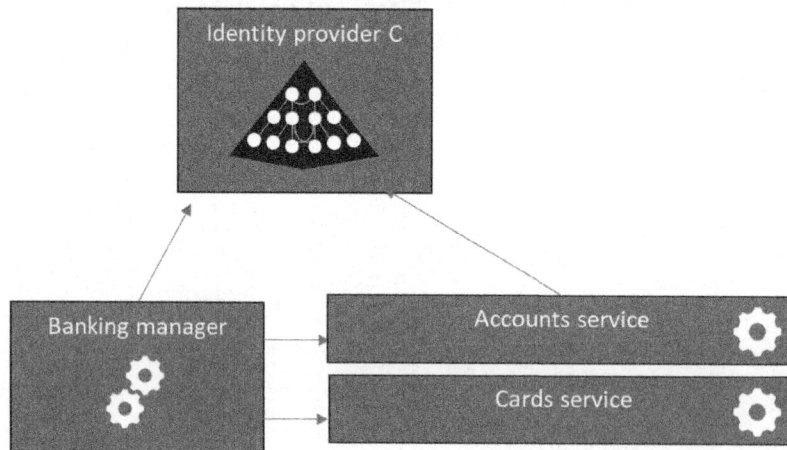

Figure 9.6 – Backend authentication sample on a modern application

In the preceding example, the banking manager is a service that calls two different services to successfully work. The assumptions in these scenarios are the following:

- The banking application is an application composed of three backend services –**Accounts**, **Cards**, and **Banking manager**

- The backend services of the bank application authenticate each other via OAuth through the client credential flow

Before extending the use case to better apply to real-world complexities, let's focus on how authentication can work in the backend components of the banking application. As explained in *Chapter 5, Exploring*

Identity Patterns, in the OAuth client credential flow, whenever the **Banking manager** service in the example needs to communicate with the **Accounts** service, then it needs to connect to the IdP to obtain an access token first. These access tokens then need to be validated for the target service (in the preceding example, the **Accounts** service or **Cards** service). When the IdP releases the access token, the **Banking manager** service can finally submit the request to the **Accounts** service, and the latter is required to validate the token.

The first question you should think about is the following:

> *How many application registrations are required against the IdP?*

As usual, it's a matter of requirements and trade-offs. If we want to fully follow the OAuth specifications, then we need to have one registration per service. Having a registration for every component of the application would require a specific token to the IdP for each component of the application. Each token will have its own *audience* (*the claim in the token named "aud"*) and *scope* fields. As such, the access token can only be spent on the specific service in the scope of the request (different IdPs may handle the *aud* claim differently). In other words, if the **Banking manager** service needs to communicate with both the **Accounts** and **Cards** services, it needs to obtain two distinct tokens from the IdP. The request for each token would be similar to the following snippet of an HTTP request:

```
POST /{tenant}/oauth2/v2.0/token HTTP/1.1
Host: hostname
Content-Type: application/x-www-form-urlencoded


client_id=1234567-8901-2345-6789-0123456678
&scope=AccountService
&client_secret=sampleCredentials
&grant_type=client_credentials
```

In this example, a service or API with a client ID of `1234567-8901-2345-6789-0123456678` (which, in our example, will be **Banking manager**) is requesting a token to be used later to authenticate itself to `AccountService`, which is given in the `scope` field. The `scope` field, as explained, should be set according to the target service where the authentication needs to occur (some IdPs do not use the `scope` field but rather the resource for this purpose). In other words, and according to what is explained in the authentication flows chapter (*Chapter 4, Authentication Flows*), the token the IdP will emit will be forged according to the scope required. This affects the audience field of the access token that will be subsequently released by the IdP. In this scenario, the **Accounts** and **Cards** services will validate two different audiences (the `aud` field in the token released and signed by the IdP), and a token obtained from one service cannot be spent on the other one.

This simple example with three basic services outlines the following facts:

- If we want to establish a full mesh of authentication (each service can be authenticated against another random service), then we need to register every component of the application against the IdP so that we can obtain different client IDs and secrets.

- In this kind of example, it is requested that more logic is implemented on the caller, as each service requests its own specific access token.

- From a security standpoint, this approach is the best, as it guarantees security (one audience for one service). The price to pay is registering and managing multiple identities on the IdP side and writing further logic from the caller.

As already outlined, the sample application represented in *Figure 9.6* is a simplified example. As a matter of fact, a typical cloud-native microservices application contains many more services.

Let's now make our diagram more complete to make our application closer to a real-world scenario. A more concrete banking application that follows a microservices architecture would look like this. The example is still simplified but closer to the reality compared to what was reported previously:

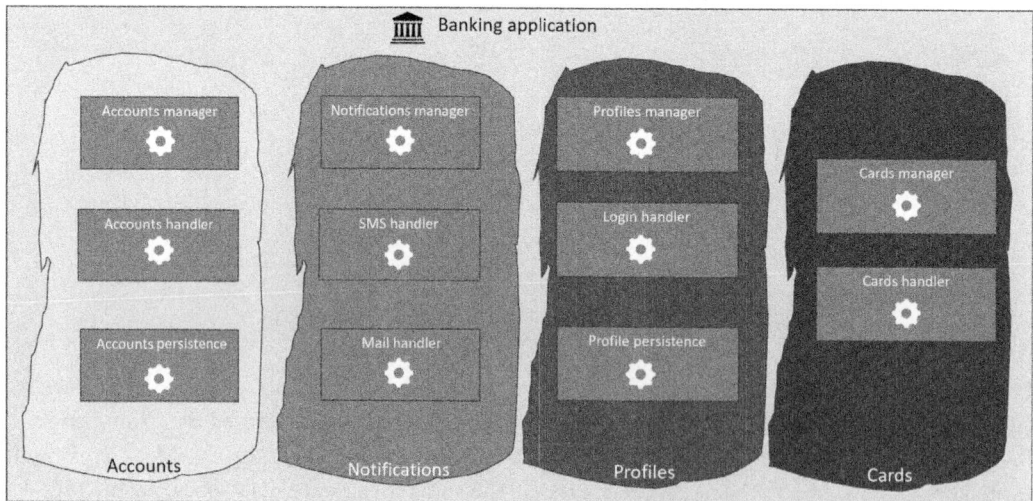

Figure 9.7 – Microservices application sample

Consistent microservices applications that follow the DDD pattern, as shown in the preceding figure, are divided into bounded contexts – in the example, four distinguished bounded contexts are present: **Cards**, **Profiles**, **Notifications**, and **Accounts**.

From a blueprint perspective, a pure microservices architecture cannot allow a service in a specific bounded context (e.g., **Accounts**) to interact with a service in a different bounded context (e.g., **Notifications**); this is to avoid the functionality of one bounded context relying on the response or functionality of a different bounded context and favor independence between the bounded domains. If domains can freely communicate with each other, then an issue on one domain can affect the functionality of another domain, and this would break the autonomous principle of a domain, as the DDD paradigm dictates. As a matter of fact, in this kind of architecture, there is usually a wide adoption of queues and publish/subscribe tools such as Kafka, Service Bus, or RabbitMQ, for example. They are adopted to enable one service to listen to the events of the others and act accordingly without any communication between the two occurring. In architecture designs, this approach is followed to increase independence across the service.

In the real world, it's very hard to find fully decoupled domains and in some circumstances, a specific microservice within a domain is promoted to query on-demand services hosted in different domains, although this practice should be an exception that is limited as much as possible to ensure good reliability within the bounded context.

Let's see, in the following sections, the implication of these designs on the IdP and the different ways to handle the identities in the service and their authentication. We are going to cover three potential identity patterns that can be applied to this application.

Pattern 1 – multiple IDPs

One benefit of the microservices approach is the ability to completely segregate the work between different teams and gain the maximum possible velocity and time to market by eliminating or mitigating all the dependencies and inefficiency across said teams.

This topic should sound familiar to you, as it directly connects to what was reported in the second section of this chapter, *The implications of the company's structure*.

If the company is mature enough to fully embrace the microservices paradigm and have different teams associated with different bounded contexts (e.g., one team that works on the **Cards** functionalities and one team that works on the **Accounts** functionalities), then the information in the previous section about standard blueprints (which includes IdP adoption) needs to be considered to prevent situations such as the one shown in the following figure:

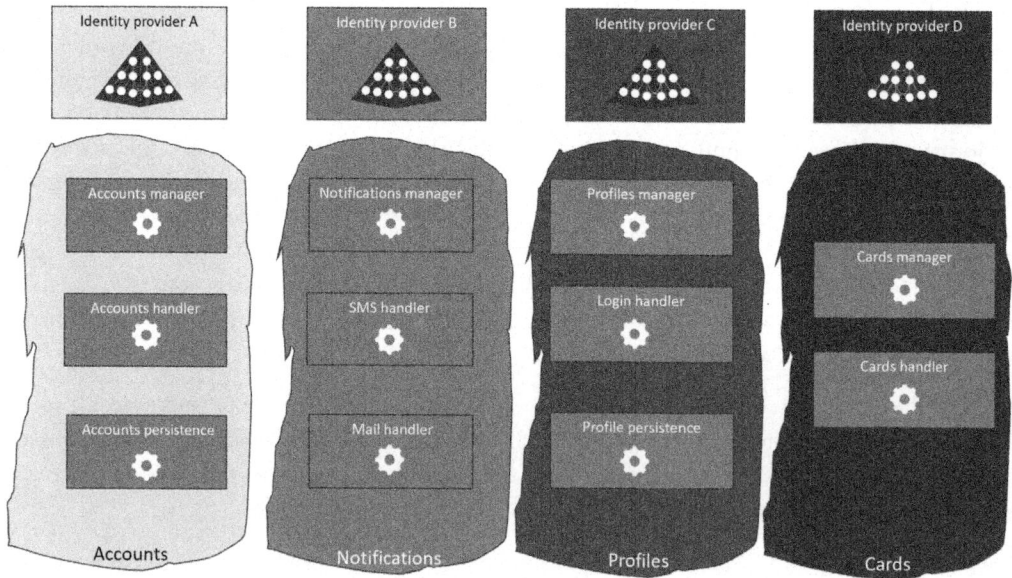

Figure 9.8 – Anti-pattern – multiple IdPs in different domain contexts

It is too easy to imagine the overhead a situation such as this would cause. These are the issues, among others:

- Multiple IdPs to maintain

- A heterogeneous registration process

- An audience field meaning changes according to the domain context

- A scope field meaning changes according to the domain context

In other words, this would cause the architecture to be unclean – the service should change the validation behavior according to the IdP.

As if that were not enough, each IdP may have its own slang and interpretation of the OAuth specs: it is common to see access tokens forged differently according to the IdP. The final result would be that the access token may contain different fields according to the source IdP and this would result in a cross-domain error when an integration test in the application included multiple bounded domains.

All in all, this kind of pattern is never recommended and should be avoided not just on the basis of the technical reasons explained in this section but also due to all the implications mentioned in the *The implications of the company's structure* section.

Pattern 2 – a single IdP

In the previous section, we had the opportunity to appreciate a concrete real-world example that showed the implications of having multiple IdPs adopted by different teams on a microservices application.

If we imagine a microservices application that takes advantage of a single IdP, and we apply the principle of the full-meshed authentication mentioned in the *Backend authentication challenges in the real world* section, the architecture will look like the following example:

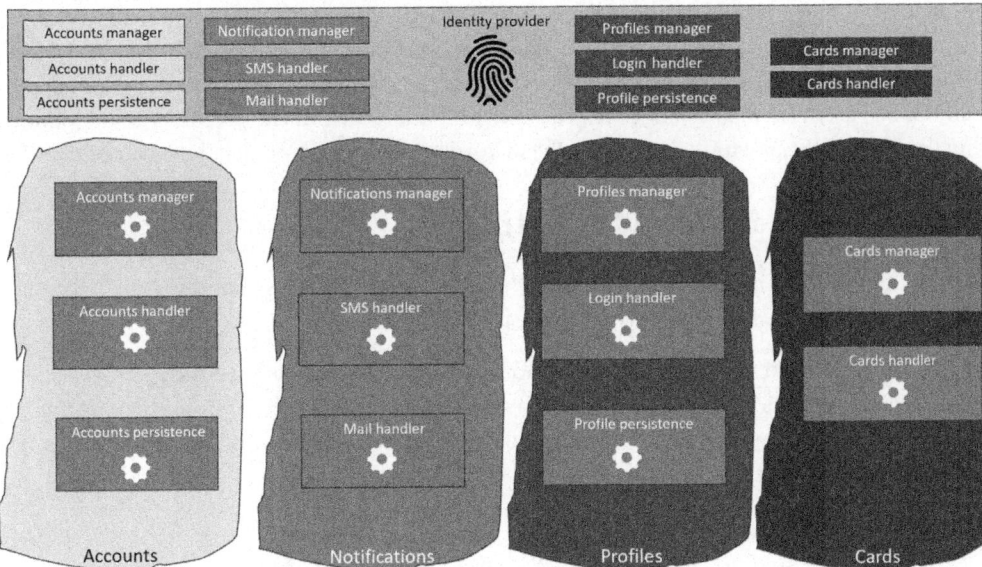

Figure 9.9 – Microservices application – single IdP

As stated in the previous section, the microservices in each domain context should have their own registration and require a specific token.

It's worth noticing that although the diagram shown in *Figure 9.9* is more complete than what was shown in *Figure 9.6*, it is a sample that may still be far from a real-world scenario: a complex and business-critical application could have dozens of domain contexts, and hundreds of microservices even. Guaranteeing all the permutations of possible authentication patterns within and, in rare cases, even across different domains will increase the complexity and the business logic that needs to be written and handled. This extension of the previous use case is not extreme: we need to consider that complex applications may rely on hundreds of microservices hosted on different functional domains. In a scenario such as this, even having a single IdP for each microservices application can become cumbersome. Registering each microservice to the IdP to ensure a full mesh of authentication within the services may not be practical and not even desirable; that's where a trade-off between productivity, reliability, and security needs to be reached.

Moreover, it is worth noticing that a well-designed DDD application requires each microservice not to communicate outside of the domain context, and as such, introducing a full-mesh authentication pattern is unnecessary, as it would generate unjustified overhead.

From the security standpoint, if the hosting system is a container orchestrator such as Kubernetes or OpenShift, where the microservices sit on top of a software-defined network that is not reachable outside the cluster, then the severity of security may be relaxed a little, and authentication can be handled in one of the patterns that will be proposed in the following subsections.

All in all, this pattern is recommended for small applications where the number of microservices and bounded domains is limited and security requirements are very high; it would also be an option wherever DDD is not closely followed and microservices require mutual authentication out of the domain. It would not be recommended to adopt it as a standard pattern due to the proliferation of identities within the IdP and the overhead required in the maintenance of the solution and the related identities.

Pattern 3 – domain-based registration

This pattern may represent the best trade-off wherever a microservices application is managed by multiple teams associated with different domain boundaries.

The idea of this pattern is to have registered identities that don't represent the microservices by themselves; instead, this pattern suggests registering domains. Each microservice that belongs to a specific domain will share its identity with the other microservices within the same domain. This approach has the following advantages:

- There is a specific audience and scope for each domain, which, on the other hand, represents the security boundaries established by the development team

- There is one registration per domain and not per microservice, which limits a lot of the required entities to be registered on the IdP

This is what it looks like:

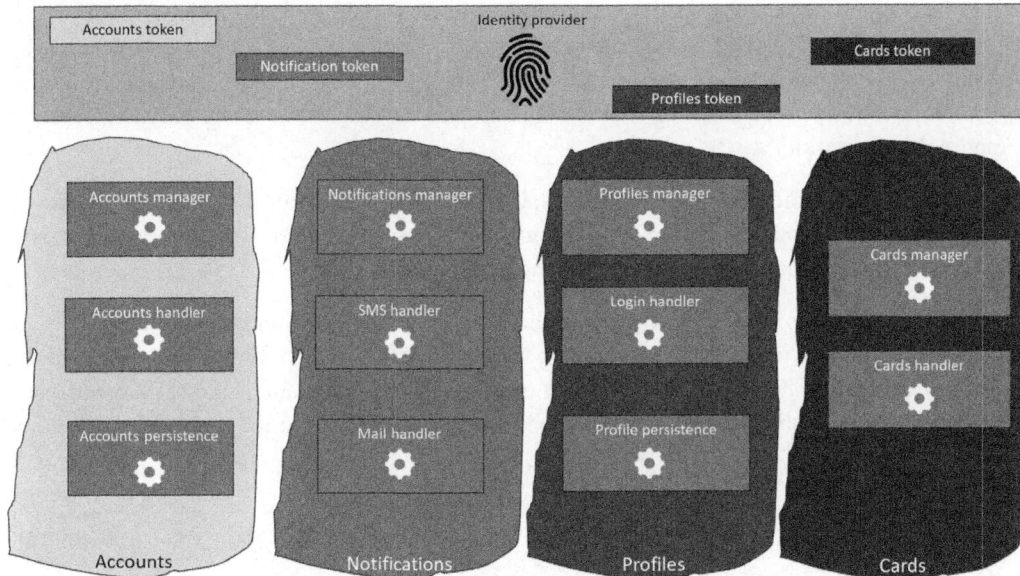

Figure 9.10 – Domain-based registration

As already explained, it's important to outline once again that cross-domain communication in a pure microservices architecture should be rare or nonexistent; this means that on average, each service should only get the token required to communicate with the other microservices that co-exist within the same functional domain.

This approach will not be as secure as the one proposed in the previous section, where each microservice required a specific token. This is because, with a single token, an attacker could potentially access all the microservices within a functional domain. Regardless, it could represent the best trade-off between productivity, maintainability, and security for most applications.

From a security standpoint, moreover, it's worth noticing that in a microservices architecture that works, the security footprint should not rely only on authentication but must be extended by a networking lockdown strategy, and as such, authentication requirements can be relaxed. As a matter of fact, functional domains in infrastructure such as Kubernetes or OpenShift should be hosted on specific namespaces and network restrictions can be paired with the authentication strategy to enhance the security footprint further and prevent unwanted cross-domain communication from both an authentication and network standpoint.

This pattern is the most practical in complex DDD architectures, as it limits the number of registrations to have and, at the same time, maintains a good degree of security.

Pattern 4 – application-based registration

This is the simplest possible pattern. It is the simplest because it requires the minimum number of registrations to the IdP. In this pattern, each application is registered once and each microservice within the application shares the same identity. In this pattern, only one identity is registered regardless of the complexity, the number of functional domains, and the magnitude of the microservices that compose the application.

This pattern is recommended in limited cases; it is advisable only when authentication between services in the same application is not required or when segregation and security are either not strict requirements or are completely handled by the networking area.

One of the advantages of the microservices application, as reported previously, is the ability to have self-sufficient teams. Having these teams adopt the same IdP is advisable. Having these teams share the same identity registration within the same IdP is not, as it may introduce an unnecessary dependency between them and involve sharing client IDs and secrets across teams, which is not advisable either.

The following figure provides a representation of this pattern:

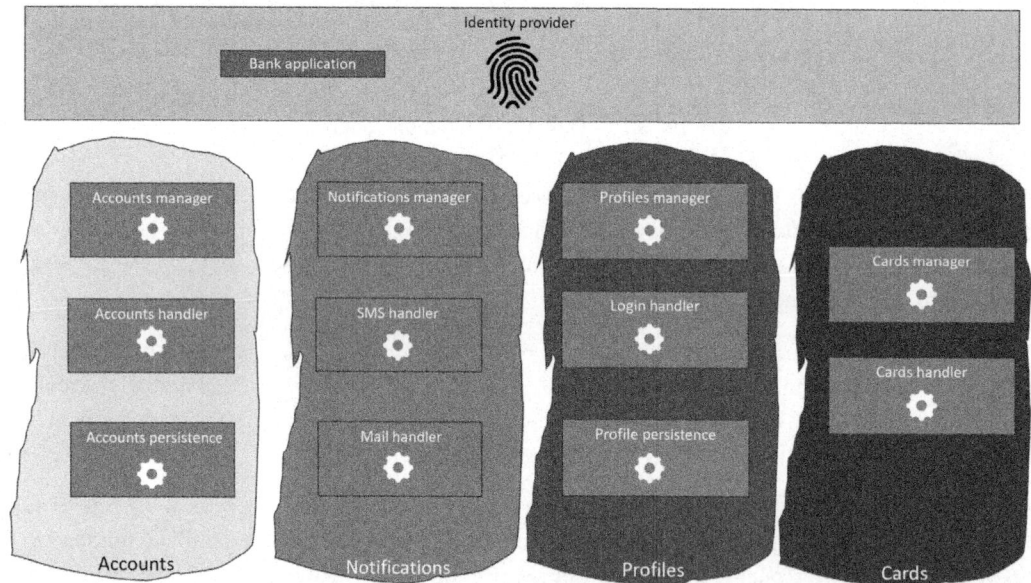

Figure 9.11 – Application-based registration

This pattern could become interesting whenever the backend service of the banking application should be accessible to an external system. This is because this external system doesn't need to know the internal details and the functional domain of the microservices application; all it needs is to have a token to access the backend service of the banking application. This facilitation, of course, has security implications if only a generic token is used for all the authentication that an enterprise architect needs to evaluate in terms of its risks and benefits. In scenarios where security is important, this pattern is not preferred. This is because the same token that external applications consume is the one used internally by an application, and if network restrictions are not in place or configured properly, a system with a token can make an undesired query to microservices that are not supposed to be exposed.

Anyway, undoubtedly, this pattern allows the application to be exposed to external systems, as they can refer to a single token and the internal complexity can be hidden.

As such, it could be interesting to see the result of mixing this pattern (application-based registration) with the domain-based registration pattern to achieve the best of both and keep security high.

The next section will focus on this kind of combination.

Authentication challenges for microservices integration

All the patterns exposed so far have focused on internal authentication within a component of an application. We have seen scenarios where we wanted to authenticate each microservice and when we wanted to authenticate them based on the domain to which they belonged.

In real-world scenarios, the context is usually way more complex and we usually come up against integration requirements that require us to consider authentication beyond the remit of the patterns described so far.

The purpose of this chapter is to situate integration within the bigger picture and review how it is possible to combine the patterns explained so far to provide a more holistic solution. This chapter will focus on inbound integrations, which are the capabilities or APIs that the application needs to expose to external or third-party systems.

Inbound integrations are the calls to which the application is expected to reply, submitted from external systems. As such, inbound integrations are supposed to be developed as part of the application itself, unlike outbound integrations, which are indeed the APIs that the application needs to call – and, as such, are external and not part of the application development.

From a high-level perspective, an inbound integration pattern looks like the following diagram:

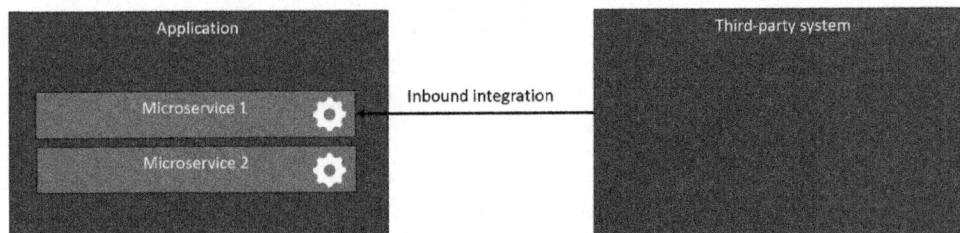

Figure 9.12 – Inbound integration

Inbound integrations are typically cumbersome during the application design. The reason behind that is that the application needs to have the capacity to scale not just for the core functionality that it needs to serve but also to serve queries from third-party components (inbound integrations). A spike of requests from third-party components should not degrade the performance of the core functionalities (which typically insist on the same database) and that's the reason why inbound integration design usually requires careful attention on the part of an experienced enterprise architect. This is because we open our application to receive a query from external systems, and these external systems may introduce a load that can affect the performance of the whole application. Strategies such as horizontal scaling and design adjustments to prevent performance overhead from being introduced by third-party systems need to be carefully considered. This design aspect requires specific attention, despite being beyond the scope of this book.

To introduce the topic of inbound integration, first, it's important to outline the full internal interactions that are needed in the application. Let's take a step back and extend the domain-based registration design to introduce a frontend component that would query the backend microservices. This aspect hasn't been outlined previously for two reasons:

- It simplifies the understanding of in-app authentication
- When it comes to discussing the design of the frontend for a microservices application, there are multiple options and permutations according to how closely the architect wishes to stick with the DDD guidance

For the sake of understanding, the example that follows will focus on the easiest approach.

The end-to-end authentication flows should look like the following:

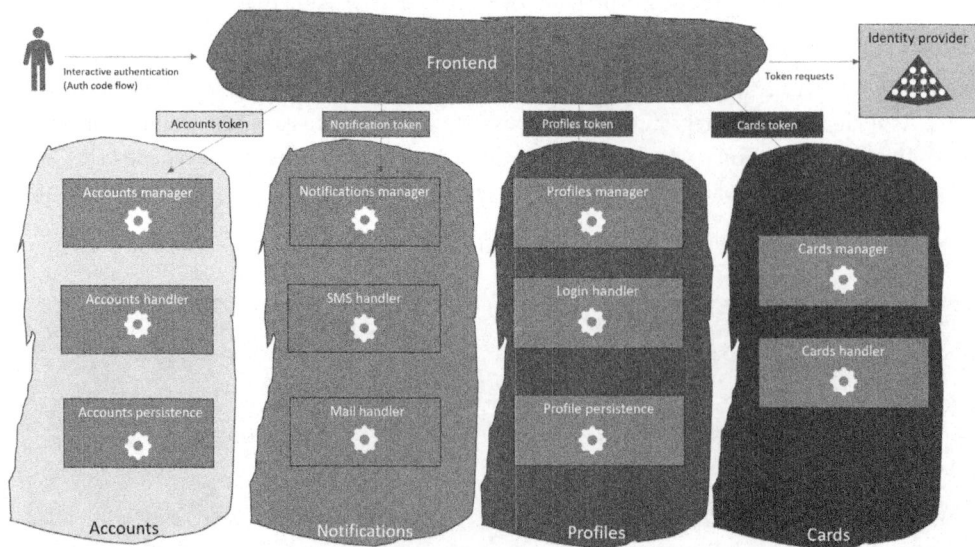

Figure 9.13 – Domain-based with a frontend component

What is shown in the preceding figure is an extension of the diagram proposed in domain-based registration; in this case, we also outline the frontend component, which is still considered an internal part of the application. It is important to understand that this kind of introduction, despite being widely adopted in real-world scenarios, drifts a little from a pure microservices design concept. The diagram shown depicts the frontend as a single entity. According to the DDD paradigm, from a design perspective, the frontend component should be divided into smaller chunks to extend the autonomy and the independence of the microservices approach to the frontend. This is usually achieved through the **micro-frontend** concept, which helps to promote the DDD paradigm further and avoid cross-domain functionality being hosted in a single component (which, in our case, is the frontend itself).

Figure 9.13 is the most common approach we have found across enterprises. As a matter of fact, most companies use it to focus on the microservices architecture on the backend side and do not extend the concept to the frontend layer. Situations in which micro-frontends could represent a benefit for your organization are out of the scope of this book; to further explore the benefits and the drawbacks of this approach, it is recommended to read this interesting article by Martin Fowler: `https://martinfowler.com/articles/micro-frontends.html`. In the case of micro-frontends, the functionality exposed to the GUI would belong to the domain itself and doesn't need to be seen as an additional layer in the architecture.

In our simpler example, we can think of the frontend component as a **backend for frontend** (**BFF**). To those familiar with the pattern, for the sake of understanding, this section will consider a standard frontend that combines multiple domains to provide responses to an SPA.

Figure 9.13 represents a frontend layer, which integrates the concept expressed in the *Pattern 3 – domain-based registration* section of this chapter. In this case, every single domain has its own identity. As a consequence, a specific access token is required to grant authentication whenever the frontend needs to query the domains. The same applies to interactive authentication on the part of the user. In other words, this diagram shows two different OAuth flows: the interactive auth code grant flow, which is used to authenticate an end user that needs to use the application as reported in the *Authorization code grant flow* section in *Chapter 4, Authentication Flows*, and the client credential flow, which has already been discussed in the current chapter for server-to-server authentication within app components and detailed in the *Client credential grant flow* section in *Chapter 4, Authentication Flows*. Despite *Figure 9.13* outlining a single IdP, it is possible, as said previously, that some organizations have one specific IdP for users/customers, and one adopted for server-to-server authentication. This aspect does not affect the understanding of this chapter, and *Figure 9.13* has been simplified for a single IdP.

The diagram outlines how the frontend component, which is supposed to be considered part of the app, requires different tokens according to the backend service it needs to access. It is uncommon in microservices architecture for the frontend to access every backend service; the most typical design is that every domain has its own service that exposes the API that the frontend needs to consume, and other microservices within the domain are designed to support this "frontend-exposed microservice." This is possible because the frontend layer is supposed to know the internal details of the application. The situation changes when the API queries are supposed to be received by an external system for inbound integration.

If we try to handle third-party systems or external applications by following the authentication pattern expressed so far, we would obtain a situation as in the figure shown here:

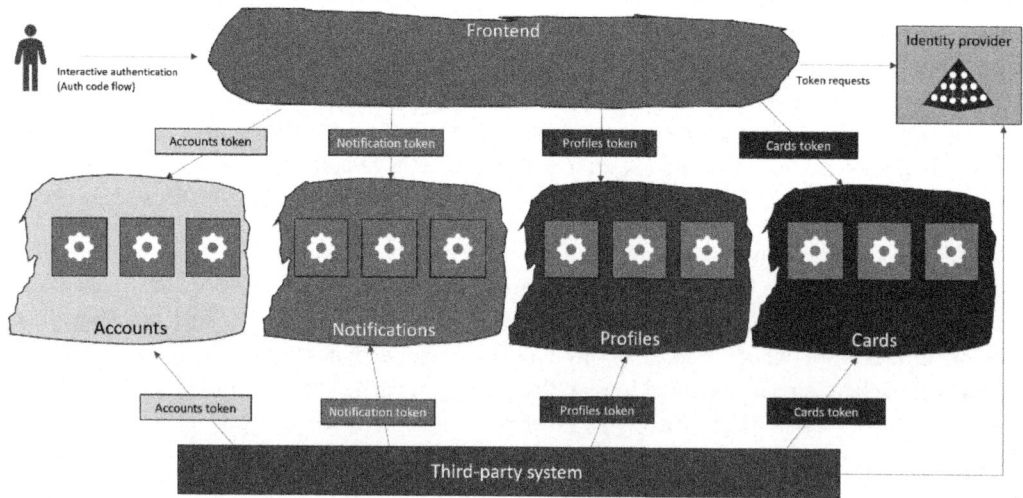

Figure 9.14 – Inbound integration anti-pattern

This design makes the integrations cumbersome for the following reasons:

- We show the application's domain design to an external system, which should belong to our organization

- We force the external system to handle multiple tokens to query a single application

- We potentially enable the third-party system (if no network restrictions are in place) to query any microservices it wants, which is not desirable from a security perspective

In this case, getting an access token for the **Cards** domain or the **Accounts** domain may not have a clear meaning for an external actor who just wants to query the banking application. This approach would require showing unnecessary complexity to an external system and breaking the segregation of duties paradigm.

The preceding bullet list should make clear why internal authentication and external authentication should not be treated in the same way.

If the backend services need to be accessed by an external application (not the frontend of the application itself), an enterprise architect should evaluate how to hide the internal details of the application by mixing multiple patterns and introducing a network appliance, as shown in the following schema:

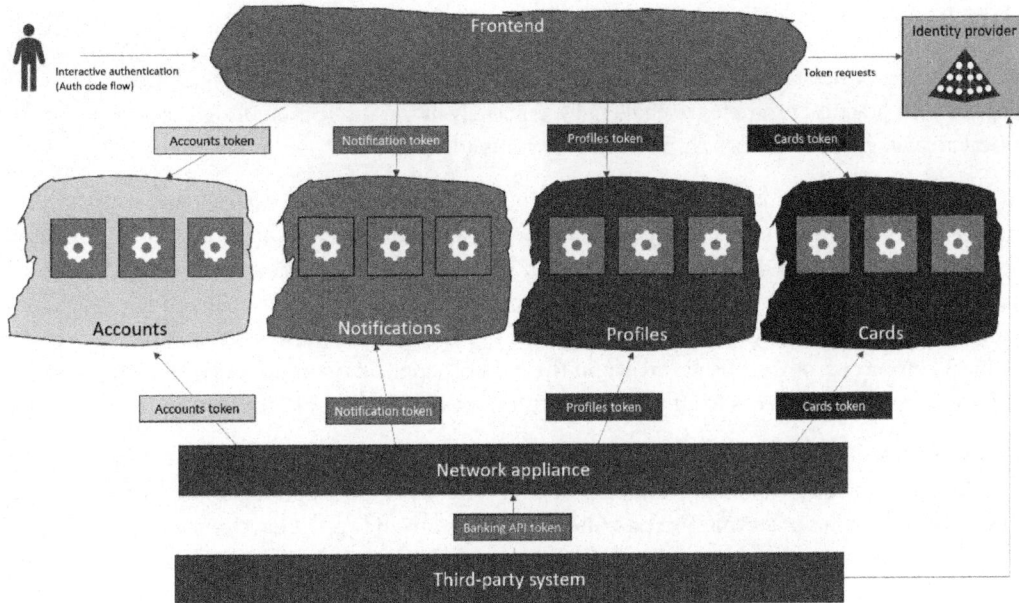

Figure 9.15 – Inbound integration pattern

This diagram shows a possible pattern to facilitate integration in a microservices application.

It enables the third-party system to not deal with the complexity of the application and not even know the application. All the third-party system needs to know is the API it needs to call and the token it needs to grab from the IdP. Moreover, the API can be exposed differently externally and internally thanks to a Level 7 network appliance, which has the goal of hiding the internal details of the application from external stakeholders. This layer, moreover, is responsible for validating a generic token for the integration and requires the proper internal token to the IdP. Some Level 7 network appliances provided by cloud providers have this capability. In the case that the Level 7 network appliance can't ask for the internal token that is needed, it is still possible to build a similar architecture and secure the communication between the network appliance and the internal application using network restrictions, which is recommended in any case.

As a side note, the network appliance layer represented in the preceding figure is a logical component that may also belong to the same cluster that hosts the microservices of the application if platforms such as Kubernetes or OpenShift are adopted.

Summary

In this chapter, we had the opportunity to complement the theoretical explanations shared in previous chapters with practical examples of challenges, especially in the application design area, which is the critical area where new business is generated by companies.

In this book, we covered many areas related to identity management and we have done so on different levels: we moved through high-level views of how a company should have a common strategy for critical topics such as identity, and we had the opportunity to share the implications of ignoring how to set up an identity strategy correctly. We then touched on more pragmatic topics, such as the implications of an identity strategy in the application designed, and we even provided low-level information about the most common protocols used today and the possible application and flows of each protocol, as well as examples and patterns to adopt when it is time to design an application.

What should be clear at this stage is that identity is a wide topic that touches on many areas we didn't even explore in this book and that we attempted to enumerate at the beginning of the current chapter; nevertheless, the focus of an enterprise architect should be on guiding the development team, who are the ones that create new business value, and avoiding pitfalls and proliferations of tools and systems such as the IdP.

A solid and robust company that wants to do good business in the cloud world should be able to focus on generating new business value, avoiding complex systems with too many layers, and limiting the overhead generated by the maintenance of unnecessary layers such as multiple IdPs that are supposed to serve common goals.

Index

‹packt›

Subscribe to our online digital library for full access to over 7,000 books and videos, as well as industry leading tools to help you plan your personal development and advance your career. For more information, please visit our website.

Why subscribe?

- Spend less time learning and more time coding with practical eBooks and Videos from over 4,000 industry professionals

- Improve your learning with Skill Plans built especially for you

- Get a free eBook or video every month

- Fully searchable for easy access to vital information

- Copy and paste, print, and bookmark content

Did you know that Packt offers eBook versions of every book published, with PDF and ePub files available? You can upgrade to the eBook version at packt.com and as a print book customer, you are entitled to a discount on the eBook copy. Get in touch with us at customercare@packtpub.com for more details.

At www.packt.com, you can also read a collection of free technical articles, sign up for a range of free newsletters, and receive exclusive discounts and offers on Packt books and eBooks.

Other Books You May Enjoy

If you enjoyed this book, you may be interested in these other books by Packt:

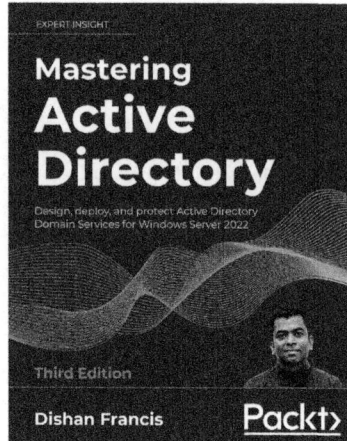

Mastering Active Directory - Third Edition

Dishan Francis

ISBN: 978-1-80107-039-3

- Install, protect, and manage Active Directory Domain Services (Windows Server 2022)
- Design your hybrid identity by evaluating business and technology requirements
- Automate administrative tasks in Active Directory using Windows PowerShell 7.x
- Protect sensitive data in a hybrid environment using Azure Information Protection
- Learn about Flexible Single Master Operation (FSMO) roles and their placement
- Manage directory objects effectively using administrative tools and PowerShell
- Centrally maintain the state of user and computer configuration by using Group Policies
- Harden your Active Directory using security best practices

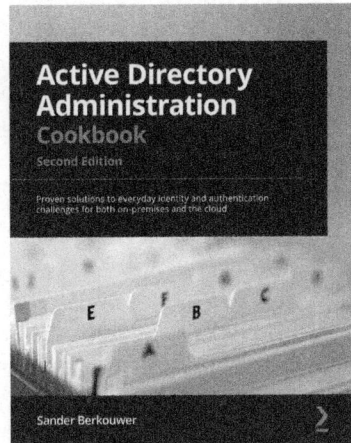

Active Directory Administration Cookbook - Second Edition

Sander Berkouwer

ISBN: 978-1-80324-250-7

- Manage the Recycle Bin, gMSAs, and fine-grained password policies
- Work with Active Directory from both the graphical user interface (GUI) and command line
- Use Windows PowerShell to automate tasks
- Create and remove forests, domains, domain controllers, and trusts
- Create groups, modify group scope and type, and manage memberships
- Delegate, view, and modify permissions
- Set up, manage, and optionally decommission certificate authorities
- Optimize Active Directory and Azure AD for security

Packt is searching for authors like you

If you're interested in becoming an author for Packt, please visit `authors.packtpub.com` and apply today. We have worked with thousands of developers and tech professionals, just like you, to help them share their insight with the global tech community. You can make a general application, apply for a specific hot topic that we are recruiting an author for, or submit your own idea.

Share your thoughts

Now you've finished *Cloud Identity Patterns and Strategies*, we'd love to hear your thoughts! Scan the QR code below to go straight to the Amazon review page for this book and share your feedback or leave a review on the site that you purchased it from.

`https://packt.link/r/1801810842`

Your review is important to us and the tech community and will help us make sure we're delivering excellent quality content.

Download a free PDF copy of this book

Thanks for purchasing this book!

Do you like to read on the go but are unable to carry your print books everywhere?

Is your eBook purchase not compatible with the device of your choice?

Don't worry, now with every Packt book you get a DRM-free PDF version of that book at no cost.

Read anywhere, any place, on any device. Search, copy, and paste code from your favorite technical books directly into your application.

The perks don't stop there, you can get exclusive access to discounts, newsletters, and great free content in your inbox daily

Follow these simple steps to get the benefits:

1. Scan the QR code or visit the link below

https://packt.link/free-ebook/9781801810845

2. Submit your proof of purchase
3. That's it! We'll send your free PDF and other benefits to your email directly

Printed in Great Britain
by Amazon